GW00391731

2,000 Years
of British Life

Plantagenet Somerset Fry

A social history of England, Wales, Scotland and Ireland

Collins Glasgow and London

Acknowledgments

There are about 300 pictures in this book. A few belong to me. The rest were provided at very short notice, with great kindness and efficiency in every case. My wife, who did the picture research (which is acknowledged elsewhere), and I are extremely grateful to all those individuals and organizations who rose to the occasion and supplied exactly what we wanted. They are listed herewith, alphabetically, with the page number, or numbers, on which the pictures appear and all are thanked for their courtesy in allowing their pictures to be reproduced.

Aberdeen Public Library, page 189; Aerofilms Ltd, 28 (top); Ashmolean Museum, 23 (left), 57 (bottom); Bath City Council, 36; Bath Evening Chronicle, 62; Batsford, 119, 144 (top); Berrows Newspapers Ltd 158 (right); Birmingham City Council, 224 (top); Bristol City Corporation, 219; Bristol (Port of Bristol Authority), 223 (bottom left); British Airways, 223 (top left, bottom right); British Museum, 11 (top right), 12 (top), 25 (bottom), 43 (top), 57 (top), 58, 61 (bottom right), 77, 78, 80 (right), 91 (top), 99, 101, 105 (top right, bottom right), 106, 121 (right), 158 (left); British Rail, 176 (top), 177; British Tourist Authority, 47, 48, 85, 86, 104, 110 (bottom), 127; Bury Free Press, 60 (top left); Cambrian Archaeological Society, 126; Cambridge University Aerial Photography Department, 31 (bottom); Cardiff City Council, 232 (left), 237 (top); Central Electricity Generating Board, 207 (right), 222; Chubb, The Reverend N., 50; Colchester Museum, 16, 35 (bottom), 59, 72 (top left); Council for Small Industries in Rural Areas, 14 (right), 17 (left); Countryside Commission, 21; Cumbernauld Development Corporation, 220; David & Charles Ltd, 39; Dean and Chapter of Durham Cathedral, 135; Department of the Environment, 17 (right), 26, 33, 35 (top), 75 (bottom), 81, 82 (top right), 89 (top left, top right); 113, 114 (left), 129 (right), 130, 133, 134 (bottom), 144 (below), 147, 172, 180 (bottom), 182 (below); East Anglia, University of (School of Fine Arts), 93; Edinburgh City Libraries, 238 (below); Edinburgh Evening News, 231; Fishbourne Roman Palace (Sussex Archaeological Trust), 37, 38; Fox Photos Ltd, 216 (below), 218, 224 (below), 226, 227; G.E.C. Ltd, 211 (right); Geffrye Museum, 178 (top); Glasgow Herald, 240 (above), 242, 244 (above); Gwynedd County Library Service, 235 (left); Hampshire Chronicle, 56; H.M.S.O., 75 (top right), 122 (below), 149 (above), 151, 184 (left); Hereford City Council, 100; Illustrated London News, 45, 176 (below), 196 (below), 197, 201, 202, 203, 205, 206, 208 (left), 216 (top), 217 (top), 246, 247 (right); Imperial War Museum, 215; Iona Community, 134 (top right), Irish Tourist Board, 22, 140 190, 192, 245; John Lewis Partnership Archives, 213 (top); London Museum, 40, 61 (top right), 72 (top right), 96, 115, 117, 149 (below), 173, 196 (above), 209 (right); Mansell Collection, 11 (bottom left), 121 (left), 163, 188; Mitchell Library, Glasgow, 239 (top), 243 (top); National Library of Scotland, 238 (top), 249; National Library of Wales, 132, 183 (top), 233; National Maritime Museum, 123 (above), 156 (top); National Monuments Record, 52 (right), 76 (top right); National Museum of Wales, 11 (bottom right), 18, 234, 236; National Portrait Gallery, 64 (top), 95, 122 (top), 143, 182 (top); Northamptonshire Evening Telegraph, 51; Norwich Castle Museum, 60 (top right), 120 (top); Phaidon Press Ltd, 64 (bottom), 71; Plaid Cymru, 230 (top); Popperfoto, 217 (below); Princess Margaret Hospital, Swindon, 223 (top right); Public Record Office, 67, 68, 80 (left), 180 (above); Radio Times Hulton Picture Library, 13, 23 (right), 25 (top), 52 (left), 74, 90, 91 (bottom left, centre, right), 94 (top left, bottom left), 103 (bottom left, bottom right), 136 (left), 154, 155; Reading Museum, 31 (top); Royal Scottish Museum, 187 (right); St Andrews University Library, 187 (left); St Paul's School, 110 (top); Science Museum, London, 102, 165, 166, 167, 168, 169, 170 (below), 174, 178 (left), 198, 207 (left), 210, 211 (left), 213 (below); Scotsman Publications Ltd, 186 (right); Scottish Development Agency (Small Business Division), 237 (below), 243 (below); Sheffield City Art Galleries, 142; Shell International Petroleum Co. Ltd, 221; Shropshire Newspapers Ltd, 170 (top); Stuart, Mr P. Maxwell, 186 (left); Swindon Borough Council, 208 (right); Tower of London, 83 (top left), University of Wales, Aberystwyth, 235 (right); Verulamium Museum, 15, 29 (left, right); Victoria and Albert Museum, 111, 112; Wales Tourist Board, 181; Wellcome Museum, 209 (left); Welsh Folk Museum, 19, 125, 129 (left), 183 (below), 230 (below), 232 (right); York Castle Museum, 212. Michael Shand drew the maps on pages 12, 21, 28, 42, 43, 108.

First published 1976
Second impression 1977
Published by William Collins Sons and Company Limited, Glasgow and London

Printed in Great Britain
ISBN 0 00 106172 0

Contents

To Fiona
my wife

Introduction

What is the difference between this book and other social histories of Britain? It is the first to tell how each of the four constituent peoples of the British Isles—the English, the Welsh, the Scots and the Irish— lived, worked and enjoyed themselves throughout their long histories. It covers the domestic, agricultural and, later, industrial developments in Wales, Scotland and Ireland from the 1st century BC, and those in England following the Anglo-Saxon invasions and settlements of the 5th and 6th centuries AD. No other social history of Britain has done this.

We are living in times when the Celtic peoples of Britain are more and more anxious to establish their national identities, and to seek self-determination, if they have not, like the Irish, already got it. And yet these aspirations are not new. They are rooted in ancient history. For centuries before joining with England, the Celtic nations had histories of their own.

This book traces briefly the individual social development of each of the four nations. It attempts to weigh the advantages with the disadvantages to the Celtic nations from their uniting with England. Above all, it sets out to underline the unique qualities and achievements of the peoples, collectively known as the British, who have pioneered so much in the history of the world but who, so often and so needlessly, undervalue themselves.

I have greatly enjoyed writing this book, but it would not have been possible without the help of my wife whose extensive research and numerous suggestions for improvement, picture research and index preparation will be remembered by me with lasting gratitude. The views expressed in the text, however, are entirely mine.

Plantagenet Somerset Fry
Burgh-next-Aylsham
Norfolk
1976

1 Before the Romans

One day in July 55 BC, more than two thousand years ago, the great Roman general, Julius Caesar, invaded Britain. He did so partly to punish some British tribes, who had been helping their cousins in Gaul try to stop the Roman advance, and partly because he was attracted by stories of rich pearl oyster beds off the island's shores. But he was also anxious to make a dramatic conquest in a hitherto almost unknown land, for this would, when reported in Rome, raise his stock considerably among his friends. It would impress his enemies too, who were already alarmed at his growing military reputation.

And so it happened. For, although the invasion can hardly be said to have been a success—he won only a skirmish or two and lost his entire fleet in a storm off the Kent coast—when the news reached Rome the Senate granted the people a twenty-day holiday of thanksgiving, called a *supplicatio*. Caesar went on to defeat all his enemies, to become master of the Roman Empire and the greatest man of the ancient world (perhaps of all time), and to be brutally murdered by men he thought were friends in 44 BC.

The inhabitants of Britain – the Celts

It has often been thought that when the civilized and cultured Romans came to Britain, they ran into a collection of barbarous tribes running about the fields half-naked, covered with blue paint, illiterate, living in primitive conditions, and possessing none of the advantages of civilization. Such was not the case at all. The inhabitants of Britain had, in their own way and in their own time, been developing for centuries. Of course they lacked many of the characteristics of the civilizations of the Mediterranean, but they had some interesting qualities of their own. Let us have a look at how far they had got by 55 BC.

The Celts were not one people. They were a group of races of similar origin, speaking a vaguely common language. Several hundred years before Caesar, they occupied many parts of central and western Europe, especially what are now Austria, Switzerland

Opposite: A bust of Julius Caesar, the greatest man of the ancient world. It is in the British Museum. For a long time it was thought to have been sculpted in or near his time. Now it is argued that it is not Roman at all, but is an 18th-century likeness produced in Italy from earlier busts.

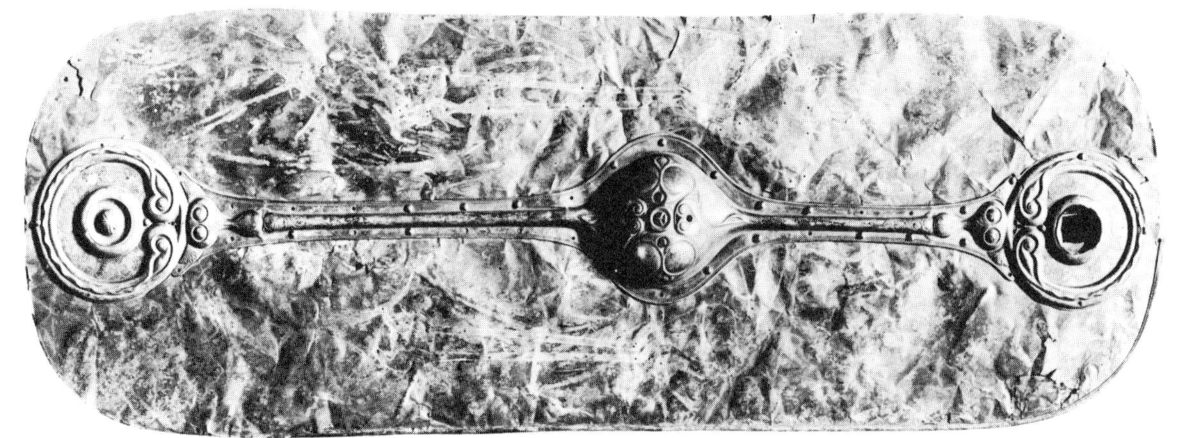

A bronze shield found in Lancashire. The decoration is La Tène style. It is probably from the 3rd century BC.

Right: A Celtic brooch from Wales, in the La Tène style. It is believed to be of the 1st century

southern France and Spain. Over the years, in wave after wave, they spread outwards, overrunning France and Belgium, and crossing to Britain. Round about the fifth century BC, when Greece was at the height of its greatness under the splendid Pericles, there was a new stage in the development of the Celts in Europe, which we call the La Tène period. This was when the Celts began to make fine articles of iron, handsomely carved and decorated. A quantity of these things was dug up in the Swiss village of La Tène, and this gave the name to the period. Some articles of the same age, like swords and armour, have also been found in Britain, which suggests that the La Tène Celts came here at about the same time. They probably brought their knowledge of how to smelt and use iron, and no doubt taught the settled Celts to make their ploughs more effective by edging the wooden shares with iron. The Celts in Britain up to then had been using bronze as well as wood and stone.

Early Celts

The Greeks of the fourth century BC knew about the Celts. It was they who coined the word *Keltoi* to describe this group of peoples with their strange but similar languages. One of the Greek navigators, Pytheas, who lived in the Greek colony city of Massilia

(present-day Marseilles), is said to have visited Britain during the reign of Alexander the Great (336–323 BC), and to have written an account of some tribes he came across in Cornwall. There, the Celts had chariots which they used in war. They knew how to extract tin from streams of earth running through rock, and they were skilled at working it into ingots for shipment to Europe, or into articles for their own use or ornament. They lived in wattle-walled houses with thatched roofs, though huts would be a better word. Pytheas also visited Kent, where he noted the tribes' farming methods. They grew corn in the fine, rich rolling plains, and stored it after threshing under cover in thatched barns, and not out-of-doors as was the custom in Mediterranean countries. They used the corn to make bread and cakes. They also fermented it to make a heavy, sweet and rather sickly liquid called mead.

Pytheas is said to have visited northern England and Scotland where he found similar people speaking similar dialects. There, the earth was less fertile and barley was the main crop.

Above: Some Celtic pottery items. These were made by Celts of the La Tène period in Europe, and they date from about 500 BC.

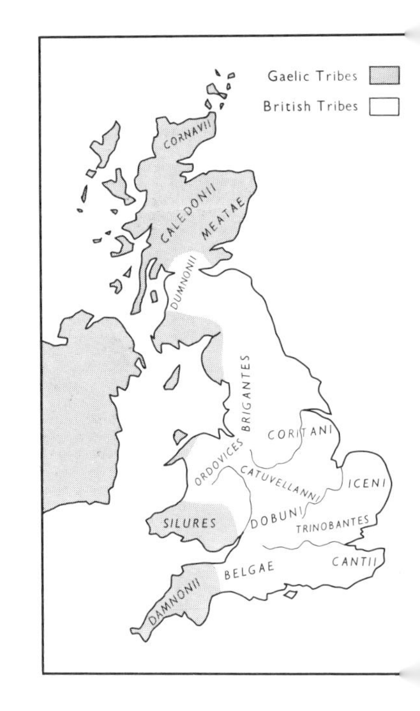

Where they came from

You will appreciate that there are still quite a lot of Celts in the British Isles today. They live for the most part in Wales, Cornwall, Scotland, the Isle of Man and Ireland. (And many live in England,

A model of a Roman trireme. This was a warship driven by oarsmen who sat in rows of three horizontally, hence the name trireme.

too!) They are from two main branches, the Britons (roughly Wales and Cornwall) and the Gaels (Scotland, Isle of Man and Ireland). There have of course been many injections of foreign blood—Roman, Saxon, Viking and Norman, and it is impossible to be precise about their differences; but they stem from the two main types of Celt who invaded Britain after about the eighth century BC. The first were the Goidelic (or Gaelic) Celts. These not quite so developed people were pushed into Ireland and the bleak highland areas of Scotland by their more civilized cousins the Brythonic (or British) Celts who came over in the fifth and fourth centuries. Perhaps some of these were of the La Tène period. They occupied present-day England and Wales.

By the time Julius Caesar was ready to launch his invasion, more Celts had crossed over from Gaul, and had settled in the south-east, in the region now called the Home Counties. These were largely the Belgic tribes, from what is now southern Belgium and northern France, and they were cousins of the Britons already here. Today we might regard one branch as more civilized than another because its art and crafts were more highly developed. But what mattered at the time was whether you could wield a sword or an axe more effectively. Of course, if you were economically better off than your neighbour at an early period of development, then it is likely that you were more civilized.

Left: This map shows roughly the division of the Celtic tribes in Britain at about the time of Caesar's invasion of 55 BC. The shaded areas were occupied by the Gaelic Celts who had come to Britain long before the Brythonic Celts. The tribal names are those given them by the Romans.

Above: In this stone relief a Gallic (Celtic) warrior in the foreground faces a Roman legionary. In the background (right) is a Celtic cottage, with wooden walls and thatched roof, such as was common in Britain at the time (1st century BC).

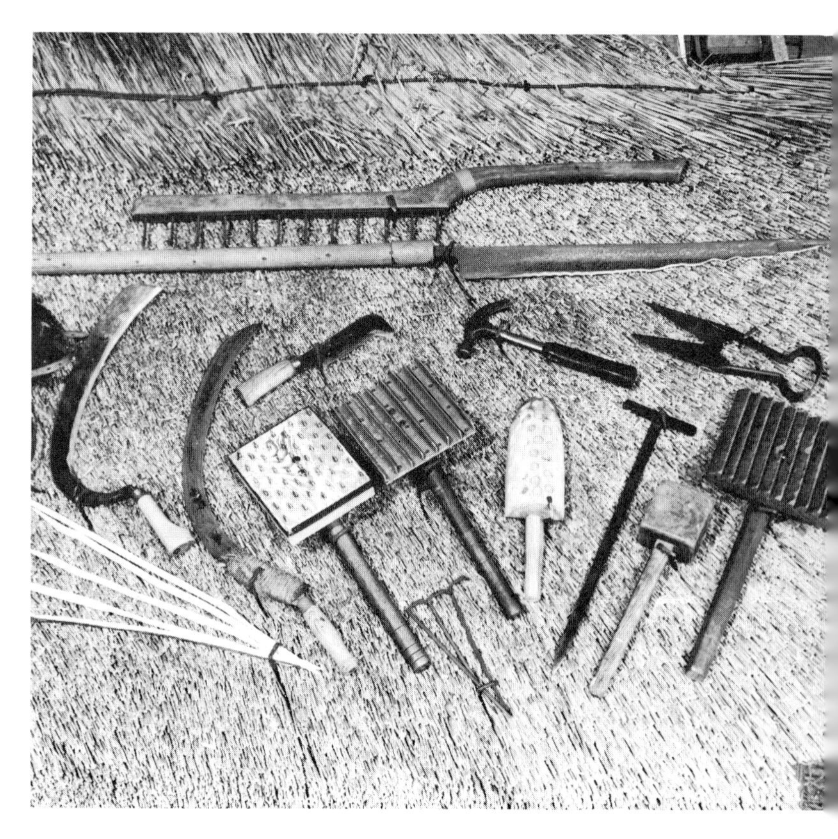

Above right: This is an array of thatching tools of the present century. They have not altered much for 2,000 years or more. You can see leggetts, for dressing the reed or straw into position (at bottom centre and right).

What they looked like

What were these assorted Celts like? Much of what we are abl to gather has come from descriptions by people who were, afte all, their enemies. Caesar, whose eight books on his wars in Gau include details of his invasion of Britain, tells a lot. But is he alway accurate or fair? He was describing an inferior people who ha had the temerity to oppose him.

It seems that the Celts wore trousers and light cloaks. Thi would have amused the Roman soldiers who prided themselve on their rugged indifference to colder climates and kept thei knees bare below their tunics. The Celts were tallish, on the whol clean-shaven, though Caesar mentions the fashion for wearin droopy moustaches and long hair. Some even had short beard Some plastered their hair down with lime wash to make it loo fairer than it really was.

The Celts loved bright, dazzling colours. Many of their clothe tunics and cloaks were decorated with golden thread woven int spidery or geometric patterns. They dyed their woollens an covered themselves with bright jewellery, much of it fine executed in bronze, gold, tin, silver, coral and enamel. The enamel work was particularly interesting. The women wore longe cloaks, sometimes fastened with ornamented brooches.

A collection of tools of Roman times, found at Verulamium (St Albans). Some are blacksmiths' implements, and all the tools will have been made by blacksmiths.

Their houses

They lived in the simplest homes, which were not very substantial as they did not use much stone or granite and knew nothing of cement or concrete. There were one or two stone-based houses in areas like Cornwall, but these were rare. Caesar's Celts built square or round huts of wattle and thatch like the cottages seen by Pytheas. They did not catch on to Roman building techniques for a long time. Some historians have said that the Celts did not attach importance to house construction. Home was where you put your head down at night or sheltered during the day if it rained or snowed. So long as it was more or less weatherproof, why bother to spend time making it grand or decorating it? But Celtic hill forts were designed with great skill and ingenuity, to the extent that the Roman occupation forces adapted and improved some of them rather than build new ones.

Inside their homes the Celts lived very simply. They had little furniture, possibly a stool or two, a chest for storage, and objects like lamps, household utensils and so on. They made much of their own pottery out of local clay, and baked it indoors in a fire on the ground. If they wanted better quality decorated articles, they could always get these from one or other of the many potters who had businesses up and down the land.

Food and drink

Celts ate a lot of meat, especially pork. They chewed roasted or boiled joints, cut it into small chunks and washed it down with their sickly-tasting mead or crude beer. The beer was probably a good bit stronger than that which you get in a pub now, and no doubt many men got very merry after a victory over a neighbouring tribe, or a wedding ceremony.

Their work

Most of the men were farmers who turned to warfare only if they had to. They cultivated small patches of land, enough to supply their family needs, and perhaps have some surplus to trade with neighbours or merchants. These farmers grew crops or raised sheep and cattle, depending on the kind of land they worked. Sometimes they did both. Their fields were ploughed in narrow rectangular strips with iron ploughshares, and the main crops were wheat, barley and rye.

Apart from farmers, there were craftsmen and merchants. The principal craft—and the one which carried the most prestige—was the blacksmith's. And no wonder, for he understood all about iron. He shaped your sword and dagger, repaired your broken ploughshare, and made all manner of everyday things you needed. It was common for these much-needed men to be held in high regard. They were usually well up the social scale in ancient civilizations. In the Hittite, for example, which flourished from about 2000 to about 1200 BC, iron was first introduced, and the Hittite blacksmiths were accorded many privileges. Blacksmiths in Britain worked locally and also travelled about from place to place to give service.

Items of Celtic pottery of the 1st century BC. They are in the Colchester Museum.

We have already mentioned the potter. He was another respected member of the community who always had plenty of work. Certainly, potters have left behind many varied examples of their skill. They had the time and expertise to produce the intricate Celtic patterns round the edges of plates or the waists of flasks, which the ordinary householder or his wife did not. In later years, when the Romans had taught some of the British how to build proper houses with tiled roofs, some potters added greatly to their incomes by making quantities of pan-tiles and occasionally glazing them.

There were also many other crafts and trades, such as carpentry and thatching. Both skills have lasted down the centuries, so that today British carpentry and thatching are very highly regarded. Possibly these trades were followed by men who were also farmers.

No society can exist for long without trading with neighbouring societies. The Celts had merchants and traders who travelled about the countryside and made frequent crossings to Gaul. Traders

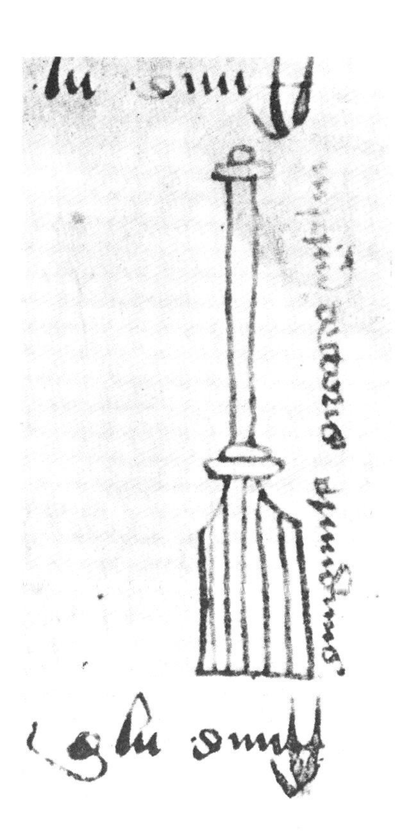

This sketch (above) is of a medieval leggett (see page 14). It is drawn in the margin of a Court Roll of 1364 for the manor of Crowle in Lincolnshire.

Above right: a view from the air of a major Celtic hill fort at Maiden Castle in Dorset. The Roman armies had to overcome several of these stoutly defended earthworks in their campaign against the British Celts.

came from many parts of Europe to Britain in search of tin, leather, coral, pearls, salt, fish and corn.

Government and social organization

When Caesar came to Britain he found Celtic society quite well organized, in much the same way as it was in Gaul. Of course it did not have the Romans' well-tried structure of government. It was probably a positive advantage to them that they did not have it at the time; by then it was badly in need of overhaul. But as Celtic contact with the Romans developed, long before Caesar's expedition, the Celts began to adopt certain Roman ideas. Their tribes were governed at first by kings, who were usually in power by virtue of their military prowess or particular bravery in battle. Generally these kings handed down their power to their sons, or other male members of the family. But it was not always as easy as that, for some of the king's chief advisers and followers became richer than the kings themselves and so insisted on having more say in running things. Thus arose the principle of electing chiefs, rather like magistrates (Caesar actually refers to them as such) as the Romans had been doing for several centuries after they expelled their last king in 510 BC. Chiefs of the Celts were still selected from the same families, as it was believed that royal families were descended from the gods. They were probably the

This is a model of a Celtic war chariot. It was a formidable vehicle and Caesar commented on it with some admiration, in his account of the invasion of Britain of 55 BC. In a battle, the chariot was driven by a warrior who was an expert in handling the vehicle, which was pulled by two horses. Beside him stood another warrior, perhaps with a third, and they jumped about flashing their spears or swords, yelling at the tops of their voices or blowing through trumpets making a terrible noise to frighten the enemy. These chariots were also used to rescue wounded chiefs from battle.

chairmen of the tribal assemblies which were gatherings of more senior Celts whose task it was to govern the tribes.

Celtic society was divided into two sections—free men, and slaves and serfs. Among the free men there were three classes, the nobles, the druids and the commons. Free men naturally had many rights and privileges not accorded to serfs. They could carry arms. They could attend the assemblies though they might not all be allowed to vote. And they had another right, to belong to a kin. It is important to understand the part the kin, or family, played in Celtic society. In the earliest times the land was shared by everybody who lived on it. Gradually, as the generations went by, people were sorted out into families and these families got together to form tribes. Some families became more powerful than others, for one reason or another (superior fighting ability, better farming methods) and these more powerful families took the others under their protection. The latter felt they belonged to them. They sent their sons to learn among them and they worked for them. In this way they became members of the family, or the kindred. The ruling royal families were probably the leading kin in the tribes, proved over the generations. So, you will see that it was a good thing to belong to a kin.

Serfs and slaves, on the other hand, had few rights. Serfs were the descendants of conquered tribes, or just strangers who had wandered over to Britain, perhaps in search of a new life. They were allotted small patches of land and sometimes given a cottage. But they could not attend ceremonies or assemblies. They were

This picture of Druids celebrating mystical rites dwells on the human sacrifice aspect of Celtic religion. While the Druids did on occasion resort to this cruel practice, it is not now thought that it played a major part in their ceremonies.

not kindred. As for slaves, they were usually prisoners taken in war and they had even fewer rights. Possibly they spent their lives in bondage, though doubtless some fled to remoter parts of the islands and made new lives for themselves.

Celtic law

On the subject of rights, Celtic law was based on the compensation of the victim for wrongs done. This was not new. Many Near Eastern civilizations had a similar basis for their laws, notably the Hittites. In Britain, most crimes and lesser offences, which today we would call misdemeanours, were sorted out by the parties involved. Every free man had what might be called his value, his 'honour price', which was what his particular kin or community put upon him. Offences were resolved by reaching agreement on terms for compensation. But there were several crimes which you could not expiate merely by paying a cash indemnity. Among them were murder, arson, and–theft of cattle! This last one is interesting as it does not seem nearly so serious as the other two. The Celts were great cattle ranchers on the hillier parts of the island, such as the West Country, Wales, the Derbyshire Peaks and the Cumbrian Hills. A great deal of cattle rustling did go on, and it seems to have been treated with the greatest seriousness, punishable by death following trial before an assembly or a panel appointed by the assembly. Perhaps this was because cattle were the principal means of livelihood of these hill tribes, and the bull

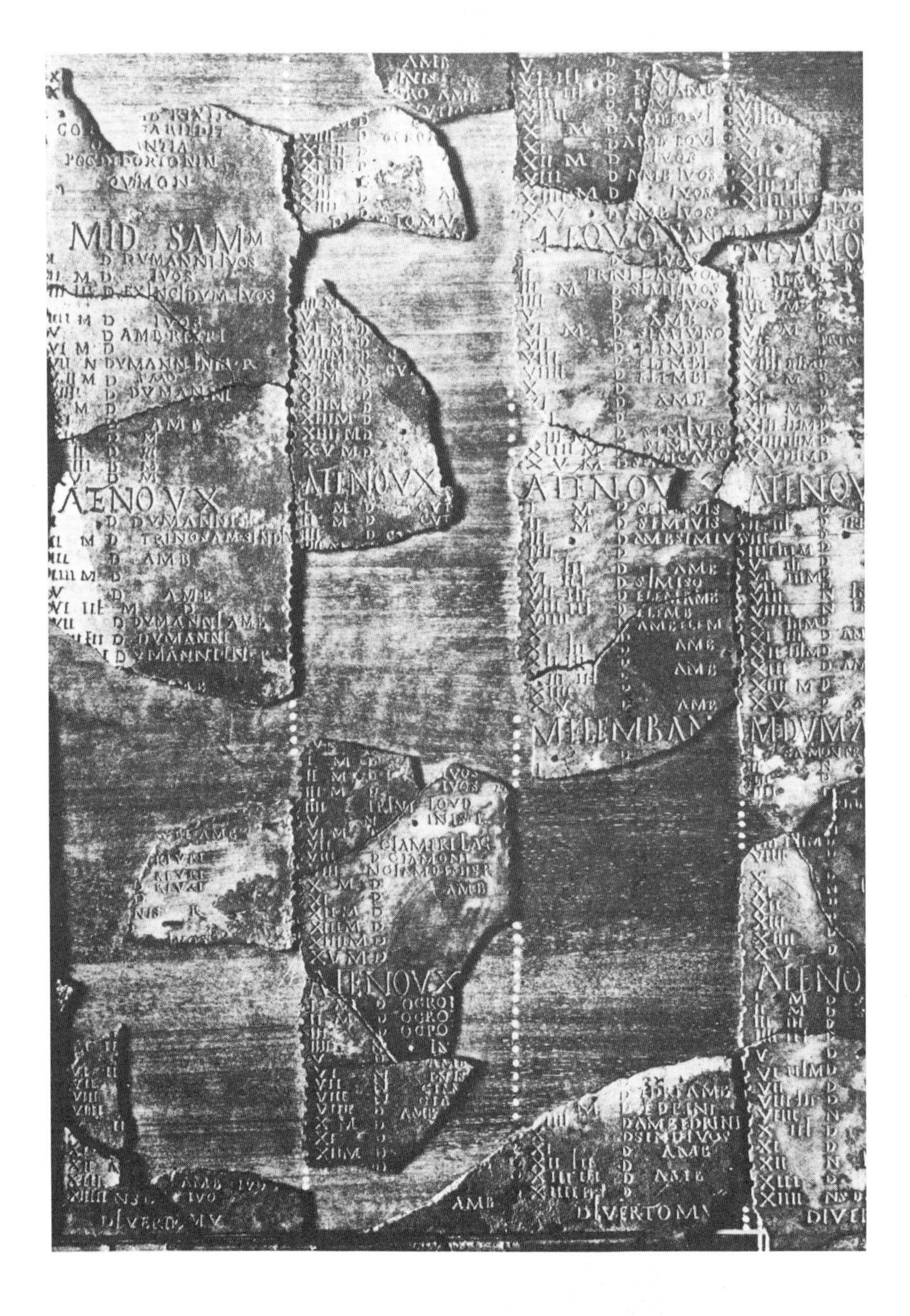

The Druids worked out calendars for religious observances and celebrations among the Celtic tribes. Here is a piece of one such calendar, which was found in France. It is probably from the 1st century BC. Though Celtic, the calendar has Latin letters.

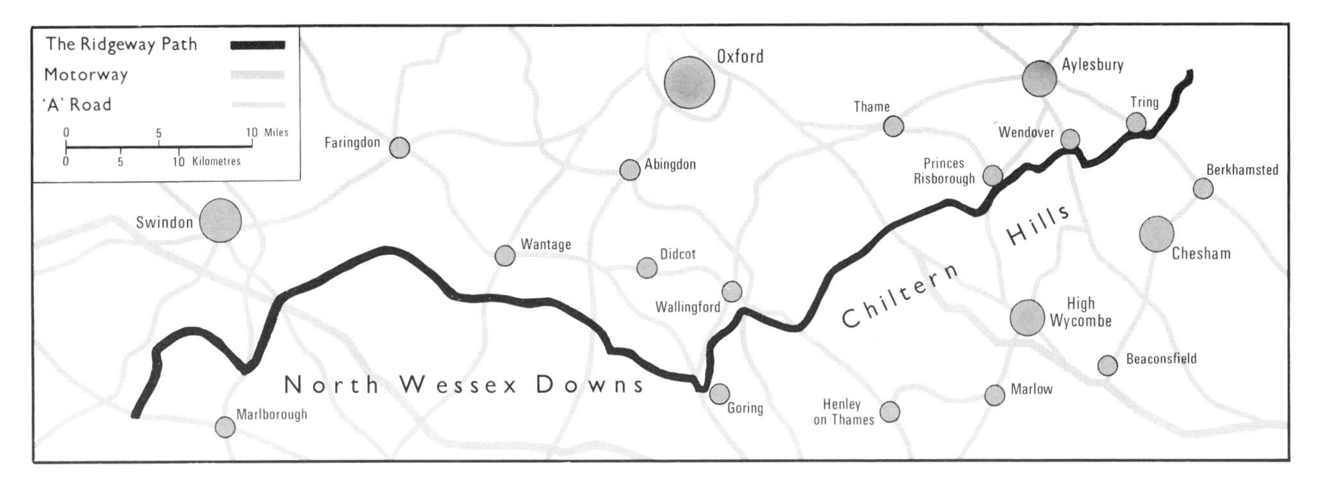

In pre-historic Britain, tracks were made across the countryside, generally along the higher levels to avoid the lower marshy areas, for people to walk to and from places, some of which had religious importance. They were later known as ridgeways. Part of one of these (shown on the map above) runs from Avebury in Wiltshire into Bedfordshire. Quite a bit of this track is still there today.

or cow was accorded some kind of religious status by them.

The laws of the Celts were largely unwritten. They developed over the centuries as a result of a growing sense of responsibility among individuals regarding their obligations to the society in which they lived. Men want order in their lives, though they do not like too much of it! The laws were usually stated by the *Druids* who handed them down by word of mouth to succeeding generations, in much the same way as the judges and priests of the Hebrews. These Druids were priests who looked after the religion and the festivals. They were men of some learning, they organized schools, and they kept the people in a state of superstitious fear with their mystical ceremonies, incantations and sacrifices (of animals and human beings) to the gods as penance for the crimes of mankind. They discussed the religious problems of the time, and gave the people a calendar, with lucky and unlucky days and so forth. And when the whole order of Celtic society was threatened with extinction at the time of the Roman conquest, it was the Druids who organized last-ditch resistance, fighting all the way back into the remoteness of Anglesey in north Wales, where they died almost to a man.

Culture

Just as the laws of the Celts were handed down rather than written down, so too were the histories and the legends and myths. You can readily understand that this is not a very good way to transmit history. Clearly, each time a heroic battle or treaty was described, it was exaggerated or possibly understated. The Celts employed poets or bards to recite these stories at meal times, feasts and ceremonies, and they were engaged as much for the dramatic quality of their voices and gesturing as for their capacity to remember the facts. These bards were important members of society, and as a type they lasted in Wales and Ireland long,

In the General Post Office building in Dublin is a splendid statue of the great Irish Celtic hero Cuchullain. It was sculpted by Oliver Sheppard and it commemorates the 1916 Easter Rising when some Irish patriots tried to overthrow the British Government. They failed, but their example inspired others who, five years later, did force Britain to create an Irish Free State.

Opposite above: the White Horse carved in Uffington Down, Berkshire. It was probably cut by British Celts in the 1st century BC. The animal may not look much like a horse, but it expresses vigorously the swift movement of a horse.

Opposite below: from the medieval manuscript of *Sir Gawaine and the Green Knight*. The Knight is showing his head to King Arthur. Arthur was not a king at all, but more probably a Romano-British general who helped to keep the early Saxon invaders at bay.

long after the conquest of both lands by the Anglo–Normans (see page 63). They used to stir the drooping spirits of the Welsh and Irish by digging back into the heroic legends and the sad truths of their early histories. The stories they loved most to tell—and their listeners loved most to hear—were those of individual heroes of bygone days, many of whom were mythical. One of these was the Irish Celtic Cuchullain, the champion warrior of the Ulstermen, who had all the virtues you associate with King Arthur's Knights of the Round Table, coupled with an overwhelming desire to be famous. Cuchullain and his father, Conchobar, and many more, all fought in single combat with their foes. You will remember that in one battle between the Hebrews and the Philistines, in ancient biblical times, the Hebrew leader David slew the Philistine general Goliath in single combat. And who has not heard of the great battle outside Troy between Greek Achilles and Trojan Hector?

All the legends of Arthur and his Knights were woven by later Celtic poets around the much more down-to-earth life story of a Romano–British cavalry commander, Artorius, who in the last years of the fifth century made heroic stands against the Anglo–Saxon invaders somewhere in the West Country.

Art

The Celts were an artistic people (they still are), and their styles and designs were different from classical and Mediterranean forms. They did not usually copy the models they found in their contacts with Greece and Rome. The La Tene period was probably the most vigorous in Celtic art, and this spread to Britain. The most notable thing was the skill with which the craftsmen executed metalwork of many kinds, especially their decorating of metal surfaces. They loved naturalistic creations, geometric designs, abstract patterns, and above all grotesque animal and even human shapes. An excellent example of this abstract approach to animal forms can be seen in the village of Uffington in Berkshire. There, cut into the chalk of the hillside, is a splendid

horse that might almost have been drawn by Picasso himself!

The Celts were skilled in enamel work. You might think that from the number of drinking vessels of many kinds of material that have survived, the Celts were obsessed with drink. But if you look at the flagons and jugs for wine that have been rescued from the earth you will see how their shapes lend themselves to intricate design and decoration, perhaps more dramatically than a flat plate.

These were the fascinating people who lived in Britain in the days before Caesar's invasion. He had, of course, come across them before in Gaul where they had fought alongside their cousins, his enemies. What did surprise him was that they were so advanced. In the next chapter we shall see what his successors did to bring them into the orbit of Roman civilization, and how the Celts reacted to the conquest of their island.

Roman Britain

The great Julius Caesar left Britain in the autumn of 54 BC to return to Gaul. The second invasion earlier in the year had been a more successful adventure than the one the previous year. He had beaten the British king, Cassivelaunus, at Wheathampstead and extracted promises of money payments, taking certain hostages as guarantees. The British could be forgiven for daring to hope it was the last they would see of him.

The second Roman invasion

It was in fact almost a century before Rome invaded Britain again. In AD 43 the emperor Claudius sent an expedition of over 40,000 troops under the general Aulus Plautius across the Channel. Within a short time this skilful strategist had beaten all that the British could send against him and had established his armies in the south-east, roughly behind a line from King's Lynn in Norfolk to Southampton. The next year Claudius came over to Britain to receive the salute of his troops and to lay the foundation stone of a temple to himself at Colchester (Camulodunum, as the Romans called it). The island was by no means overcome, however, and many years more were needed to bring the various tribes under control. Several times they rose in revolt, and the rising led by Queen Boudicea (or Boudicca) in 60–61 bade fair to drive the Romans out of the island altogether.

By 84 nearly all of what is now England and Wales was in Roman hands and garrisoned, and the governor of the province, Julius Agricola, had made substantial conquests in Scotland, as far as a line from the Forth to the Clyde. He is believed to have thought about invading Ireland, though he did not actually set out. Some time in the early years of the next century Roman arms were badly defeated when the Ninth Legion was wiped out. This brought the emperor Hadrian over to Britain in person, and it was he who ordered a tactical retreat to a line from the Solway Firth to the Tyne. There he built his famous wall, much of which still stands.

For the next three hundred years the Romans occupied Britain

Opposite above: here is an artist's impression of Caesar's landing near Romney in Kent, in 55 BC. You can see the tough resistance which the British offered, and which Caesar mentions in his account. Caesar himself is standing at right.

Opposite below: bronze head of the Roman emperor Claudius, who reigned from AD 41 to 54. Claudius visited Britain in AD 44, a year after his general Aulus Plautius had invaded and overrun the southern part of the country. The Romans set up a base at Colchester, an old British village, which came to be called Camulodunum. Some scholars have argued that Camelot, the capital of the legendary King Arthur, was Camulodunum.

south of this line, and from time to time some districts above it. There were many difficulties. On and off, the island was subjected to invasions by the Irish, the Picts in northern Scotland, and Saxons from Denmark and Germany. These last raids were particularly heavy in the closing years of the third century, and led to the creation of a special official, called the Count of the Saxon Shore, whose job it was to organize the policing of the coast from Norfolk to the Isle of Wight.

Then, at the beginning of the fifth century, the very heart of the western Roman Empire was itself in dire trouble. Barbarian Goths, Visigoths and Vandals were pressing upon and breaking through an ever decreasing imperial boundary. In 410, Alaric the

Looking eastwards along Hadrian's Wall from Cuddy's Crag. The wall was about 120 kilometres (75 miles) long, and at every mile there was a fortress with gates, and a barrack for about 25 soldiers. There were also a number of larger forts along or near its length. Much of this remarkable structure is still standing, cared for by the Department of the Environment.

Goth actually sacked Rome. In the same year the Roman emperor Honorius, when asked by the Roman authorities in Britain to send aid to keep out the barbarians, replied that the British would have to look after themselves. How had the British and the Romans lived together in those four hundred years?

Romans and Britons

Although no Roman army came to Britain for a century after Caesar, his invasion had opened up many new points of contact between the British tribes and the Romans in Gaul. Trade across the Channel, which had up to then been on a small scale, quite quickly grew into a profitable business. The Romans introduced the British to their wines, both those made in Gaul and those from Italy. Traders also introduced silverware, Samian pottery, glass, ivory, bronze-veneered furniture and many other things which the British took to with relish. After all, it was probably the first time they had seen glass or silver on any scale.

Britain became an imperial province, ruled by the emperors through a governor and troops who were for the most part Roman—or at least Continental European. The governor had executive power over all matters, except raising taxes and administering finance, which was handled by another official, the procurator.

To all intents and purposes the island was managed just like other Roman provinces. The Romans' policy was always to cooperate with native peoples whenever possible. They believed that their civilization was the best in the world, but they also believed it would be more acceptable if it were not imposed without regard for native institutions. Native people who did cooperate were given every encouragement to develop, and in many instances local kings or chiefs were allowed to go on ruling their own people, subject to the overall dominion of Rome. Occasionally, conquered tribes would not cooperate, and to them Rome showed little mercy. The people would be forced into slavery, conscripted in gangs to build roads or harbours, to clear forests and so forth.

Roman roads

When the Romans came, they found very few towns of any size, and there were no roads as they knew them. Here and there were tracks like the ridgeways, one of which, from Dorset to East Anglia, is still traceable today. It was Roman policy to build straight roads in their provinces to make it easier for troops, police, tax collectors and other officials to get from one place to another. The roads were planned in a network, and along the major routes towns were put up to provide stopping posts for travellers. Most towns began as such posts, supplying food and water for men and for beasts of burden. As the number of officials and business people using the roads grew, so did the size of the towns. They were usually sited at important geographical points—river mouths (Deva, or Chester), valleys (Calleva, or Silchester), rising ground dominating large areas of countryside (Eboracum, or York). But to begin with they were generally intended to serve the road system.

Their roads have become one of the most famous features of Roman civilization. All over Europe there are long stretches of modern road laid down on top of, or alongside, the Roman original. Look at the picture of part of the well-known A5 in the Midlands of England and at the original stretch of Roman road

Above: aerial view of the famous A5 main road from London to Holyhead in Anglesey, north Wales, as it runs through Stony Stratford in Buckinghamshire. This stretch was built along an ancient Roman road.

Below: an artist's drawing of the major roads built in Britain during the Roman occupation. Note how straight they were and how they linked the various main towns and military centres together.

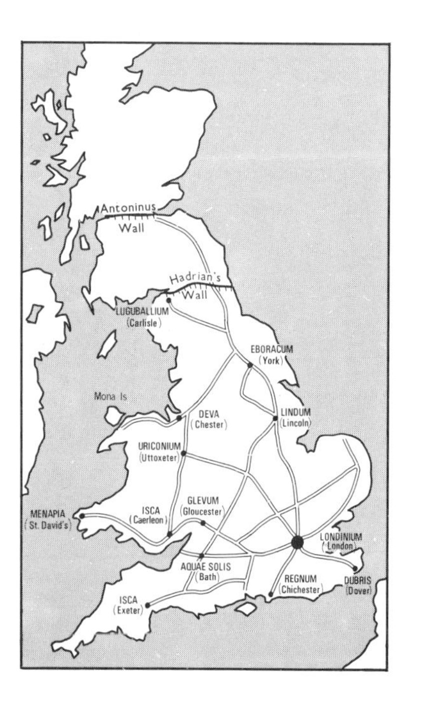

that you can still see at Silchester (p. 31). The building of thes roads was a wonderful feat of engineering when you remembe that the surveyors had no compasses or Ordnance Survey maps This is how they were planned.

To begin with, the road builders refused to be put off by natura difficulties. Hills, ravines, rivers and lakes were not thought of a obstacles. You merely cut through them, skirted them or bridge them. The route of a road was determined by standing at th top of rising ground and selecting the direction it would take Fast horsemen were sent off in a straight line, marking it of here and there, until they came to another bit of rising ground The engineers and road gangs followed behind. They dug out th earth and raised embankments about one and a half to two metre (five or six feet) high, to allow water to drain out. On top of th earth heap they laid a base of large stones, and on this they pu down the surface which might be crushed small stones or sla from iron mines.

We do not know how smooth the roads were, but they wer probably like an ordinary gravelled farm drive that has bee covered with a layer of hoggin (sifted gravel) and flattened b usage. It seems they were good enough to enable a four-wheele cart to travel fully laden, pulled by mules, at about eight kilometre (five miles) an hour. A fast-riding messenger on horseback however, could cover over twice the distance in an hour, whic meant he could get from London to York in a day. But he woul not be able to do this on one horse. He would change at regula intervals at staging posts along the roads.

Above: The ruins of a theatre at Verulamium. These were excavated in the 1930s and you can see them today, along with many other uncovered remains of buildings in this important Roman town.

Above right: an artist's reconstruction of the theatre at Verulamium. Most of the major Roman towns had theatres.

If you look at the road map of Roman Britain you will see it is a complex network, linking up a fair number of towns. These towns were not of course all built at the same time. Colchester (Camulodunum) was probably the earliest. St Albans was another early one. Caernarvon was later. These towns are interesting. They began as links in the road network, then became bases for Roman provincial organization.

Roman towns

Roman provincial organization rested on two main types of town, the colonial and the municipal. The colonial town was really a township created for retired soldiers. It was somewhere for troops, who had been paid off by victorious generals for their services in a war, to enjoy the rest of their days. Caesar, for example, created several colonies in north Africa (like Carthage), Greece (Corinth), Spain and Gaul for re-settling veteran troops, especially those who had fought with and for him in his Gallic campaigns and in the civil war that followed. These townships were usually walled, and the lands immediately outside were parcelled up and shared by the inhabitants. Perhaps you could liken a colonial township such as Colchester, Lincoln (Lindum) or Gloucester (Glevum) to a modern city or metropolitan council. The town had considerable self-governing powers, controlled by its own senate, or council, of elected men, a popular assembly, elected magistrates and so on, rather like Rome itself in miniature. One of the duties of the senate was to arrange for the collection of taxes for the procurator, for the capital of the empire was kept going largely on the revenue it drew from the provinces.

The other type of township, the municipality, was similar to a colony, but was not regarded by the Roman government as quite so important. Generally, the municipalities were smaller. St Albans (Verulamium), an early municipality, appears, over four hundred years, to have gone through several periods of prosperity interspersed with times of decline.

Outside the colonies and municipalities the country districts were divided into cantons and further broken down into pagi. These were what used to be rural district council areas, with villages and hamlets. In Britain they were left largely in the hands of the natives. Rural areas provided much of the food for the towns. Romans, of course, like us today, often wanted to get away from it all and go into the countryside on a fine weekend or for a few weeks after many months of work. So they had their country homes or villas. Remains of many of these can still be seen today. Excavations at Brading on the Isle of Wight and Bignor in Sussex have revealed fine examples.

Let us look briefly at the layout of a typical Roman town. The plan was a square, rectangle or polygon (like Silchester) with straight sides. The whole was surrounded by stone walling with turrets and gates here and there guarding bridges across a moat dug outside the wall. Some towns had only earth ramparts for walls. The gates were usually on the north, east, south and west sides.

Inside, the streets were arranged on a grid system, with main thoroughfares running through from north to south and east to west and crossing at the centre. This crossing point was the heart of the town. It was here that the main buildings, such as the forum, the basilica or town hall, local government offices, theatre, public baths, temple or temples, and even the odd hotel or guest house were situated.

This is a map of the Roman town of Calleva Atrebatum, now Silchester, near Reading, in Berkshire. From it you can see the kind of facilities Romans enjoyed in Britain during their occupation.

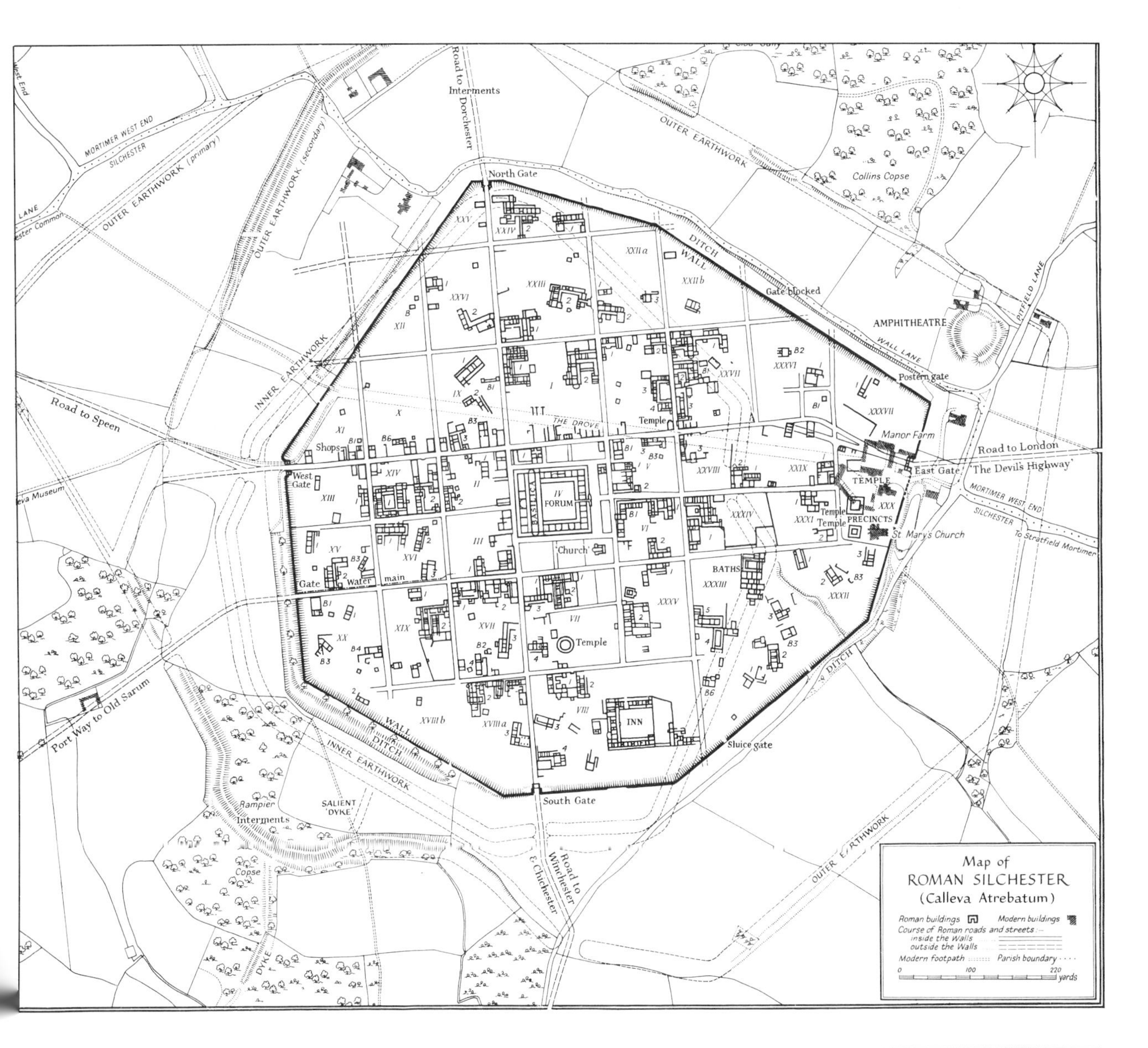

Here is an interesting aerial picture. It is of Calleva, and the ancient Roman street plan can be seen through the crops and grass of the fields of to-day.

The streets running off the centre of the main road axes had shops, houses and blocks of flats. Larger private houses standing in their own grounds were usually sited nearer the walls.

The forum was always the hub of any Roman city or town. It consisted of a square which was a public meeting place. The square would be flanked on two or three sides by colonnades of pillars. Sometimes a forum would have a splendid arch at one end as an entrance. This might be built to celebrate some great military event or commemorate an important man. In the forum at Rome, for instance, there are arches dedicated to the emperors Titus, Septimius Severus, and Constantine the Great.

Shops and houses

Roman shops were sometimes like our modern detached private garages, with one or two storeys under a gabled, tiled roof. The back part of the building might have living quarters either for the owner or for a family (possibly slaves) who managed it. The top storey was really an attic and was used for storage. These shops were put up in all parts of the town. The ones which sold goods likely to be needed by travellers stopping at the town would probably be nearer one or other of the gates.

Roman private houses were single- or double-storeyed, and they looked a little like modern bungalows with pitched roofs. A house was planned on a square. There were rooms on each side, and the middle of the square was usually an open courtyard with paved paths or patios and there was often a pond. In Italy, where it was much warmer than in Britain, the courtyards were small and the four sides often had extensions to the roof projecting inwards over large areas of the paving, to keep off the sun. But in Britain the Romans built their houses with larger courtyards to get what sun they could.

Roman houses were usually built of brick, but some were constructed using the rural technique of wattle and daub. Some villas have been found where the bottom walls were of brick and the top walls were of wattle. Presumably the outside of the

Above: Alan Sorrell, one of the most famous artists specializing in reconstructions of ancient buildings, drew this picture of Lullingstone Villa as it might have looked in about AD 350. Lullingstone Villa is near Eynsford in Kent. It was one of the larger Roman villas in Britain.

Above right: this is a mosaic floor at Lullingstone. It is called the Europa panel because it portrays the seizing of Europa by Jupiter, the king of the gods, who disguised himself as a bull to get her to sit on his back so that he might run off with her.

top storey looked something like those medieval half-timbered houses that are still to be seen at Tewkesbury in Gloucestershire, Lavenham in Suffolk or Thaxted in Essex.

One of the most interesting features of Roman houses was their flooring. In the lesser rooms such as bedrooms (which were not considered very important), floors were covered with a mixture of chalk, stone and tile chippings set in concrete. But the best public rooms had mosaic floors. There are some very picturesque examples from Roman times at Lullingstone, Bignor, Brading and Fishbourne.

Mosaic floors owe their patterns to an ordered assembly of tiny cubes of different coloured stone. These floors were prepared to look like woollen carpeting. The individual cubes, cut by hand and tapered into wedge shapes, were laid in position in a background of soft plaster of lime and plaster dust. When the plaster set, the stone surfaces were polished. There was a great variety of patterns. As floors like these could be very cold, they were, in most villas, heated from underneath.

Walls were covered with plaster, with or without decoration. The Romans were fond of painting nature scenes, animals, town views and so forth on their walls, in gay colours, with a strong leaning towards red shades. Windows were made with glass which often came in moulds from Gaul. It appears that windows were set high up in the wall, so that on darker days, ground floor rooms would be quite gloomy. For additional light a variety of oil lamps were used, some of which are in the British Museum.

Rooms were not extensively furnished. But in Roman times the furniture was more interesting, and better made, than that which our medieval ancestors had to live with. The Roman couch, for example, was a most graceful thing, with a scroll headboard, a bronze veneered, wooden framework with webbing to support a

A Roman couch, about 2000 years old, from Boscoreale in Italy. It looks uncomfortable, but it would have been covered with soft cushions, or a mattress if you wanted to lie down and go to sleep.

mattress, standing on four short legs. These were turned to look like candlesticks, or they might have been shaped like animal hooves or lions' paws. People reclined on couches a lot in their spare time. They even reclined at meal times and ate off metal or Samian pottery plates on broad low tables.

This Samian pottery was not only used for plates. In the better houses Samian ware was regarded for a long time as the best pottery you could own. It was reddish brown in colour, and at first had been made in northern Italy. As Roman civilization advanced westwards, potters in Gaul began to reproduce it, and for some time Romans in Britain imported the Gallic variety. Then, some potters in the Nene valley, near Peterborough in East Anglia, produced what is called castor ware, a pottery in copper or slate colour. The Romans in Britain came to prefer this to Samian ware. They decorated it by squeezing threads of clay round the article, like icing sugar, and firing it. This enabled them to produce all sorts of natural designs—hunting scenes, and so on. A similar ware was made in the New Forest.

The Romans introduced a variety of techniques of clay usage. They brought tile making to Britain, and specialized in what we call the pan-tile, which they used to clad the roofs of villas, shops and public buildings.

A stone relief of a Roman basket-work chair of the 3rd century AD. Basket-work chairs are still made and sold in many parts of the world, including Britain.

Roman baths

Some private houses had their own bath systems—that is, series of rooms producing different temperatures for bathing and washing. But for the most part, people went to public baths. Every town had at least one such building. It was a main meeting place for the community. It often contained games room, lounges for people to sit about in and talk, shops and restaurants. Some historians have said that the public bath was perhaps the most important building in Roman Britain. Whether it was or not, it was certainly an imposing structure. You approached it through a colonnaded courtyard leading to the entrance hall. Here you selected your attendant and perhaps paid your fee if

Some items of Samian ware found at Lullingstone.

Castor ware pottery was made in the Nene valley, in and near Peterborough. These pots and the lid are castor ware, and are now in the Colchester Museum.

there was one. You were escorted to the dressing rooms where you disrobed and handed your things to him. Then you wandered into the frigidarium or cold room, where you had a shivering splash down with cold water. This toned you up, ready for the next room, the tepidarium. Here you bathed in medium temperature water, which started off the business of getting you to perspire, opening up the pores of the skin. From there you walked on to the caldarium, or hot room, which was like a Turkish bath. A servant rubbed oil into your skin, and with a strigil (scraper) he removed the dirt which was literally sweated out of you. If you wanted a massage, you would have one in this room.

Then you wandered back to the frigidarium to have another cold water dowse. This got you ready to face the lower temperature outside. You might of course like to hang about a bit in the baths, discussing some point of law with a fellow advocate if you were a lawyer, or just picking up the latest gossip about the emperor Hadrian's new young boyfriend. You could lounge about on couches just as if you were in the foyer of a hotel or a modern hospital.

One of the best kept examples of Roman baths, using natural waters from local springs, is at Bath in Somerset. This picture shows one of the bath rooms, still in a good state of preservation.

How were the rooms heated? A furnace fired by burning wood was generated in an out-building. Warm air and steam passed through a flue leading into channels running under the marble or stone floors of the hot room which was on brick or stone stilts. The warm air rose up through the thickness of the hot room walls which were hollow, and escaped through chimneys. The tepidarium operated in the same way, the amount of heat being controlled by the thickness of the floor. This simple system operated as central heating in most larger Roman houses and villas in Britain. It was new to the British. It was not new to Rome. And indeed it had been employed by the Indus Indians in Mohenjo-Daro and Harappa in north-west India in about 2000 BC!

Clothes

After you had got yourself clean and played some games or discussed your business with your colleagues in the lounge, you got dressed again. What sort of clothes did you wear? If you were adult and free, you almost certainly wore a toga. This was made of white wool, and was a circular cloak which was wound round you in a particular way. Under your toga you wore a tunic, a sort of sleeveless long shirt, though Caesar's tunics always had sleeves with frilly ends. If you were a workman or stallholder, you wore a rough sort of tunic without a toga, and occasionally a hood. On your feet you wore sandals with a toga, and heavy leather shoes with nail studs with rougher clothes. If you lived in the highlands of Scotland you would probably refuse the benefits of Roman civilization, but you might enjoy wearing a Roman officer's red cloak and studded belt.

The toga was white and showed the dirt quickly. In those times laundry was done by fullers. A toga was put into a barrel of warm water and trodden down. Then it was washed with fuller's earth powder to remove all grease and oil. If it was particularly dirty, the launderers might put it over a bubbling vat of sulphur to be bleached by the fumes. Then it was rinsed in another vat.

These are traces of Roman box hedge beds. They are at Fishbourne Roman Palace near Chichester in Sussex.

Trades and crafts

We have seen that the Celts had their own craftsmen (page 22) and that men like carpenters and blacksmiths had full lives, not only making tools and instruments in their small communities but also travelling about the countryside carrying out commissions elsewhere. The coming of the Romans provided native craftsmen with a lot more work, if they were good. For although the Romans employed their own, they often did not have enough of them in the provinces. Blacksmiths were particularly in demand, to forge more weaponry and armour for the occupying forces, and also to make the hosts of tools needed by so many other craftsmen and labourers who were to get involved in the great engineering and building works. Think, for example, of the number of picks and shovels required for work on the great network of roads that was being constructed, many hundreds of kilometres of them, and on the forts, walls and other structures that were to transform the face of Celtic Britain. You can see the sort of tools that were

Here, box hedges have been planted in the tracks of the old Roman hedges at Fishbourne Roman Palace.

used in Roman times, and that in many cases they are not very different from those we use today. They even had to make garden tools, for the Romans introduced gardening into Britain. At the villa at Fishbourne there is a reconstruction of what the garden looked like two thousand years ago.

The Romans also introduced a variety of mechanical aids to get things done more quickly. One of these was the water pump. This was an arm rocking on a central pivot on a post. At each end of it was a lever with a piston at the other end which slid up and down a tube projecting into the source of water. The tubes had valves and when you moved one end of the arm down the other end came up, drawing water up the tube through the valve and into a discharge pipe. It was very simple. Another machine was a crane for lifting masonry and other heavy things. This was motivated by a treadmill which, when it was turned round, pulled ropes up over pulley wheels and lifted the load. The Romans even had water clocks which turned hour hands on dials.

The Roman countryside

So far we have looked at Roman Britain as it appeared to the town dweller of the time. Most Romans lived in, or just on the outskirts of, towns, and so far as they were concerned the countryside was there to serve the town—providing its corn, meat, clay and labour force. The Celts, however, were predominantly country people, and many never really got to like the new arrangement in Britain. They found there was little Rome could teach them about farming, except perhaps the use of a heavier and better cutting plough, the two-handled scythe and the iron-bladed digging spade. So, most of them tended to stay on the land in isolation or in very small communities, an arrangement the occupying power seemed happy to allow, in return for getting supplies for their towns.

The occupation, once the serious opposition was quelled and a general calm had settled on the land, brought the country folk much prosperity. The Roman troops were not the great meat-

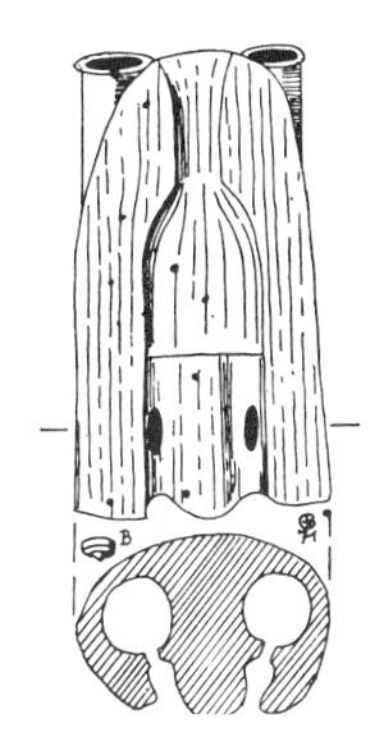

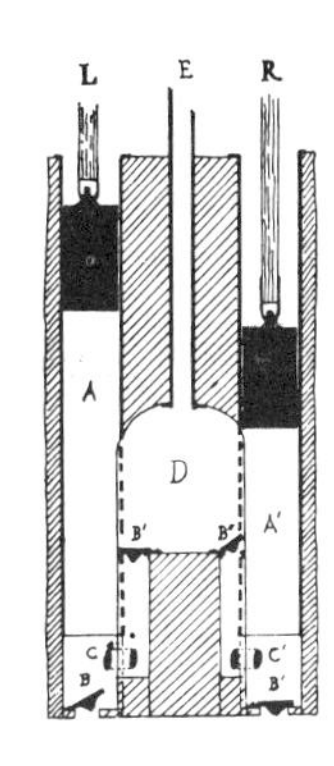

The left hand drawing is of a wooden force pump with lead cylinders, approximately as it was found at Calleva. The drawing at right is an illustration of what it would have looked like in section when in operation. Using the righthand diagram, this is how it worked: Pistons L and R were moved up and down alternately by a hand lever above. When piston L was lifted up cylinder A, water came up through valve B at the bottom into A. At the same time piston R pushed down cylinder A' which closed valve B' at the bottom and opened valve B' into the central reservoir D. This forced water up and through pipe E outwards. When piston L was pushed down valve B closed, water rushed into D and up through pipe E – and so on.
The cylinders in this pump were about 55 cm long and 7·5 cm in diameter. They probably delivered water at the rate of about 5 gallons a minute. It is thought that a pump like this would have been used to lift water from a ground floor tank to an overhead cistern for a bath house or for domestic uses.

eaters that the British are now—or indeed the Celts were then. They, like present-day Italians, ate a lot of pasta or corn-based pies, puddings, cakes and so forth. The cornfields were in great demand. So were hides for leather for all manner of uses—tents, shields, tunics, carrier bags, helmets, hats, and so on.

Another commodity produced in the country was wine. At first, wines for the Romans were imported from Gaul. But after the middle of the 3rd century wine growing was allowed in what is now England and it soon began to flourish in the south.

The growing demand for agricultural produce meant that British farmers had to become more efficient and more land had to be worked. In what is now East Anglia there was some of the most fertile ground in the whole country, in what we know as the Fens. These areas were often submerged beneath the sea or swollen rivers. So the Romans began to drain them by cutting canals. One is said to have been more than eighty kilometres (fifty miles) long, between Lincoln and the river Trent. On it barges carried corn from the rich fields to main centres. Perhaps, to visit someone in Leicestershire or Nottinghamshire, you might have 'thumbed a lift' on one of these barges. But in fact few seem to have used the water for passenger transport.

Transport

If you wanted to get from one place to another, there were various vehicles. Which one you took depended on the distance you wanted to go. In town, the Roman taxi was a *lectica*, or litter, rather like the 18th-century sedan chair, a portable covered chair for one, in a box carried on poles by two men. Caesar used one which had two seats. The second seat was often occupied by a secretary to whom he would dictate dispatches, letters, orders, perhaps even chapters of his famous eight-volume work on his war in Gaul. If you had luggage and wanted to go from, say, Ratae (Leicester) to Corinium (Cirencester), you might use a *roeda*, or four-wheeled wagon pulled by mules. Somewhat faster was the two-wheeled cart, also drawn by a mule. But as the Romans

An Alan Sorrell reconstruction of Roman London as it was in the 2nd century AD.

had not invented suspension, any journey was uncomfortable. So perhaps you did not travel unless you really had to.

Decline of the empire

In the 5th century the great Roman Empire in the west of Europe began to break up under continual and growing pressure of barbarian invasion from central and eastern Europe. The British outpost had itself been afflicted for years by raids from Angles, Saxons and Jutes from north-west Europe, who in turn were being pressed by other peoples from the east. By about 430 Roman administration had come to an end. For a generation, calls for help from the mother country of Italy had robbed Britain of its best Roman officers and men. In 410, the emperor Honorius had said that Britain could expect no more help from Italy. What followed is almost entirely lost to history.

Here and there over the next 150 years we know of isolated events, struggles, personalities, comings and goings of different invaders. But we cannot draw the whole picture. What is clear is that, despite 400 years of Roman occupation, the British seem to have been little influenced by Roman civilization. When the administration collapsed, the British were quite unable to fend for themselves. So it was not hard for the Jutes, the Saxons and the Angles to make inroads into the country and overturn most of what they found. They seem studiously to have ignored the road system and those splendid lines of communication became overgrown and ultimately lost. Nor did they bother much with the towns, which they often left in ruins. The inhabitants of the British Isles, whether Celt or Saxon, had perforce to learn all over again how to do many things. In this they were not alone. It was the fate of most of western Europe.

3 Anglo-Saxon England

There are great gaps in our knowledge of what happened in Britain for the hundred years or so after Roman administration broke down. But there were many events which were recorded, very briefly it is true, in that splendid calendar of early English history, the Anglo—Saxon Chronicle (see page 61). It tells how the Angles, the Jutes, and the Saxons took a long time to settle down in what is now England. In 449, a British king, Vortigern (which is probably a Celtic word for chief) begged the Jutish warrior brothers Hengist and Horsa to come over from Denmark to help him stop the Picts ravaging the south-east of the country. When they came they found they liked the land, but had little use for the Britons whom they considered 'worthless'. They stayed on, and invited more of their kinsman over from the continent. This was probably the first settlement. There were to be many others.

It took the invaders nearly two centuries to get established in England. By the first years of the seventh century, there were seven kingdoms—Kent, Sussex, Wessex, Mercia (Midlands), East Anglia, Bernicia and Deira (in the north-east). About two centuries later, these had been reduced to three—Wessex, Mercia and Northumbria, and by 900 the great Wessex King Alfred had emerged as overlord king of all Englishmen, except for those parts which were under Danish (Viking) domination. The Viking invasions and settlements (see page 55) had begun in about 787, and, despite the ferociousness of the invaders' attacks, proved in many ways beneficial to England. Indeed, one of their kings, Canute the Great, who was also ruler of Denmark, Norway and Sweden, turned out to be one of the best kings England ever had.

The six centuries of the Anglo–Saxon period were painful years, but they were illuminated by the spread of Christianity, the development of local government, the growth of the English legal system, and the expansion of trade and commerce. And the pages of their history were made more fascinating still by the careers of many remarkable men, such as Alfred the Great, Canute, St Dunstan, Bede, and, at the end of the period, Godwine of Wessex.

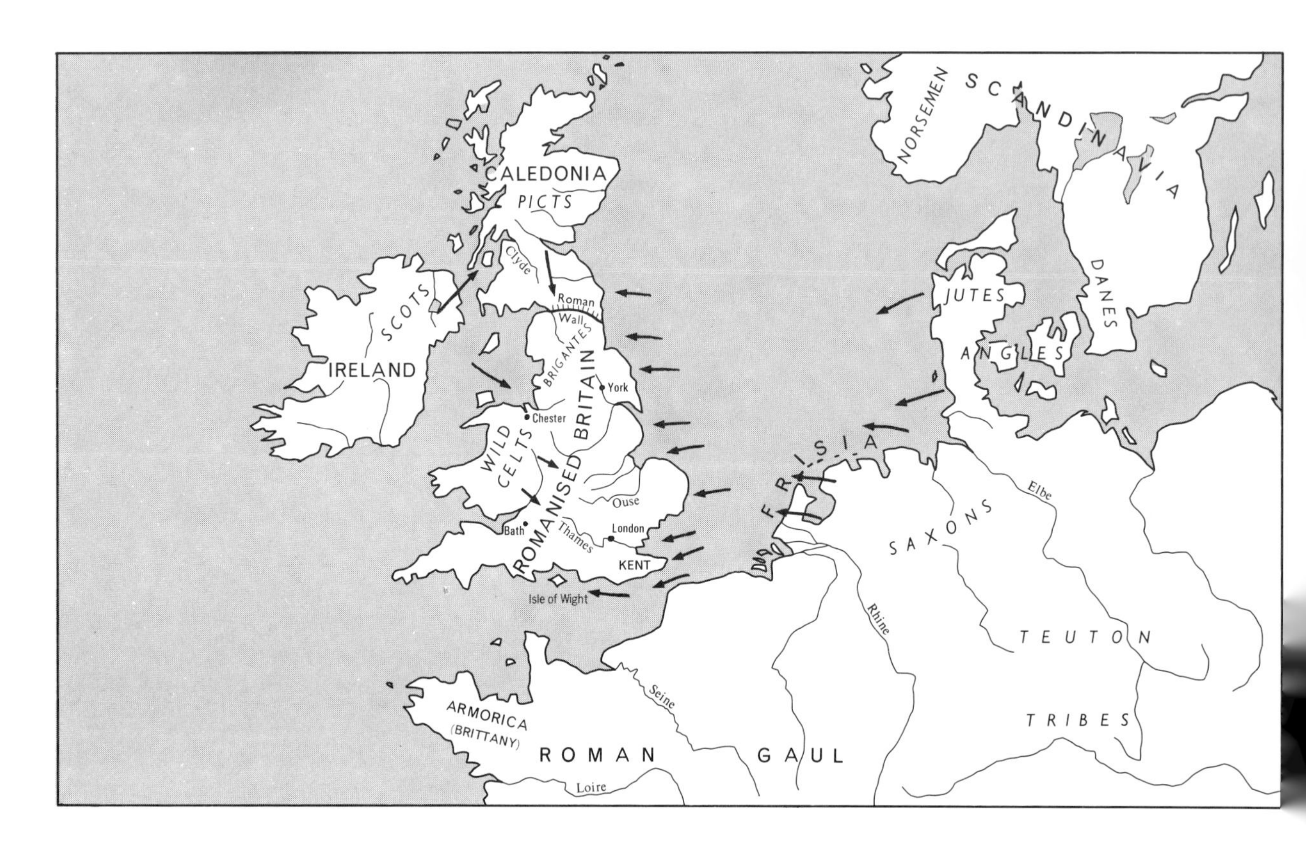

Roman Britain was invaded in the 5th century AD by Jutes from Denmark, Angles from south Denmark and Saxons from north-western Germany and Holland. At the same time Picts from the Highlands of Scotland and Gaelic Celts from Northern Ireland (called Scots) attacked Britain from north and west.

The political and military history of the time you can read in one or other of many excellent books (see page 251 for a list). This is how our Anglo–Saxon ancestors lived and managed their everyday business

The invaders

What sort of people were these Jutes, Saxons and Angles, who harried the shores of Britain and then decided to come here and live?

They were tallish men, taller than the British, and they were rugged-featured. About every other one coming up the Dover to

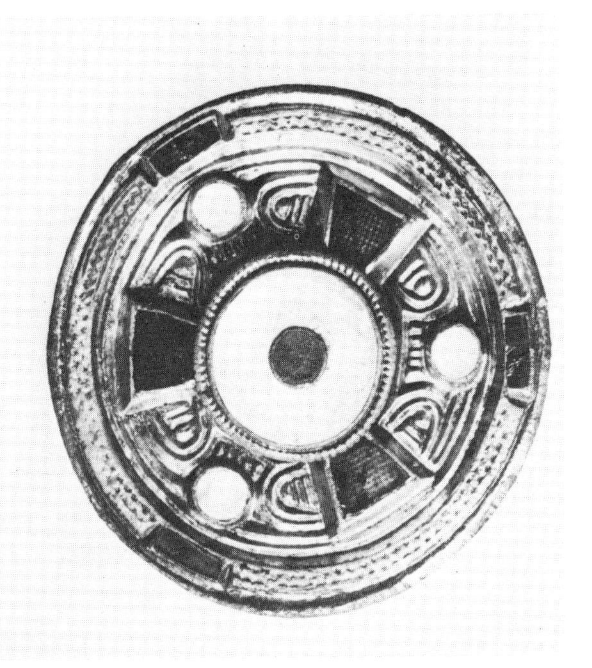

Two Anglo-Saxon brooches of the early 7th century AD found at Faversham in Kent.

London road would have blue eyes and flaxen hair, not unlike the Danes of today. But in fact if you were British you would probably not stay around long enough to see the colour of their eyes, for they were a very warlike people. They regarded fighting as the supreme activity for able-bodied men. It was degrading to work. They left that to the women, the old, and to weaklings who were unable to shoulder arms or ride horses into combat. Even the necessary business of providing food was too much like hard work. Either they stole food from a neighbour or an enemy, or actually fought for it. As a great authority has put it, the Saxon 'would rather challenge an enemy and be wounded than plough land and wait for the harvest.' But of course crops were grown, chiefly wheat and barley.

And when the men were not at war they would idle their time away drinking, often for prolonged periods, singing, gambling, quarrelling and challenging each other to duels, often fighting to the death. It is surprising to find that few Saxons ever bothered even to hunt wild animals either for food or for sport. But these strange people, who usually gathered in gangs around elected chiefs, were on the whole good to their wives and women-folk. They did not believe in having lots of wives or mistresses. Their homes were important to them, and so the people who cared for them had to be treated properly.

The Saxons wore very simple clothing, really just enough to keep out the cold in winter and to cover the body decently. The ordinary warrior sported a short cloak fastened by a brooch. Chiefs and wealthy men had tunics with fur trimming. Some had

Here is a map of England at the time of the Seven Kingdoms, that is, in the 7th and 8th centuries AD.

horses and they would travel everywhere on horseback.

Their people were not governed in the sense the Romans understood it. They were divided into tribes, each of which had its chief, its nobles (who were advisers and who probably got together to elect the chief), and a general assembly which anyone could attend, provided he was a warrior and had his own weapons. This assembly had quite extensive influence. It could overrule a decision made by the chief with his nobles in council. But it could not bring in ideas for the chief and council to act on. It could only take this vetoing action once the decision had been made.

These assemblies also used to deal with serious crimes on a kind of jury basis. The accused was heard by the whole assembly, a judgment was made and a sentence or acquittal pronounced. For some crimes, particularly those where the penalties were paying sums of money in compensation, the assemblies would delegate a group of their number to hear and decide.

These were the people who came over to Britain, some looking for new living space, for they were being pressed hard at home in Europe by other barbarian hordes like the Avars and the Huns. And when they came they made little effort to mix with the British people whose homeland it was. We do not know fully why this was so. Partly, of course, the British, who were Christian, had acquired at least a veneer of Roman civilization, were very jealous of their own language and culture, and did not want them here. From the beginning there was really very little cooperation between the invaders and the invaded. The Anglo–Saxon Chronicle tells us that Hengist and Horsa had helped Vortigern in 449, but by 455 they were fighting the British leader. In a battle at Aylesford, Horsa was slain, but the next line says that Hengist succeeded to the kingdom. So Vortigern perhaps was killed, too? Two years later Hengist defeated the Britons at Crayford and slew 4,000 of them. And in 465 Hengist was again fighting, this time against the Welsh in a battle when he slew twelve Welsh nobles. This is the sort of picture the Chronicle gives of the early years of the Anglo–Saxon invasions.

Another of Alan Sorrell's reconstructions, this is the king's palace at Cheddar in Somerset. It was probably one of the residences of King Athelstan (924–940), grandson of Alfred the Great, who was King of all England. The hall at right was possibly like the one mentioned in *Beowulf*.

Royal families

The chiefs who came over may have been no more than tough local gang leaders who commanded the respect of their immediate neighbours, but when they came to Britain they set themselves up as kings, possibly even forging a sort of family tree showing them to be descended from the gods, especially Woden, the Saxon king of the Gods. Hengist, for example, was said to have been the great-great-grandson of Woden. And Cerdic, king of the West Saxons, who came to Southampton in 495, was also a direct descendant of Woden.

Once the chief was accepted as king, the nobles were often glad enough to select a successor from the same family when he died. Even at that time they understood the advantages of continuity, though there was never any rule that the first-born should succeed.

As more chiefs came over and settled, there was of course more excuse for fighting, not only with the British (or Welsh, as they came to be called from the Saxon word *waelesc*, meaning foreigner) but also among themselves. By the middle of the 7th century Kent, East Anglia, Mercia, Northumbria and Wessex all had royal families. In these kingdoms the king wielded much power, though he could always be murdered by his followers. He might also be subservient to the next kingdom. For example, after about 730, the Kent kings were really no better than dependants of the rulers of Mercia or Wessex, whichever of these two happened to be in the ascendant.

Royal courts

The Saxon kings spent as much time fighting as anyone else, but when they were not at war, they set up splendid courts at which great feasts and drinking bouts were held. They entertained neighbouring chiefs on a grand scale. They provided them with gifts and mementos. They had bards who sang songs boasting of their prowess in war, or of their possessions. These feasts were held in substantial halls, which were made of wood and thatch. Halls became the centres of gatherings of buildings which in time grew into villages.

A Saxon hall, such as that mentioned in the famous poem *Beowulf*, was rectangular, tall and long, not unlike the great tithe barn at Bradford-on-Avon in Wiltshire. Around the main building were gathered a number of smaller ones, used as sleeping quarters, stores, stabling and so on. The building was made of timber posts hammered into a foundation trench and clamped together with iron bands. The posts might be round, square or semi-circular. The roof was steep-sloping and thatch-covered. To prevent the weight of the roof pushing the walls outwards, a row of buttresses was erected outside the walls.

Inside, the walls were lined with benches which were used for sitting, sleeping or storing things. Extra trestle tables were provided for meals. The walls might be hung with tapestries, some containing gold thread in the design.

This hall would be used for a multitude of things. The king would entertain there. He also had his own quarters at one end, called in later years a solar. Sometimes it would be used for council meetings or meetings of the assembly of the people. The other buildings provided all the things a community should have, such as a mill for the corn, an inn for rest and refreshment and, after the conversion to Christianity, a chapel. If the king felt his position was not entirely safe, he might dig a ditch and erect a wall or palisade round the whole group of buildings. There are some remains of such a hall at Yeavering in Northumberland.

We have been talking of Anglo–Saxon England up to the seventh century. Things began to change after that, due largely to the introduction of Christianity and to the new ideas and techniques which its believers brought over from Europe. Let us look at the part the Church played in Anglo–Saxon life.

The church and education

Today, many people believe in God and go to Church, if not regularly, at least several times a year, such as at Christmas, Easter, on Ascension Day, Whit Sunday and so on. Some people become priests. But the fact is the church in this century does not dominate our lives.

It was quite different in Anglo–Saxon England, after the conversion of the English to Christianity. The new religion pervaded everything. It also led to the introduction of many new things, he most important by far being education.

In 597, Saint Augustine came to Kent, with the blessing of Pope Gregory I, to establish a Christian church among the pagan English. It was no easy task. The English understood no Latin, and St Augustine and his followers did not know Anglo–Saxon. So he had to think of ways of getting his message across. He used music, chanting, and pictures of Christ, the Saints, and scenes from the Bible. Meanwhile, he began to learn their language. But he had also to persuade them to scrap their large catalogue of gods. One god only was allowed. He had to get them to use their existing

When Saint Augustine came to Kent in 597, to try to convert the pagan English to Christianity, he began his mission at Canterbury. There stood the ruins of a church built in Romano-British times, and it was in its shell that he held the first church services and blessings. Some time after his death, a stone chair was made which has been called St Augustine's Chair and which is now in Canterbury Cathedral.

The tomb of Bede, the celebrated scholar, in Durham Cathedral. You can also see something of the 'zig-zag' type design in the arches at Durham, which are of Norman origin.

temples as churches, and to make them remove all their idols, images and other paraphernalia dedicated to Woden, Thor, Tiw, Frigor and a host of others.

Augustine was greatly helped, however, by the fortunate fact that the wife of Ethelbert, the king of Kent, was herself a Christian. The kings of East Anglia and Essex of the time, moreover, were under-lords of his and would do what they were told. Possibly Augustine knew this before he came.

One of the vital things that these missionaries had to do was to establish places where children could be taught Christianity. They knew that it was one thing to convert a handful of enthusiastic adult Saxons who may have been looking for a new god anyway. It was quite another to bring up a whole new generation of people to accept the faith. So Augustine set up school rooms wherever he established a church or monastery. There, children between seven and eight years old were taken from their homes and brought up by the church authorities. They learned not only about Christianity but, what was more important still, they learned how to read and write. Imagine it – before Augustine came, only a handful of people in England anywhere could write a line.

Children were also taught Latin, and to converse and argue about religious and other matters. Some who were exceptionally bright were allowed to learn arithmetic, and even a little astronomy.

Over the next two centuries the church acquired a firm footing among the English. The people were not by any means converted overnight. And Christian kings were not always successful against their still pagan neighbours. Edwin of Northumbria, for example, was converted by Paulinus, an early bishop, in about 627. Six years later he was killed in battle against the pagan Penda, king of Mercia. The battle was so decisive that the Anglo–Saxon Chronicle says that Bishop Paulinus left Northumbria and settled in Kent where he was offered the bishopric of Rochester.

But in those two centuries nearly all the learning, poetry, historical writing, codifying of law, art, and book production, was produced by or under the direct sponsorship of the church. Canterbury, the capital of Ethelbert of Kent, became a centre for advanced studies, rather like a university. In time it also became the see of an archbishop. But Northumbria was to be the main centre of learning in England for about a hundred and fifty years, from about 630 to 780. There, the scholars and historians and their works were the wonder of Europe. Benedict Biscop founded two splendid monasteries, at Monkwearmouth and Jarrow. And it was at Jarrow that one of England's greatest scholars spent his whole academic life, the Venerable Bede (673–736). Biscop re-introduced stone building into the north, for the first time since Roman days, and his monasteries had glass in the windows.

These monasteries were equipped with the best books obtainable in Europe, and there the scholarly Bede trained a handful of almost equally clever young men, especially Egbert of York, to go out and spread learning.

One of Egbert's pupils was Alcuin, said to have become one of the brightest brains in Europe, who reorganized the educational system in the empire of the Frankish emperor Charlemagne.

It was not only in the north, however, that the church re-introduced stone for building. Brixworth church in Northampton-

Brixworth Minster, a parish church near Northampton, is perhaps the earliest – and certainly the finest – late 7th- early 8th-century Anglo-Saxon church architecture anywhere. Not all of the building is original, such as the spire and the roof over the nave, but the tower and turret are as they were in the 700s.

shire is thought to have been begun in the 7th century. Later Anglo–Saxon chapels were built largely of stone and flint rubble. The walls might be as much as a yard wide. One feature of design was what we call 'long and short work', that is, the stones on the outside angles of towers are set upright and horizontal alternately. Another feature was the triangular doorway. There were towers supporting church bells as early as about 950.

When they were building churches, the Christian builders also erected stone crosses here and there to mark the sites of important events, or as monuments to the dead. There is one surviving from Bewcastle near Hexham in Northumberland. It has scenes featuring John the Baptist carved into its main trunk. These crosses were not invented by the Anglo–Saxons. The Celtic Irish had been putting them up for many years.

Earl's Barton Church, also in Northamptonshire, is another good example of Anglo-Saxon architecture. This church and Brixworth, and a few others as well, show that the Anglo-Saxons certainly knew how to build in stone. Most of the tower in this picture is Anglo-Saxon. The battlements at the top are later.

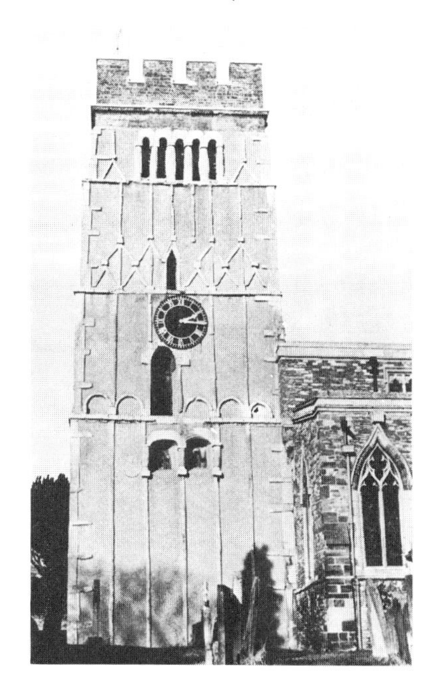

The law

We said that the church was responsible for making some kind of order out of the laws of the various kingdoms. Up to the arrival of St Augustine, none of the laws of the kingdoms had been written down, not surprisingly, for there was no-one who could do it. But within a few years of the beginning of the 7th century, Ethelbert of Kent's laws had in part been written down. They were not laws made by him, for the kings were guardians of the law and not law-makers. Rules of behaviour among tribes grew up more through habit and usage, and through the decisions of the council or the assemblies of the armsbearing people. In the same century King Ine of Wessex had his laws written down, and by the time of Alfred (871–900) there was a considerable collection of laws which needed codifying. This was to be one of the many contributions this splendid ruler made to his country.

The early laws established clearly the dominant position of the kings in Anglo–Saxon society. They defined the rights and privileges of freemen and they also set out the special position of the church and its staff. The penalties for offences against the

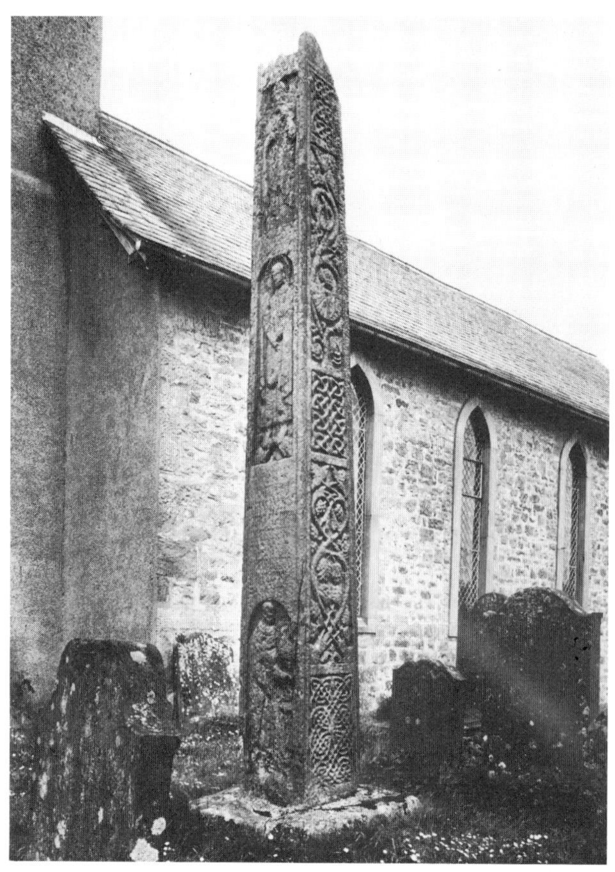

Above: an early Christian stone cross. This is in the churchyard at Bewcastle in Cumberland.

Above left: a variation of trial by ordeal. If the accused sank after the water had been exorcised by a priest, his innocence was considered divinely proved. If he floated, he was judged guilty.

king were severe. If you were caught brawling on his land or in any building belonging to him, you could lose all your possessions, or your life if he felt like it. Brawling on a Saxon noble's estate, however, might only cost you a fine of sixty shillings. The church had the same sort of protection as the kings. If you stole from the church you could be compelled to pay compensation up to twelve times the value of what you had stolen, whereas if it was from the king it would be up to nine times the amount.

Offenders brought to trial by local courts were likely to be put to what is known as trial by ordeal. There were three main kinds of ordeal. If you were a freeman, that is, not a slave or a villein, (you would probably be a thegn (noble) or a ceorl (free farmer or craftsman)), you would be expected to carry a burning hot iron rod for about three yards, or plunge your arm into boiling water up to the elbow to pick out a stone. If your injuries healed within three days, you were pronounced not guilty. If you were a villein, that is, a farmer who owed part of your working time to a ceorl or a thegn, or had to pay a food rent to a landlord, you would be bound and thrown into a pool of cold water. If you sank, you were declared innocent and, if you were lucky, they got you out before you drowned.

Members of the clergy were ordered to eat a piece of bread or cheese. If they choked they were adjudged guilty.

The administration of the country's law was for a long time very much a hit or miss business. The kings had great power, which they exercised through their nobles (gesiths as they were called at first, and later on, thegns), individually or through the council of nobles. These nobles were members, usually chairmen, of the local courts, and they could enforce the laws by exercising their delegated authority. What the kings tried to do was to make each local area, whether it was a village or a cluster of villages, responsible for peace and order in it. This collective responsibility went hand in hand with a spirit among villagers who worked together for the communal good.

Eighth-century administration

The eighth century was one of more rapid development in England. The Christian faith had become more or less universally accepted. There were numerous churches and monasteries up and down the land. Wessex and parts of southern and eastern England were already being divided into shires, which represented either the older and smaller kingdoms of Sussex, Essex, Kent, and so on, or the tribal regions like Norfolk and Suffolk (so-named from two main groupings of Angles who came over in about the 6th century, the north folk and the south folk). These shires were governed by ealdormen, who were thegns put in command by the kings. The ealdorman's responsibility was extensive, and his office gradually became hereditary.

By the end of the 800s, many of the shires were being divided into hundreds, with their own courts, called hundred moots. A moot was a meeting where local business was dealt with and local justice dispensed. If agreement could not be reached at a moot, the matter would be taken to the higher shire moot or court. The hundred moots met once a month.

The origin of the term hundred has not yet been accurately traced, but it is believed to mean 100 hides. This could be

An artist's impression of a Viking raid along the English coast in the 9th century. At first the Vikings came solely for plunder. Then, after a while, they decided to settle in Britain.

anything from 100 times forty acres to 100 times 100 acres of land. The hide, a basic measure of land determined by how much earth could be ploughed by one plough pulled by one team of oxen in one season, naturally varied from area to area. The soft and light earth of East Anglia was clearly easier and so quicker to plough than the heavier and more clay-bound earth of parts of Devonshire.

This progress in England, and the different but nonetheless interesting developments going on at the same time in Wales, Scotland and Ireland (page 124), were significantly interrupted toward the end of the 8th century by the Viking raids, the first of a series that were to afflict the whole British Isles for another two and a half centuries.

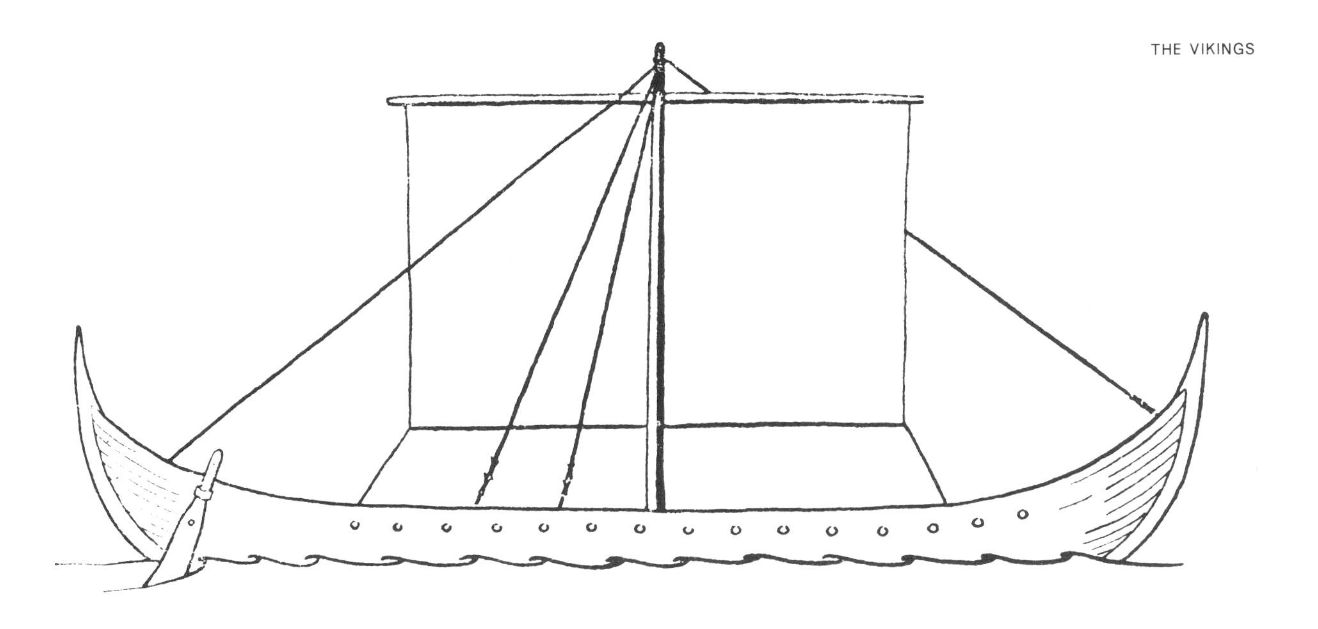

This is a simple drawing of what the famous 9th century Viking ship, called the Gokstad ship, looked like. Remains of it were found at Gokstad in Norway. It had been 23 metres (70 feet) long and 5·25 metres (16 feet) broad. Some seventy men were carried in it.

The Vikings

It is easy to write off the Vikings as savage marauders, burning and pillaging everywhere they went, with no thought for the future, no ideas and no positive contribution to make to the development of the lands they invaded. This is how they began, it is true, and the Chronicle is full of gloomy reports of the invaders' doings. In 787, '. . . came for the first time three ships. These were the first ships of the Danes to come to England'. In 793, '. . . the harrying of the heathen miserably destroyed God's Church in Lindisfarne, rapine and slaughter'. 794 saw '. . . Northumbria . . . ravaged by the heathen and Ecgfrith's monastery at Jarrow looted . . .'. Where did they come from?

The Vikings were fierce, bold, dauntless warriors who lived in Scandinavia, that is, Norway, Sweden and Denmark. They were known as the Northmen, and, setting out in their sleek, swift, high-prowed ships, they came unsuspected on churches and monasteries situated on off-shore islands, like Lindisfarne, on the coast or up rivers. They slew all who came against them and seized everything of value or use that they could find. Then they went home. For many years the coasts of the whole British Isles were subjected to these raids, some areas suffering more frequently than others. Although there were both Norwegians and Danes on these expeditions, it was the Danes who predominated. To begin with they came in small fleets of three or four ships. Then the fleets got bigger and, it is said, contained over three hundred men. This is probably what the Chronicle means when it talks about the 'host' visiting and storming Winchester in 860.

Statue of King Alfred the Great (871–901) by Sir Hamo Thornycroft at Winchester in Hampshire. It was put up 1000 years after the king's burial there. Alfred was without doubt the greatest king England has ever had in its long history.

By the middle of the 9th century the Vikings began to settle in England, chiefly in the Midlands, East Anglia, the North Country, and of course in Scotland, Wales and Ireland. They settled in well, and have left many traces of their particular civilization. Place names on or near the Yorkshire coast with *by* at the end, like Whitby and Wetherby, suggest Viking origin. Many of the words they used in everyday speech have become part of our language, words such as law, husband, anger, sky, although and fellow.

There has been much research into the story of these remarkable people—for remarkable they were. It was a Viking ship which actually sailed as far as Labrador, off the east Canadian coast, five hundred years before Columbus discovered the West Indies. And it seems that they were not anti-Christian. The monasteries were looted because that was where the riches lay. These were freedom-loving warriors who had the strictest regard for order, whose own society was governed by a severe but in many ways sensible system of laws. They were very hard workers, good builders and intelligent farmers. Their craftsmen were first rate, and their ship-building experience was second to none in all Europe. Such indeed was their nautical skill that they sailed via the rivers of Russia and east Europe right to the gates of Constantinople, down the Atlantic to north Africa, and even into the Mediterranean where they attacked and burnt the Lombard town of Pisa.

In 878, the Danes met their match in Alfred the Great who defeated a host of them at Slaughterford, near Chippenham, in Wiltshire. The victory was decisive, but Alfred, a generous victor, recognized the sort of contribution the Danes could make to England, and granted them leave to stay in an area they already occupied, which came to be called the Danelagh. This was a huge area between a line running from London to Chester up as far as the Tees in Durham. There, the Danes had their own laws, language and way of life, which gradually became merged with the longer-settled Anglo–Saxon model, so that by the middle of the 10th century the Danes were no longer an independent power in England.

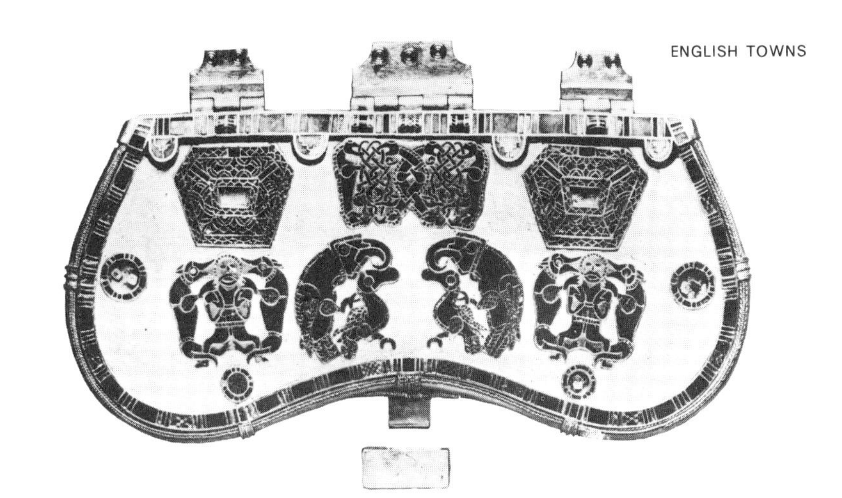

A fine purse lid, with gold decoration, inlaid with garnet stones and glass. This came from the Sutton Hoo burial ship, of the 7th century AD.

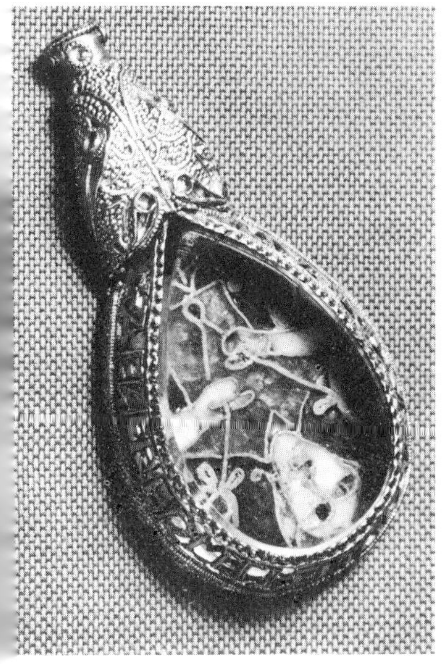

This is a remarkable piece of Anglo-Saxon jewellery. Called Alfred's Jewel because it has inscribed around it the phrase (in Anglo-Saxon) 'Alfred had me made', it is of gold, the portrait is of enamel and the cover crystal. It was found at Athelney in Somerset over 300 years ago. It was in Athelney marshes that young Alfred hid after a defeat by the Danes, and there he planned how he would mobilize the men of Wessex to avenge the defeat and bring the Danes to their knees. He accomplished this at Ethandune in 878, in one of the most glorious victories in English history.

Once the Vikings began to settle down, they started to fit in with English ways. Despite some differences, they lived much the same kind of town and village life as their neighbours.

English towns

The English had neglected many of the Roman towns they found when they came to Britain in the fifth and sixth centuries, but they used a number as well. Canterbury, for example, an early Roman colonial town, became Ethelbert of Kent's royal capital. Paulinus, who converted King Edwin of Northumbria, had a church at York, once the headquarters of the Roman administration in the northern half of Britain. And many towns of Roman origin are mentioned in the Anglo–Saxon Chronicle, such as Dorchester (in 639), Cirencester (577), Lincoln (627) and Colchester (921). London, a clearing house for trade and a sizeable port in Roman times, never lost its importance, and in 886 Alfred occupied it and handed it to a thegn to govern for him. The English built several new towns for themselves too, including Southampton, which was given a harbour, and a new small town near the old site of Verulamium (St Albans), some of which was constructed of the old stone and brick from Roman ruins.

The English towns were usually of three types, a burh (or borough as it came to be called), a port, and a caister. A borough was a town fortified by a bank and ditch, or a wooden wall. In some cases, such as Winchester, where it was on the site of a Roman town, the old walls would be re-built of stone. A port was a market town, perpetuated today in places like Littleport (Cambridgeshire), Newport (Essex) and Stockport (Cheshire). A caister was usually an old Roman town, for example Dorchester.

A coin of Offa, who was King of Mercia from 757 to 796. It is a silver penny, and was perhaps the first English coin to carry a portrait of a ruler. Offa ruled well, built a dyke between England and Wales to mark the border and keep the Welsh out, and made a name for himself in Europe.

Trade

These towns were important because they contained markets. Trading of all kinds was invariably done in markets, indeed it was not supposed to be done anywhere else, except on the king's own lands. The king would undertake to provide some kind of protection for traders and market places in return for a percentage of the takings from sales, whether these were in goods, as in the earlier days, or in coinage, when it became widely used after about 700. The variety of goods was very wide, but the biggest demand was for salt for preserving foods, fish, iron, pottery, pitch (for boat hulls, some types of roof, barrels, and so on), cattle, sheep, corn, eggs, wool, butter, vegetables, leather, clothes, and jewellery (the English were very fond of bright and colourful brooches, necklets, bracelets, and so on). These were brought into market by farmers, craftsmen and traders, and changed hands rapidly. There was also, at some of the more important towns like London, Southampton and Norwich, a big import and export business. English wool, hides, Cornish tin, silver and lead were sought by many European countries and by visiting Arab, Viking and Byzantine traders. In return, the English imported gold, dyes, wine in some quantity, ivory, sulphur and glass. Fur and timber were imported from Scandinavia, amber for decoration from Baltic lands, and weapons from Germany.

When the goods were not bartered, they were paid for with coins. By the time of Offa, King of Mercia (757–796), the English coinage had become limited to pennies with his portrait, with half and quarter pennies for change. Coins were not supposed to be minted anywhere except in recognized mint towns, and the dies were to be cut only in London from the time of Eadgar (969–976).

A silver penny of Canute (1016–1035). This was made at a mint in Maldon, ssex. Canute, who was also king of enmark and Norway where he is emembered as Canute the Great, was ne of the best rulers England has ad. Starting as little more than a eathen warrior interested only in avaging English coasts with his father weyn Forkbeard, he became a hristian, founded schools, ncouraged education, trade and griculture, and died, still hardly 40, evered by his subjects.

Villages

Meanwhile, the Anglo–Saxon village had been developing, too, into an economic and social unit. By the time of Ethelred the Unready (978–1016), in whose reign England was beset by a fresh and more savage bout of raids from the Danes, there were numerous villages scattered over the countryside. They were usually made up from a string of farms of small enclosed fields, or of arable areas laid out in large open fields. Beyond the land was the woodland and the scrub area. These were all clearly marked, either by man-made boundaries such as dug banks or grown hedges, or by natural features like streams, woodland edges and rises in the ground. The houses were dotted around a square or a less precise green, like Cavendish in Suffolk, or strung out in long streets like Ramsbury in Wiltshire. The roads, paths and lanes were protected here and there by hurdle gates and fences, for one ever-present menace was the wild wolf which could in a night destroy a great deal of livestock—hens, sheep or young cattle. Some villages had additional lanes behind the rows of cottages, and this practice is perpetuated in the name Back Lane found today in many villages. These lanes were for protection against wild animals, especially wolves.

Everyday life

What kind of houses did our Anglo–Saxon ancestors occupy? They were excellent thatchers and could use stone and flint. But they were not used to working with brick. We have briefly described a king's hall, on page 45. The smaller house may have had stone foundations, and perhaps a stone wall, up as high as the first metre (three or four feet) or so, but the usual construction was of timber, like the medieval barns outlined in chapter 5. The houses were simple. They were shared by humans and animals, separated only by low walls like pens in pigsties today. Heating

Above left: Near Bury St Edmunds in Suffolk, some archaeological students have been reconstructing simple one-room dwellings of Anglo-Saxon design, with tree trunks and thatch covering a wide pit in the earth. This is the kind of home in which it is thought an Anglo-Saxon peasant farmer lived.

Above right: the Anglo-Saxons knew how to make glass, and this is a surviving example of a beaker with no base, called a cone beaker. It comes from the Norwich Castle Museum.

Opposite below: a page from the famous Anglo-Saxon Chronicle. This amazing work of the history of Britain from Julius Caesar to the 5th century AD and thenceforth of England until 1154, was started by Alfred the Great. There is more than one version of the text: this one is in the British Museum. No other country in Europe has its early history so well documented as this. It is but one more of the legion of accomplishments for which all English people have reason to thank Alfred.

such as it was came from a fire in the middle of the floor and th smoke went upwards to find its way out of whatever window openings there were, or a hole in the ceiling which in winter o in rain had to be covered. All the meals were cooked over thi fire. Probably a house smelled all the time rather like the kitchen in a modern home after someone has left the joint in the oven gone out for the afternoon and forgotten to turn the oven of

The English had hardly any furniture, and slept on the floor o rushes or hides. But they had quite an assortment of pottery an glass utensils and ornaments. Pottery was made by hand at first but in the 8th century the potter's wheel arrived in England afte centuries of absence, and this led to a great increase in manufac ture. The English made and imported a lot of glassware. It wa usually coloured, blue, green or amber, and was often decorate in very attractive styles. Some cups had spidery threads on th bowl outside, rather like the Romano–British castor ware potter (page 35). Apparently few glasses were made to stand uprigh which meant you either had to hold them in your hand all th time or throw back the drink in one or two gulps and then pu them down.

Alfred, who, along with all his many other skills was a inventor, introduced a lantern. Candles were known, but it was h who had them enclosed in wooden frames panelled with thi translucent sheets of ox-horn. He also invented the candle clock, candle marked with divisions to last four hours. When one ha reached the bottom, another was lit, and so on, and when six ha been consumed, another day had passed.

Above right: King Alfred invented ox-horn lanterns. None of these is known to have survived, but the metal lanterns in the picture, of the 13th century, had an ox-horn panel in the empty side.

Above left: an 18th-century engraving of what the ruins of Glastonbury Abbey in Somerset looked like then. Since that time more of the buildings have deteriorated, but it is possible to see how big an abbey it once was.

lfred and the church

n the 9th century the church suffered a decline in its great vigour nd drive, largely through the depressing effects of the Viking aids. It must have been terrible, for example, to have lived and vorked at the monastery at Jarrow, the very centre of learning n England, during the Viking descents. How grievous it must ave been to see all those manuscripts, so lovingly copied and luminated, flung out of the windows or into the fire, along with recious carvings of wood or stone, jewelled chalices and crucifixes nd so forth. Years of devoted skill would be destroyed in an istant. You would need the highest endurance to create these iings all over again, knowing that your monastery could—and robably would—be raided again. We shall never know how much f Alcuin's famous library was destroyed.

But if the church relinquished its dominion over education in ngland, it was not allowed to die, for Alfred saved it. He injected ew life into it. He organized new translations of valuable works ito English, actually writing some of them himself, so that more eople, especially young people, could learn to read and to under-tand a little more about the world outside, past and present. e gathered round him many of the leading scholars of the day, nglish, Welsh and Irish—and some Europeans, too. And the esult was more books, lives of saints, text books, translations of ede's *Ecclesiastical History of England* and Latin classics. His xample spurred on a revival of enthusiasm in the monasteries, id once more the church dominated the education of Englishmen.

This early Anglo-Saxon church, in Wiltshire, is St Lawrence's, Bradford-upon-Avon.

William the Conqueror

Some time in the reign of Edward the Confessor (1042–1066), Harold, son of Godwine, Earl of Wessex, who was the king's most powerful noble, was shipwrecked off the French coast and brought to William, Duke of Normandy. William said that Edward had promised to name him heir to the English throne, and he ordered Harold to swear an oath promising to help him succeed when the old king died. Harold did so, probably under pressure, and was released.

In January 1066, Edward died, and at once the English Council elected Harold king. He was not of the blood royal, but he was a strong and determined leader, such as England needed at the time as the nation was threatened by a Norwegian Viking invasion led by Harold's brother Tostig and the king of Norway, Hardraada. When William heard of Harold's betrayal—as he saw it—he planned an invasion to stake his claim, and in October, a few days after Harold had defeated his brother and Hardraada at Stamford Bridge in Yorkshire, William set sail and landed at Pevensey in Sussex. Harold came racing down the length of England and reached the Sussex downs about a week later, to do battle. But his men were tired, and William had had time to prepare a strong beachhead and train his men. On 14th October a great battle was fought which William won decisively. Its results were no less than the transformation of England and its society.

4 Norman England

When the Viking Normans conquered England in the years following the battle of Hastings, in 1066, they brought about a decisive change in the social structure of the land. Their chief, Duke William of Normandy, known to us as the Conqueror, was a conqueror indeed, and few men in history have overrun a country and so completely bent its people to his ways. The structure he built lasted for centuries, but it could only work under strong and determined kings, such as his sons William II (Rufus) and Henry I (Beauclerc), and it had to be modified from time to time by legal and administrative changes such as those introduced by, or in the times of, Henry II (Curtmantle), John (Lackland) and Edward I (Longshanks).

The structure was based on the feudal system, not itself something new to Anglo–Saxon England. It was Duke William's interpretation of feudalism that was new. And it was, above all, the way in which every man in the kingdom, high and low, was honour-bound to serve William that ensured its smooth operation.

The Normans

Where did these Normans come from? They were descendants of Viking warriors led by a chief, Rollo, who settled in northern France in the 10th century. This band of warriors had been granted land in the hope that they would settle down, and perhaps prevent more of their warlike comrades descending on France. They were expected to recognize the kings of France as overlords.

They very soon got accustomed to French ways. They learned and used the French language (which was somewhat different from modern French), they adopted many French habits, and they became Christians. But they were also tough and disciplined warriors and built up a powerful army of cavalry and foot soldiers. They learned all about building and became very skilled at it, particularly in the use of stone. Stone from Caen (known as ashlar) was used for dressing in many cathedrals and castles. They proved to be good businessmen too, with a remarkable grasp of trading conditions throughout most of Europe.

A coin of William I. It was probably designed by an artist called Theoderic. Its date is 1068 and it is now in the National Portrait Gallery.

In the middle of the eleventh century these Normans had the good fortune to be led by one of the most masterful men in European history, William.

William

Once William had decided, he planned his campaign with great thoroughness. He got the support of the Pope on the grounds that he would, if successful, bring the English church more into line with Roman religious teaching and practice. He secured the support of a number of rich and adventurous earls and barons in Europe, chiefly, though not entirely, Norman, by offering them lands in England in return for their help. He trained his cavalry and his

This Bayeux Tapestry panel shows Norman knights and archers rushing in against the Anglo-Saxons at Hastings.

archers relentlessly for months in advance, so that they would be equipped to match anything the English could marshal against them. He even had wooden forts prefabricated in Normandy, to be shipped to England once he had made a beachhead and occupied some land. These forts were to be put on the tops of small natural hills or mounds of earth built by his teams of diggers—or Englishmen if he could force them to work for him. This was the beginning of a programme of castle building by the Normans once they had conquered England.

Above all, William had a clear idea of the system of government and the order of society he intended to impose on England—his brand of feudalism. And in October 1066 he made a successful landing in Sussex, and defeated the English army in a glorious victory in which King Harold and the flower of his nobles were slain. The way was clear for William to change the face of the country.

Norman feudalism

What was feudalism? To begin with, the word was not coined until the 16th century, by which time the system it described had virtually disappeared in England. (It had not disappeared in France, Russia and many other lands.) It came from the Latin *feudum*, meaning tenure of land. That is what the system was based on, a holding of land in return for which you gave the owner services of one kind or another. In the unsettled days of the 7th, 8th and 9th centuries in Europe, following the collapse of law and order when the western Roman Empire fell to the barbarians, men used to make agreements with one another to guarantee their mutual security. An owner of land, for example, would offer a portion of it to a man who had none, or perhaps very little, and ask in return a promise to fight with him if he was attacked by a neighbouring landowner. Europe was full of people parcelling out land for themselves, either peacefully or by force, and there were always enough men around who had no interest in farming and who lived from day to day by wielding a sword for someone else. Gradually, kingdoms large and small grew up, kings were elected or seized power, or were deposed or assassinated and new ones took their place. The hereditary principle did not take root at once.

The kings—and the bigger landowners whom we shall call lords—found that the best type of man to hire for their defence was the armed cavalryman, an expert horseman who could fight while still in the stirrups. Later on, these men were known as chevaliers or knights. But they were not cheap to hire or train, to clothe or equip. And swift horses were expensive, too, so there were not many kings or lords who could afford to employ a troop of cavalry. What was much worse, the knights were often aimless and irresponsible men who cared for nothing except fighting. When they were not fighting for a king in some war the justification for which they never questioned, they would fight among themselves. Their loyalties, too, were shallow, and sometimes non-existent. It was only in the time of a strong king like Charlemagne or Otto the Great or William that it was possible to get them to serve in any way, and it was done by offering them land. The knights swore oaths to serve the king, or the lords, in return for land and in the right hands these contracts were kept. This arrangement was called vassalage, and a lord was obliged to help a vassal if the latter were attacked from outside. The vassal, for his part, had to wait on his lord at court. The land given to a vassal by a lord was called a fief, and at first the land was held only during the vassal's lifetime. It reverted to the lord on the vassal's death. Eventually, however, the practice of passing the land on to a son was allowed, but the son also inherited the obligations of service to the lord. If there was no son or heir, the lord got the land back. He also got it back if the vassal proved treacherous—as some did.

The arrangement was, as you can see, a reciprocal one. There were privileges and obligations on both sides. In the hands of a masterful lord like William, the lord and vassal compact could be extremely effective. In his case he looked after them both, but in return he demanded forty days a year service in the army, but only for the protection of his duchy. He also extracted an oath

The two volumes of the famous Domesday Book. They were re-bound by the Public Record Office not long ago. The smaller volume contains the survey returns for Norfolk, Suffolk and Essex, written in one column. The larger volume, written in two columns, has all the remaining parts of England except counties and areas in the extreme north.

from both lord and vassal that they would be faithful to him first. And when he brought them all over to England, he gave them their lands as rewards—with the English peasants and serfs on them as well. He reinforced his control by making everyone on the social scale swear loyalty to him first. In this respect, he was different, and more positive, than the European kings and lords who did not bind their tenants tightly enough to them.

William now used a number of devices to consolidate his newly-won kingdom, and to keep bound to him his own followers, the Anglo–Saxon lords (there were not many of them left), the tenants and the serfs, in other words, to enforce his feudal system. He organized a vast survey of nearly all the land in England. This came to be known as the Domesday Book. At the Oath of Salisbury he made all his lords and many of their vassals publicly swear fealty to him, and so confirm the arrangement whereby he came first. He took over all the manors and villages in England. And he built castles at strategic points up and down the country. These were to garrison troops and police, to keep order and to frighten the peasantry into submission. And in order to prevent his own lords from rebelling, he carefully gave them their lands broken up into estates scattered far and wide. The lands on the east and south coast went to his close friends and relatives. These men could be most relied on to help resist any invasion which, if it came, would most likely occur in these areas. But no lord had all his lands together, which meant that if he was disposed to rebel and summon the aid of all his vassals and tenants, it would be quite a job to get them all together before William heard about it and put a stop to it.

7 viii. uitti 7 iii. bord cu̅ .i. car. Ibi .ii. serui. 7 vi. pars molini. 7 tcia pars alteri molini. 7 x. ac̅ p̅ti. 7 de pasnag 7 de herbag. xiii. porc. De molin. vi. sol 7 dimid.
T.R.E. 7 m̅. ualt. lx. sol. Cu̅ recep: l. solid.

Nigellus ten̅ de ep̅o COTELESHAM. Anfrigus tenuit de rege. E. Te 7 m̅ se defd̅ p̅ v. hid. Tra. e̅ .iiii. car. In dn̅io sunt .ii. car. 7 iii. uitti 7 iiii. bord 7 ii. serui. Ibi eccta. 7 ii. ac̅ p̅ti. Silua: de .iii. porc.
T.R.E. ualb .iii. lib. 7 post: l. sol. Modo: iiii. lib.

Hugo de port ten̅ de ep̅o BEROE. Tres libi hoes tenuer. 7 quo uoluer ire potuer. Te se defd̅ p̅ v. hid. Modo p̅ .ii. hid 7 dim. H .iii. maner ten̅ hugo p̅ uno m̅. In Waleton hund appciatu̅ e̅. IN AMELEBRIGE HUND.

Isde̅ hugo ten̅ de ep̅o .i. hida in ~~Aissela~~ libam 7 qda̅ femina de eo. Ibi .e̅ un̅ uitts. Val. v. sol. Xdo hugo hanc tra̅ saisiuit. non habuit inde libatore̅ uel breue̅ regis. sic hund testat.

Herfrid ten̅ de ep̅o WERPESDONE. Duę sorores tenuer. T.R.E. 7 quo uoluer cu̅ tra se uertere potuer. Te se defd̅ p̅ .iiii. hid. modo p̅ .ii. hid. Ibi .e̅ un̅ uitts. 7 i. bord. 7 xvi. ac̅ p̅ti. Silua: de .v. porc. Val 7 ualuit .xl. sol. Xdo ep̅s hanc tra̅ saisiuit: libatore̅ t breue̅ regis inde n̅ habuer. sic hund testat.

Wadard ten̅ de ep̅o DITONE. IN CHINGESTUN HUND. Leuegar tenuit de heraldo. 7 seruiebat ei. s; quo uoluisset cu̅ tra ire potuisset. Xdo obiit. hanc tra̅ trib; filiis suis dispti uit. T.R.E. Te se defd̅ p̅ vi. hid. modo p̅ .ii. hid 7 dim. Tra. e̅ .ii. car. Ibi .e̅ car 7 dim. 7 iii. bord. 7 iiii. serui. 7 pars molini de .xv. den. 7 iii. ac̅ p̅ti. Silua: xx. porc.
T.R.E. ualb .iiii. lib. 7 post: xl. sol. Modo: iiii. lib. Ille q̅ ten̅ de Wadardo: redd ei .l. sol. 7 seruitiu̅ uni militis.

Ipse ep̅s h̅t in SUDWERCHE un̅ monasteriu̅ 7 un̅ aque fluctu̅. Rex .E. teneb die qua mortuus fuit. Qui ecctam habebat: de rege tenebat. De exitu aque ubi naues applicabant: rex habeb .ii. partes. Goduin tcia. Testant u̅ hoes de hund franci 7 angli. qd ep̅s baiocsis cu̅ Rannulfo uicec de his placitu̅ inierit. sed ille intelligens placitu̅ n̅ duci p̅ rectitudine̅ ad p̅ficiu̅ regis. placitu̅ deseruit. Ep̅s aut̅ ded ecctam 7 fluctu̅ primu̅ Adeloldo. deinde Radulfo p̅ excabio uni dom. Vicecomes q̅q; negat se p̅ceptu̅ uel sigillu̅ regis de hac re unq̅ p̅cepisse. Hoes de Suduuerca testant. qd T.R.E. null capieb thelo neu̅ in strande t in uico aque. nisi rex. 7 siqs forisfaciens ibi calu̅pniat fuisset: regi emdabat. Si u̅ non calu̅pniatus abiisset sub eo qui saca 7 soca̅ habuisset: ille emdam habebat. Ipsi hoes de Suduuerche deprecati sunt una̅ haga̅ 7 the loneu̅ ei̅ ad firma̅ de Chingestone. hanc Eustachius com teneb. Qd rex ht in Suduuerche: appciat .xvi. lib.

In Wodetone hund 7 in m̅ Sudtone habet ep̅s baiocsis .ii. hid 7 dim. Brixsi tenuit T.R.E. 7 quolut ire potuit. Te se defd̅ p̅ .ii. hid 7 dim. modo p̅ nichilo. H appciata 7 annumerata sunt in Brunlei m̅ ep̅i.

VI. TERRA ECCLE WESTMONAST. IN BRICSISTAN HD.

Scs PETRUS de Westmonast. ten̅ PATRICESY. Herald com tenuit. Te se defd̅ p̅ lxx .ii. hid. 7 m̅ p̅ xviii. hid. Tra. e̅ In dn̅io sunt .iii. car. 7 xl v. uitti 7 xvi. bord cu̅ xiiii. car. Ibi .viii. serui. 7 vii. molini de .xl .ii. lib. 7 ix. sol. 7 viii. den. aut frumtu̅ eide̅ p̅cii. 7 qt xx. 7 ii. ac̅ p̅ti. 7 Silua: de .l. porc de pasnag. In Suduuerche .i. bord de .xii. den. De theloneo Wandelesorde .vi. lib. De uitto hnte .x. porc. un̅ porc. Si min̅: nil dat.
De tra hui m̅ ten̅ un̅ miles .iii. hid. Ei pecunia co̅putat supius cu̅ alia. 7 x. sol. 7 viii. den.
Tot T.R.E. ualeb q̅ter .xx. lib. 7 post: xxx. lib. Modo: lxxx. lib.
Hoc m̅ ded rex .W. sco petro p̅ excabio de Wandelesorde.
De tra hui m̅ ten̅ com moriton .i. hid 7 dimid. quę ibi erat T.R.E. 7 post aliqua̅diu. Gislebt p̅br ten̅ .iii. hid. eod m̅ fuerunt. Ep̅s Lisoiensis .ii. hid. de q̅b; fuit eccta saisita T.R. Witti. 7 post desaisiuit ea̅ ep̅s baiocsis.
Abb de Certesi ten̅ una̅ hid. qua̅ p̅fect uille hui p̅pt inimicitia̅ qda̅ ab isto m̅ abstulit. 7 misit in Certesi.

Ipsa abbatia de Westmonast ten̅ IN WALETONE HD. MORDONE. T.R.E. se defd̅ p̅ xii. hid. modo p̅ .iii. hid. Tra. e̅ In dn̅io sunt .iii. car. 7 viii. uitti 7 v. cot cu̅ .iii. car. Ibi un̅ seruus. 7 un̅ molin̅ de .xl. solid.
T.R.E. ualb .vi. lib. Modo .x. lib. 7 tam̅ redd .xv. lib.

Ipsa abbatia ten̅ CLAIGATE. IN CHINGESTUN HD. T.R.E. se defd̅ p̅ .ii. hid 7 dim. m̅ p̅ dim hida. Tra. e̅ .ii. car. In dn̅io est una. 7 iii. uitti 7 ii. bord. cu̅ una car. Ibi .v. ac̅ p̅ti. Silua: de .i. porc. T.R.E. ualb .xl. sol. Modo: l. sol.

Ipsa abbatia ten̅ TOTINGES. IN BRICSISTAN HUND. Suam tenuit de rege .E. 7 defd se p̅ .iii. hid. Tra. e̅ .i. car 7 dimid. Ibi sunt .ii. uitti cu̅ dim car. 7 iii. ac̅ p̅ti.
T.R.E. 7 m̅: ual .xl. sol. Cu̅ recep: xx. sol.
Hanc tra̅ accep Wallef com de Suan. p̅ morte regis .E. 7 inuadiauit p̅ .ii. mark auri Alnodo lundoniensi. Qui co̅cessit s̅ petro p̅ sua anima. scilicet qd ibi habeb. Osbert ten̅ de s̅ petro. 7 nichil redd p̅ geldo.

Ipsa abbatia ten̅ PETEFORDE. IN GODELEI HUND. Herald tenuit de rege .E. Antequa̅ herald habuisset. defd se p̅ xx vii. hid. Postq̅ habuit: p̅ xvi. hid. ad libitu̅ heraldi. Hoes de hund nunq̅ audier nec uider breue̅ ex parte regis qui ad tant posuisset. Tra: xiii. car. Modo geld p̅ viii. hid.
In dn̅io .e̅ una car. 7 xxx vii. uitti 7 xiiii. bord cu̅ vi. car. Ibi .iii. serui. 7 ii. molini de .x. sol. 7 xv. ac̅ p̅ti. De pasnagio 7 herbagio: qt xx. porc.
T.R.E. ualb .xii. lib. 7 post: x. lib. Modo: xviii. lib.
De hac tra. h̅t rex .iii. hidas in foresta sua.

VII. TERRA SCI PETRI WINTON. IN WALETONE HUND.

ABBATIA SCI PETRI WINTON. ten̅ SANDESTEDE. T.R.E. se defd̅ p̅ xviii. hid. m̅ p̅ v. hid. Tra e̅ .x. car. In dn̅io .e̅ una. 7 xxi. uitti 7 un̅ cot cu̅ viii. car.

As for the Anglo–Saxon lords, their lands were generally confiscated. A few joined their conquerors and were allowed to keep them. More were reduced to much humbler positions. One or two, like Waltheof and Hereward, rebelled. Waltheof was caught and executed; Hereward was spared after giving William a lot of trouble in the Fens of East Anglia.

Let us look at the main devices William used, for they affected everyone in the land.

The Domesday Book

This great survey is said to have been called the Domesday survey because many people resented it and regarded it as heralding the Day of Judgment. It was by any standards a remarkable administrative undertaking. For an age in which more than nine-tenths of the population were illiterate (even William himself could not write) it was amazing in its thoroughness. It was no less than an assessment of the land and agricultural resources of the whole nation (barring Cumberland, Westmoreland and Northumberland, which were considered too wild to be worth surveying!). Special commissioners were sent out to every shire, where at the shire court every owner of land was asked a lot of questions. The answers supplied details of every hundred and every village. What was the name of this or that village? Who owned it in 1066? To whom did the Conqueror give it after Hastings? Who owns it now? How many hides had it in 1066? How many now? How much woodland and pasture land is there? Has it any water mills or fishponds? How many ploughing teams work on this or that stretch? How many people live in it? What livestock do they possess?

All these and many more were asked time and again as the procession of owners went through. The answers were given on oath and recorded in Latin by tireless clerks scribbling away on rolls of parchment. In some cases the answers were put to special juries for verification. It was more thorough-going even than a 20th-century census.

This is a page from the larger volume of the Domesday Book. It relates to properties in Surrey (Sudrie). Some of the names are familiar.

Castles

The programme of castle-building was another device. William did not introduce the motte-and-bailey kind of castle into England. This had been brought over by some Norman lords, invited to live in England by Edward the Confessor (1042–1066). But William and his lords put up a veritable network of them all round the country, in such places as York, Lincoln, Norwich, Oxford and Dover. It is thought that at least a hundred had been erected by the year 1100.

The motte-and-bailey was a mound of earth surrounded by a strong wooden fence made of sharp timbers side by side, anchored every so often by a stout wooden pillar. There was a ditch round the outside of the fence. On the top of the mound (the motte) was erected a wooden fort with a look-out tower. This was not very big and it was not meant for people to live in for any length of time. It was surrounded by a wooden wall and here and there were observation slits.

At the bottom of the motte at one point there was a gate in the fence, with a simple drawbridge whose flap lowered over the ditch. This led into a walled courtyard, surrounded by a ditch, also with gate and drawbridge. This was called the bailey.

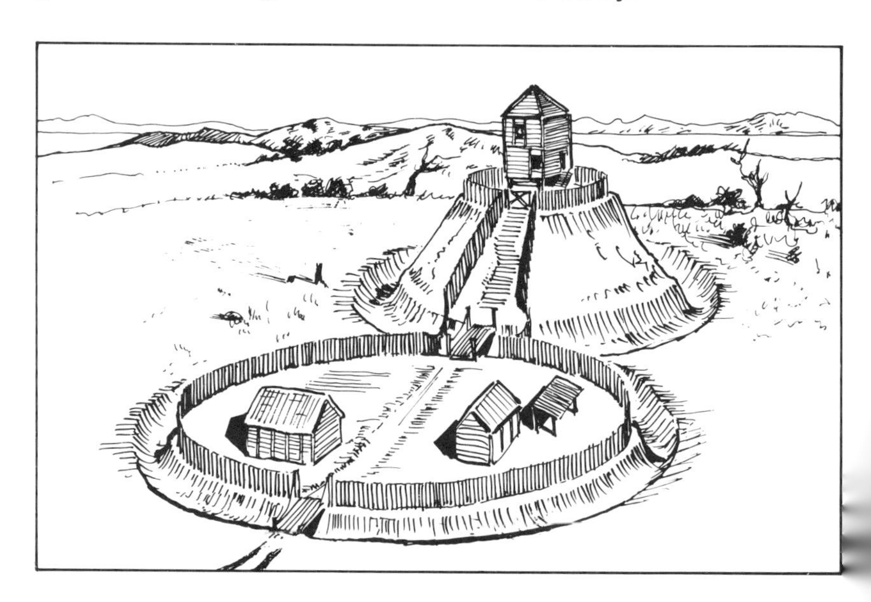

An artist's drawing of a motte-and-bailey. One or two of these were erected in England in the last years of Edward the Confessor (1042–1066), but it was William I who put up probably more than 100 in his time as king, or instructed his army commanders to do so.

These castles were put up on existing mounds, such as the one at York, or they were made from scratch by scooping out earth in a ring about three to four metres (ten to fifteen feet) wide and heaping it up inside the ring. Many of these mounds can still be seen today. The average height was about twelve metres (forty feet), but there were higher ones. At Thetford, for example, the mound is over twenty-five metres (eighty feet) high. The earth was strengthened with harder materials like stones, sand, flint and rubble tightly compressed.

The sides of the mound were very steep, and in wet weather extremely slippery. Besieging a castle of this kind was a dangerous job. Even if you got across the ditch round the motte and broke through the gate or wall, the climb up the slope was extremely difficult. The defenders lined the slopes with polished timber planks and poured water over them to make them like a skating rink. A motte-and-bailey was usually sited by a well or other water supply, and the defenders could boil water and throw it down on you.

These castles could generally be built very quickly. The one at York was supposed to have gone up in eight days. A lot of labour was required, but the conquering Normans pressed the defeated Anglo–Saxons into service as diggers, carpenters, carriers, and so on. No obstacle was allowed to stand in the way of a motte if a lord or king wanted it in a certain place. At Lincoln 166 houses

A motte-and-bailey in northern France, besieged by William, Duke of Normandy. It is the kind of castle built by William when he came to England, before he began the construction work on the stone towers at Colchester and London.

Above: Colchester Castle as seen from the south-west. This enormous tower was originally over 30 metres (90 feet) high. It was built in the style of the White Tower of London, though it is much larger, and it may have been supervised by the same architect, Gundulf. It was almost certainly built at much the same time.

Right: here is a picture of William the Conqueror (right, on horseback) watching the construction of the White Tower of London. Beside him in clerical garb is the architect. This was probably Gundulf, who was an abbot from Normandy and who later became bishop of Rochester. In those times the architects of great buildings, like men in other professions such as lawyers, usually belonged to holy orders, for they were the only people who were educated.

were simply demolished to make room for a motte by the river.

They were often so well sited that in the next century or two their mounds were used for the positioning of rectangular stone great towers which we shall look at in the next chapter.

William also began the construction of two important stone great towers, at Colchester, and the White Tower of the Tower of London.

These castles were not liked by the English. The Anglo–Saxon Chronicle, in its tribute to William on the news of his death in 1087, recorded how unpopular they were. 'He caused castles to be built which were a sore burden to the poor.'

The law and the church

The Conqueror did not meddle much with the English legal system as he found it. He used it, improved it and occasionally added to it. One introduction was a set of laws regarding forests. He is reputed to have wanted to lay aside huge areas of forest for himself to indulge his favourite sport of hunting. In fact, he was considerably concerned by the growing shortage of wild game available for food, because hunters had for years been hacking down trees and shrubs in the pursuit of deer and boar. So, to save the forests and encourage fresh growth, he declared certain woodland areas as royal forests, with heavy penalties for hunting on or damaging them. These areas included Epping Forest, the New Forest and an extensive stretch of woodland running from Oxford to Stamford in Lincolnshire. These forest laws are said to have led to many families being dispossessed of their homes and land, but probably no more than a few hundred people were much affected.

William introduced a new feature of the trial-by-ordeal procedure. This was an old Germanic custom, trial by battle. It was a duel between a plaintiff and the defendant fought under a tight code of rules. They fought with batons or poles with hammer-shaped heads made of horn. Iron was not allowed. If the weapons were broken, they carried on with fists, nails and teeth, if need be. The first to be knocked unconscious lost his case. It was very rough justice by our standards, but it was accepted then.

You will remember that William had the Pope's blessing for his invasion of England. When he had conquered the country, he re-organized the Church. He began by replacing Anglo–Saxon bishops and abbots with Norman ones. Even the English Archbishop of Canterbury, Stigand, was not exempt, and he was superseded by Lanfranc. Then William and Lanfranc altered many of the actual bishoprics themselves. There had been bishops at small places like Dorchester-on-Thames and Sherborne, but now there were to be sees at major towns like Norwich, Chester and Salisbury, and many of the cathedrals were to have their own deans and chapters, that is, a fair measure of self-government. The bishops and the priests were lords of their lands as tenants-in-chief or tenants of the king; the feudal system was extended into the church. Because he guaranteed the church protection, and upheld its particular privileges in law, he expected to be consulted over the appointment of archbishops and bishops.

The Normans took their religion very seriously. Although they were on the whole an illiterate, rough-mannered, violent people, they believed passionately in God and in the afterlife. These coarse men went to mass every day. Their castles and houses had chapels. They continually begged monks to pray for their souls. Even their oaths of fealty were sworn over the bones or relics of saints. And they believed that the supreme power of their king was held directly as a charge from God.

From Royal Manuscript, 14 E iii, a medieval picture of trial by battle.

The church was only one of the institutions of England which enjoyed the energizing spirit of the Conqueror. Nowhere was this more obvious than in the upsurge of cathedral- and church-building which marks the years of William and his sons. You have only to look at Durham to see something of the Norman achievement in cathedrals.

Norman cathedrals and churches are recognizable by their styles, although there is no cathedral that is entirely Norman without later additions or improvements. Norman arches were usually rounded. One familiar pattern of decoration was 'zig-zag' or 'dog-toothed', as it is called. Inside, the pillars were very thick, with rounded surfaces, often unnecessarily massive for the roof structure or towers they were intended to support. This style gave way at the beginning of the 13th century to what is called the Early English style. The buildings were higher, the columns more slender, the arches pointed, the windows were narrower, and late in the period often grouped together. The whole building seemed to be pointing to heaven. This was the exact intention of the masons, who often spent their whole lives on one or two cathedrals which, in many cases, took nearly a century to build.

These cathedrals and the smaller churches were meant to last forever. Unfortunately the enthusiasm was in one or two cases not matched by technical skill. Towers were blown down in high winds at Bury St Edmunds. The central tower at Ely collapsed, and at St Albans the roof caved in and crashed into the nave. Doorways

Opposite Below: Hedingham Castle is in north Essex. Its great tower was built early in the 12th century. The staircase outside was once covered by a fore-building whose roof marks can be seen on the tower wall over the steps. The castle belonged for generations to the de Vere family, who were for a time earls of Oxford. One earl, early in the time of Henry VII, entertained the king there, and he had many of his servants and armed retainers dressed in the Oxford livery. But the king had forbidden his barons to have private armies of any kind, and though he accepted the dinner, he brought Oxford to court for breaking his laws.

and windows began to subside and fracture away from the walls at St David's Cathedral in Pembrokeshire, Wales.

The Chapel of St John in the Tower of London is in the south-east corner of the White Tower. It is a fine example of early Norman ecclesiastical architecture in England, and was probably finished in the early 1080s. Note the heavy use of stonework for arches and pillars.

The effect of the conquest

What effect did the Norman Conquest have on English villagers and their lives? It was probably not as bad as has often been said. While William was quite ruthless in his policy of keeping the conquered English down, he was no less strict with his own Norman followers. On the whole, king's justice was dealt out equitably to all. It was said that at the end of his reign there was only a fraction of the number of slaves working on the land that there had been at the beginning. The Domesday survey may have irritated or frightened the tenants-in-chief, the vassals and the sub-tenants, but the villagers were not severely affected. The results of the survey reveal a remarkable state of prosperity in many parts of the country.

By the arrival of the Conqueror, the English villages, of which here were thousands, consisted of three or four huge fields, usually sited near a stream. The fields were divided into many one-acre strips, separated by ditches or turf paths. Outside the fields were the meadows for the cattle and other livestock and beyond them the woodland areas. The land belonged to the village communally. The livestock belonged to the villagers, and they were tended by cowherds or swineherds. Three of the fields would be given over to arable land. Each was divided into furlongs, and these into smaller one-acre strips. An equal number of these strips was allotted to each householder so that each had only a third of his total holding in any one field. No two strips lying side by side were owned by the same man. One field was sown in winter with wheat. The second was sown with barley or oats in spring-time. The third lay fallow. In the next autumn the wheat and barley were harvested but when the winter came the fallow field was sown with wheat, and so on, in rotation.

These villages were independent in many ways. While some might nominally belong to a great earl or lord, many were not

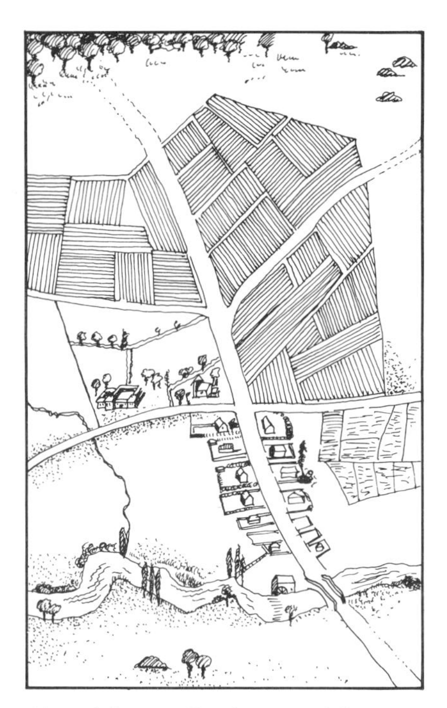

Above left: a medieval manor might have looked something like this from the air.

Above Right: at Boothby Pagnell in Lincolnshire there is a fine building of Norman origin. It is a hall house, built of stone. The main hall part is on the first floor, above the ground level row of windows and doorway. The lord's solar is at the right of the building, at the end of the main hall.

so tied. Everything the villager needed could be obtained within the village confines. Clothes were woven by the womenfolk who spun the wool from the shearings of the sheep. Furniture was made from timber in the woodland where the deer and the pigs roamed. Everything everybody ate came from the fields. About the only commodity that had to be imported was salt for preserving.

The manors were much the same as the villages. It was the ownership which differed. When the Conqueror came, the ownership of manors and villages was in great confusion. There were some manors where the tenants had as many privileges as the lord. There were others where the tenants owed a very loose allegiance to the lord and a stronger one to a neighbouring lord. The term manor might mean a huge area with land enough for 120 ploughing teams, that is, 120 hides, or it could mean a handful of strips worth a few shillings farmed by a few peasants.

William changed all that. He made every village belong to a manor under a lord. The lord kept some of the land, called his demesne. The villagers kept the rest, but no longer on such independent terms. They had to pay a rent, not of money but of service. All of them had to work some time, generally at sowing and harvest time, on the lord's demesne. They might also have to work on other days. Few of the villagers were allowed to remain absolutely free men. They were in the main bound to the lord for the whole of their lives. They could not marry without his consent. They had not only to work some days on his land. They had also to pay money, food rents (that is, give him a proportion of their harvest), and they had to pay him for using his mill to grind their corn (probably there was no other mill anywhere nearby).

A charter of Waleran Fitz Ranulf granting the church of Bures St Mary in Suffolk. The charter has crosses at the bottom, indicating agreement by William I, his wife Matilda, and John Archbishop of Rouen. This was drawn up in about 1075. A scribe wrote in the names.

It seems a harsh settlement, but we need not feel it was the action of a cruel and unfeeling ruler. It was much more a manifestation of the Conqueror's passion for order, and there is little doubt that that is what English society needed.

Leisure time

How did the villagers spend their time when they were not working? They had their meals. Breakfast was a hunk of bread with a cup of ale. Lunch was more bread, with cheese perhaps and an onion, and another mug of beer. Their main meal was supper. For this they had a plate of gruel or pottage, probably filled out with peas or beans. There might be more bread and cheese to follow and the inevitable beer. It does not seem a very exciting diet, but we do not know how much of it they ate, or what variety of cheeses they had. Did the Normans bring over their delicious brie? Meat was eaten as a treat, perhaps twice a week. People did not eat meat on Wednesdays, Fridays or Saturdays, as part of their Christian duties, and they gave it up altogether during Lent. They could have fish or eels, even then very popular in England. The meat most widely eaten was pork. Now and again a

Some chessmen of ivory, believed to be of the 12th century.
They were found in the Isle of Lewis, off the west coast of Scotland, but they may be Norman rather than Viking.

sheep might be killed, but only if it looked as if it was dying anyway. And there were poultry products, such as chickens and eggs.

They ate and drank this fare from pottery plates and cups, much like their Saxon ancestors. The utensils were made either in hearth kilns at home, or by one or other of the enterprising potters who now had potter's wheels and who set up in business in more prosperous villages.

There were several local entertainments. Apart from anything organized by the villagers, the church had its festivals to be celebrated. Manorial lords often gave sumptuous feasts at Christmas time, and they would ask their tenants to come and collect the 'left-overs'. The tenants armed themselves with a plate, a mug and a bowl to take away whatever the lord and his friends did not want. Harvest time was always an excuse for a party, with folk-dancing, sports, and much drinking of cider and local ale In William's day, the men sang old Anglo–Saxon songs, and perhaps a few Norman tunes brought over from Europe by his knights.

The average person in England in the second part of the 11th century was quite uneducated, not very good-mannered, but devoutly worshipping God at all times expected of him. He was superstitious in a way we would not understand today, and content if not happy with a hard-working but (by our standards unhurried life. Life would occasionally be disturbed by the clatter of horses' hooves, and the shrieks and yells of people being harried by Norman knights on their way back through the village to the manor house. They were no doubt fresh from a drunken spree to celebrate a successful castle siege or to mark the elevation of one of their number into the king's councils.

William died in 1087. His second son, William II (Rufus) succeeded as king of England though not as Duke of Normandy This much maligned king endeavoured to maintain his father's new order and probably did so much better than the historians of the time said. They were, after all, churchmen who were no high up on his list of favourites, and so distorted the truth abou his reign.

5 Medieval England

Under the Norman and Plantagenet kings, England began to become a nation. The early hostility between Normans and Anglo–Saxons mellowed with time, and by the middle of the 14th century English was the national language. There were of course many problems. The feudal lords continually gave trouble as they fought among themselves, or ganged up against the kings. When the king was masterful, like the Conqueror or his two sons, or like Henry II (Plantagenet) or Edward I (Plantagenet), the lords were usually tamed. Under weak kings like Stephen or Henry III, however, there was often civil war in which everybody suffered. The Anglo–Saxon Chronicle tells how the people endured awful miseries during Stephen's reign. The kings and the barons also bickered incessantly over their respective rights. This came to a head several times, the most famous being when John was forced, in 1215, to agree to Magna Carta, which was really a string of promises to grant more power to the lords. Simon de Montfort went one better, when in 1265 he called a Parliament of lords, Church, and elected citizens and knights from the towns and shires, to decide national issues. Simon was killed the same year, but his idea lived on and is with us today, in Britain and in many other parts of the world.

Many of the kings spent a large part of their time fighting abroad, or in Scotland, Wales and Ireland. They were either battling to keep their possessions in France against a nation that was becoming increasingly determined to unify itself and expel the English altogether, or they were trying to hold down the Celtic peoples in the remaining parts of the British Isles. All these campaigns cost money, and the English at all levels of society had to contribute. If the lords were more heavily taxed, they raised their rents or the amounts they expected the villeins to pay. England was for much of the period a prosperous land, chiefly because of the high quality and great quantity of the wool it produced, wool which all Europe wanted. This prosperity brought changes in the feudal system, and these were greatly accelerated by the Black Death in 1348–9, in which between a third and half of the population perished. After it, labour became scarce,

Above: after King John agreed to the terms of Magna Carta in 1215, sealed copies were sent to different parts of England. Four original copies have survived. This is not one of them, but is a document of 1225, in which the terms of Magna Carta were re-issued for the third time. It included amendments made to the 1215 charter, and is the definitive text.

Above Right: one of the earliest detailed maps of Britain that has survived. It was drawn by the 13th century historian Matthew Paris in about 1250. He is evidently impressed by rivers. Near the top you can see Hadrian's wall. It would be interesting to know how much of it was still standing in 1250.

and labourers could afford to tout round for the best wages they could find. Grievances grew as a result of the Government's attempts to stop this mobility of labour, and when these were combined with other deep-seated grievances, they exploded into rebellion in 1381. These grievances were summed up by the Essex priest John Ball in his rhyme

> When Adam delved and Eve span
> Who was then the gentleman?

a text he used for every one of countless sermons he preached up and down the Home Counties. The uprising was known as the Peasants' Revolt and was a serious affair. Concentrated chiefly in

An aerial view of the Tower of London. It is perhaps the most famous castle in the world. For five centuries (about 1100 to the early 17th century) it was used as a royal residence much more than a prison. And a good many prisoners in those days enjoyed quite a full life, with servants, books, good food, and sometimes members of their family with them.

the Home Counties, it affected twenty-two others. It was eventually crushed, but the result was the quickening end of feudalism and serfdom. The rebels' points had been made and some lessons learned.

But the Middle Ages were not entirely times of gloom. People had their belief in God. Witness the breathtaking achievement of cathedral-building, possible only by men who loved a Superior Being somewhere above their heads beyond the sky. The age saw the steady development of towns, improvements in the legal system, the growth of local government, the beginnings of English literature, and at the end of the age, the crucial contribution to the spread of learning—the printing press. Above all, the age held the years in which the English character was moulded, when other Europeans recognized the country as more than just a group of islands, with people who could make a real contribution to the expansion of Western civilization.

Castles and towers

Only two stone castles of any size, the White Tower of London and the great tower at Colchester, had been completed before the

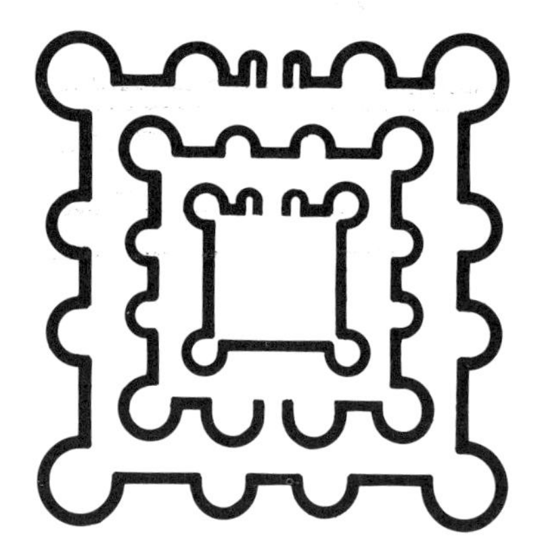

Above right: Orford Castle is in Suffolk, almost on the sea. It was built by Henry II as a stronghold from which to control the activities of one of his more dangerous barons, Roger Bigod. The tower has 21 sides. It would have been much more difficult to bring this tower down by undermining it, than to bring down a rectangular great tower like Hedingham (picture on page 75).

Above: Plan of an ideal concentric castle.

Opposite above left: This is a medieval drawing from the Tower of London showing a battering ram, used in sieges. The artist makes it look easy, but in fact it was very hard to break down a castle's gates. They were often extremely thick and high.

end of the 11th century. But in the next century the Normans began to build stone castles all over England. This programme went on right into the 14th century, and over the 250 or so years their shape and fortifications changed considerably. Towers are now called keeps, but that word did not come into use until the 16th century.

The first castles of stone consisted of great towers, rectangular in plan, surrounded by high stone walls. The towers were tall: for example London, 30 metres (90 feet); Dover, 32 metres (95 feet); Richmond, over 35 metres (100 feet); Rochester, 40 metres (113 feet). These massive buildings had three or four storeys, thick walls (Dover's were over 6 metres (20 feet) in some places), and in several cases the entrance was protected by what is called a forebuilding, a stout structure covering a staircase from the ground to the gate at first-floor level. The trouble with rectangular great towers, however, was that you could have the corners brought down quite effectively by mining—that is, your enemy dug a tunnel from outside under a corner, erected a wooden platform held up by props, removed the earth under the corner, and set fire to the props. It gave way, leaving a goping hole into which he could send his troops. Exactly this happened at Rochester in 1215.

To get round this problem, castle-builders designed new types of great tower, circular in plan or with many angles, that is polygonal or multangular. (The Celtic Scots had thought of this twelve hundred years before!) At Orford in Suffolk in the 1160s, Henry II erected a splendid twenty-one sided tower which still stands in fine condition today. You could not easily bring this type down with a mine. Nor could you have made much impression on cylinder towers like Conisbrough in Yorkshire, Pembroke in Wales and Bothwell, near Glasgow, in Scotland.

Above: A mantlet provided protection for archers who were attacking a castle. It was a moveable sloping screen.

Another type of castle that was difficult to capture was the curtain wall type with flanking towers. A very good early example was Framlingham in Suffolk, which has a many-sided wall round an enclosure in which buildings like dining hall, chapel, stables, storehouses, and so on were erected. Along the wall, at intervals, are thirteen square or rectangular towers, each an independent structure. So you could not be sure of capturing the whole castle just by taking one tower. The defenders would go on fighting in all the other twelve until one after the other they fell. Framlingham's wall was over 13 metres (40 feet) high, and its towers more like 20 metres (60 feet). This kind of castle was put up in many places, like Corfe in Dorset, Conway in north Wales (which has round towers), Carreg Cennen in south Wales, and Tantallon in Scotland.

But castle-builders were not satisfied with the designs, for they did not enable the defenders to go over to the offensive and attack the besiegers. So, following the example of the Crusaders in the Near East, they began to build what are called concentric castles. These are castles which have two or three rings of walls or ramparts, each one a unit in itself, with towers and a gatehouse. In Britain, concentric castles were built from new, like Beaumaris in Anglesey in Wales, Harlech and Caerphilly, also in Wales, and Caerlaverock in Scotland; or they were older castles improved by adding rings of walls or ramparts or moats, like the Tower of London, Dover, Goodrich in Herefordshire, or Castle Rushen on the Isle of Man. If you garrisoned the inner ring and its towers and the next ring, too, and then drew up a force of attacking troops inside the outermost ring, you could send these men out through the outer main gate against the besieging army. If they were driven back inside or slaughtered where they stood, there were the two inner rings which would have to be fought for, tower by tower, gatehouse by gatehouse.

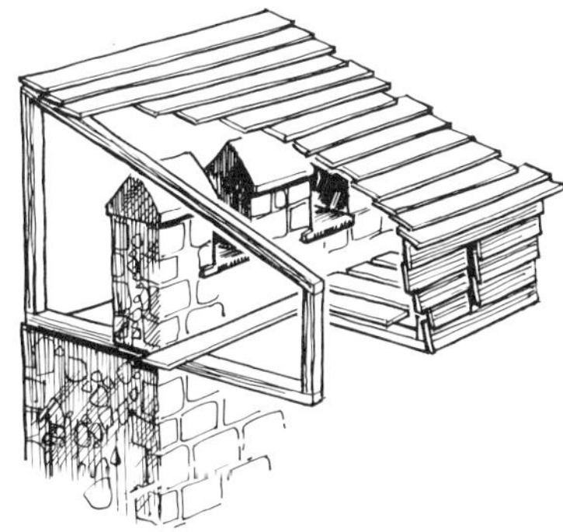

Defenders of castles sometimes built wooden hoardings round the tops of the walls. From there they dropped missiles through slats in the floor on to attackers below.

Below: A trebuchet was a mechanical sling operated by a counterweight at one end of the arm. It was used for firing a variety of missiles, stones, even rotting carcases of animals to spread disease, against castles in medieval sieges.

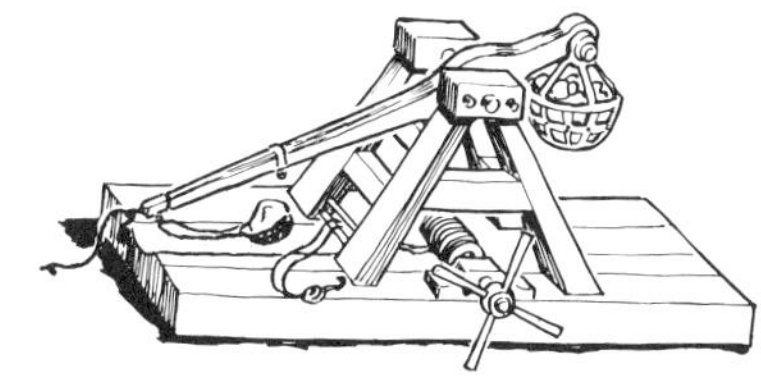

The great tower at Tattershall Castle, Lincolnshire. It was built of brick in the middle of the 15th century. It is over 30 metres (100 ft) high.

That was the theory, but it did not work on one occasion at Château Gaillard, near Rouen in France, a supposedly impregnable concentric castle built by Richard the Lionheart in the last years of the 12th century. It fell to Philip Augustus, king of France, in 1204, and the shock ran through Europe.

Nearly all the concentric castles built in Britain were never put to the test of impregnability. By the time the biggest and best of them were ready, siege warfare was rapidly going out of fashion. Armies preferred to fight it out in open fields, as at Creçy and Bannockburn. Thereafter, castles principally became residences of great lords and landowners—and what uncomfortable places they were—claustrophobic, damp, dark, smelly, very chilly, and extremely noisy every time anyone went upstairs or crossed a floor. In the next century, some new castles like Tattershall in Lincolnshire and Oxburgh in Norfolk were built mainly of brick. Handsome and imposing though these and others were, and in many cases still are (Tattershall's red brick great tower dominates the Lincolnshire landscape for miles around), they would not have lasted long against the newly developed cannons which armies were now using. But they were more comfortable to live in.

If you wonder why castles seem to be built of different kinds and colours of stone or brick according to where they are, this is because in the days of slow and cumbersome transport, builders had to use as much local building material as they could find. Having chosen to put up a great tower at an important river crossing like Goodrich on the Wye, or Rochester on the Medway, the builders had to ask several important questions. Where was the nearest quarry? Was the stone suitable for buildings of such

Norwich Cathedral is one of the oldest in England. Much of it is Norman, built in the late 11th, and throughout the 12th, centuries. The tower is a good example of Norman tower architecture, but the spire was added much later.

massiveness? Who owned the quarry and how much would the stone cost? Was there any rock on the site? (Rock was a good foundation and you could not mine it.)

The great medieval cathedrals

We have seen that, while churches and monasteries had been built of stone as far back as the 8th century (or even earlier in the case of Jarrow), it was the Normans who showed Britain how to put up those splendid, massive houses of God which still adorn the towns, the cathedrals. Apart from Durham, perhaps the finest of them, parts of Norwich, Ely and Peterborough stand out as marvellous examples of the Norman style of thick walls, small windows, and massive pillars. You might think these features seem less attractive when compared with those of the next two or three periods of church architecture, the Early English, the Decorated

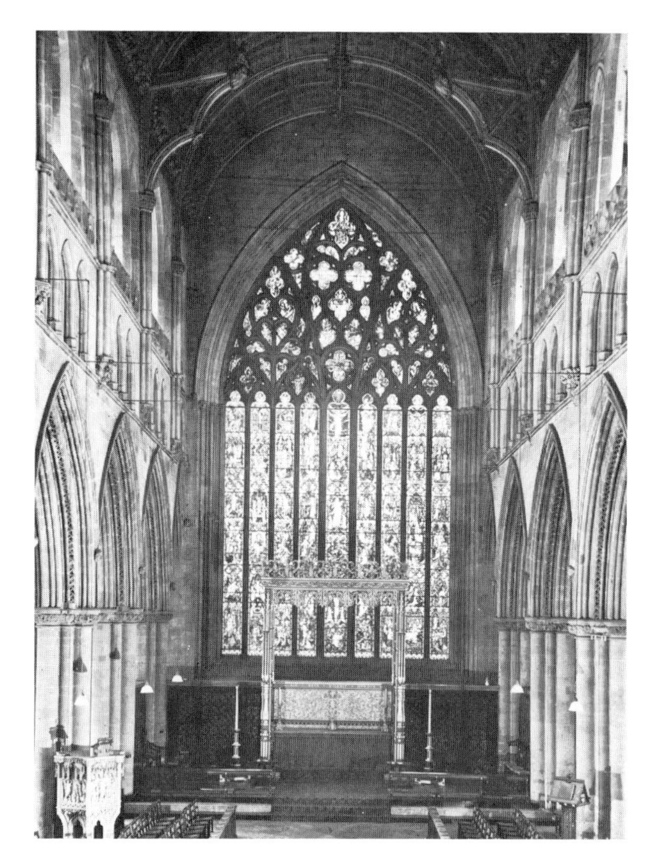

and the Perpendicular, but this is largely because the Normans did not rate the appearance of their buildings as highly as their successors did. Stone masons were given the job of erecting a suitable cathedral or church at a chosen place and told to get on with it. So, they played safe and used far more stone than was necessary.

Then, in the middle of the 12th century, when England had recovered from the awful civil wars of Stephen's reign, the Early English style of architecture began to appear. Parts of Canterbury and Ripon were rebuilt in this style, with more pointed arches, larger windows, and thinner walls supported by deep buttresses. A number of new cathedrals were begun, notably Lincoln and Wells. This new style was the result of a growing respect for masons who were, after all, the nearest equivalent to architects that the Middle Ages had. Masons of long standing and proven skill were appointed master-masons, sometimes to the king, and they acted as consultants to cathedral-building projects.

In the 13th century, the Early English style developed into what is called the Decorated style. Cathedrals and churches built in this mode had much more ornament and decoration. The windows were wider still, obtained without weakening the walls by being divided by upright and curved mouldings into

Above left: The tracery in the East Window in Carlisle Cathedral is made up of 86 pieces of stone. The work was executed in the middle of the 14th century, and it is a fine example of Decorated Architecture.

Above right: Fan vaulting in Henry VII's Chapel at Westminster Abbey. The effect, even in a photograph, is breathtaking.

patterns so that they look like lace. This is called tracery; the tracery in the east window of Carlisle Cathedral is said to be made from more than eighty pieces of carved stone. The pillars of these buildings were more slender, and the carving and moulding more delicate. A fine example of Decorated style is the west window of York Minster, finished early in Edward III's reign.

This Decorated style was a luxury that even the Church could often ill afford, and before long it gave way to a simpler mode called the Perpendicular style. The important features of this style were that its lines were straight rather than curved, in windows and elsewhere, and the pillars were still slender and less 'clustered'. Arches were flatter, windows were higher to give more light, and the widths of naves, aisles and choirs were increased. There are many wonderful examples of the Perpendicular style in Britain, including Gloucester, Winchester and St George's Chapel, Windsor. The style, by the way, lasted until the 1570s or so, after which the first of the Renaissance-influenced buildings went up. Though the Perpendicular style is basically simpler, we must not overlook the wonderful feature of fan vaulting, which is so much easier to illustrate than to describe. The picture here of the roof of Henry VII's Chapel at Westminster Abbey speaks better than words.

Cathedral builders had the same building problems as the castle masons. Local stone had to be used where possible. Quarries at Shepton Mallet in Somerset supplied the masons at Wells, and Lincoln was built largely from stone from nearby Ancaster. Norwich got much of its stone from Caen, across the sea in France. Masons had no drawings such as our architects or engineers have today. Their plans were in their heads: and they had to do a great deal by judging on the spot. Mouldings, pillar segments, arch members and so on were cut in stone to wooden templates at the quarry and then numbered or lettered before being moved to the building site, by water transport if possible for that was cheaper and less troublesome. Masons and their gangs had nothing like the range of equipment our builders have, and of course there was no machinery at all. They relied on chisels, adzes and axes, with mallets and crow bars, made for them by local blacksmiths. The sharp edges were constantly worn down and had to be honed or ground every day or so.

Monks and friars

The first monks in England were missionaries who came with St Augustine at the end of the 6th century to convert the heathen English to Christianity. They were Benedictine monks, that is, they belonged to the order of monks founded by St Benedict whose system was based on a combination of work and prayer. Prayer was necessary if one was eventually to reach Heaven at the end of one's life on earth; work was good for the soul, too, for it kept one's mind off the wickedness of the world and it also resulted in benefits for one's neighbours. Monks, therefore, were good men who aimed to improve the moral standards of their fellow men not so much by instructing them but by setting an example through their own way of life. This is not to say that early monks did not go out and preach—many of them did. How else could St Columba have brought Christianity to Scotland, or St Augustine to England?

By the Middle Ages the monasteries had become rich and influential. They were havens of refuge for men who did not like warfare or commercial trading. They provided the thinkers, the teachers and many of the statesmen of the time. Their wealth had been built up through careful working of their lands for agriculture and, more importantly, sheep-rearing, Many had also received substantial gifts of money and land from wealthy nobles and warriors who towards the end of their lives believed they might purchase salvation and eventual admission to the Kingdom of God by offering these gifts.

But even monks could be tempted by worldly pleasures, and, sad to relate, many monasteries became better known for high living, good cheer and occasionally worse. Several attempts were made to reform them, and in the 11th century a new order, called the Cistercian order, named after their first abbey at Cîteaux in

Above left: The ruins of Fountains Abbey are about 5 kilometres (3 miles) from Ripon in Yorkshire. The abbey, founded early in the 12th century, was Cistercian.

Above right: Tintern Abbey, in Monmouthshire, is another Cistercian foundation.

France, introduced a new religious discipline. This was much simpler and more austere. Cistercians preferred to live in the country, far from the temptations offered by towns where most of the Benedictine monasteries were. Some of the Cistercian abbeys must have been astonishingly beautiful, to judge from their ruins, such as Fountains in Yorkshire, and Tintern in Monmouthshire.

Whatever our view of the monastic way of life, we must not forget that for centuries it was in the monasteries and in their schools that nearly all learning in England was to be had. King Alfred's famous Anglo–Saxon Chronicle was written by monks, and the last two centres where it was compiled were at monasteries at Worcester and at Peterborough.

By about 1200, many monasteries had acquired, from one source or another, considerable lands, on which the monks and their employees raised sheep. This provided them with enormous wealth from the wool which they sold in England and more especially abroad. It was said that by the time of Henry VII (1485–1509), nearly one third of the wealth of England was in the hands of monasteries. But despite the enormous contribution they were making to the national economy and to learning of all kinds, men's souls were being neglected. This was even more true outside England in Europe. In the small town of Assisi, in Tuscany, an Italian state, a merchant's son, Francis, decided suddenly to give up his comfortable life and spend the rest of his days helping the poor and the sick. To do this properly, he believed, he had to be poor himself, and so he abandoned everything he had, even his clothes, and set out on the road as a beggar, helping everyone less fortunate than himself whom he happened to meet.

A panel painting of St Francis of Assisi being reprimanded for stealing money for rebuilding the church of St Damian in Assisi. The stolen bag of money is in a cache under the crucifix.

It was not long before he gathered round him a band of men of similar ideals, and they formed themselves into a new order not of monks but of friars (from the Latin for brothers, *fratres*). This order was called the Franciscan order. They were known everywhere for their good works, their plain dress (simple grey robes) and their refusal to wear shoes. They concentrated in towns where they believed their work lay among the dirty, ill-kept poor homes, and unswept, rubbish-strewn streets and alleys. They studied, they taught, and most important of all, they preached, often in fiery emotional language, calling their fellow men back from the ways of wickedness to God. They preached well, often illustrating their message with stories from the Bible or parables they made up themselves. They lived, meanwhile, entirely on what they could beg from strangers and from people they got to know. For many of them it must have been a very hard life, not knowing whether they would eat that day or the next. But they were kept going by their amazing faith.

Another new order was created at much the same time, the Dominicans. This order was founded by St Dominic, a Spanish merchant who also gave up his life for a poor one. He was particularly concerned by the ignorance of people and his order sought to spread education rather than comfort and help to the needy. So there was room for both orders, and in the 1220s friars of both kinds began to come to England, settling at Canterbury and at Oxford. Indeed, they came to Oxford at just the time that the new university was being built up, under the supervision of the Bishop of Lincoln and his chancellor.

You can see that the friars would not exactly be welcomed by the monks. Their approach to life was different; their methods were quite foreign. They did not bother with fine churches or abbeys or other buildings. They refused gifts of money from rich conscience-stricken knights. And there was great friction between the orders, especially when the friars began to recruit many followers among those from whom the monks would generally expect to find support. It is thought that by 1300 there were over 5,000 friars in England, one to every 900 inhabitants.

Some boys being taught at a medieval school. This is from a medieval manuscript. The boys do not seem to be paying much attention to the teacher.

In time, the friars began to become like the monks, who had fallen from their high ideals. This was one of the underlying causes of great upheaval within the whole church which we shall look at in the next chapter.

Schools and colleges

Nowadays you have to go to school whether you like it or not. In the Middle Ages school was a privilege for only a very few children. To begin with, the family would have to pay, unless they

An artist's drawing of how men of three religious orders of the Middle Ages dressed: (left to right) a Franciscan friar, a Benedictine monk, and a Dominican friar.

could find some rich man willing to be generous and give you an education. Most of the country's education was run by the church, and the church was not concerned about what is called primary education—that is, reading, writing and arithmetic. If you were the son of a lord, your parents taught you these subjects or got some local parish priest to do it. If you were the daughter of the same parents, you might be packed off to a convent or have a private tutor. After that, boys went on to become pupils on the estates of other lords where they learned manners, and after the age of about thirteen, were instructed in field sports like riding, hawking, and fighting with sword or stick. Now and again they would have a lesson in Latin and in Norman French (in the earlier centuries). Girls might be taught a little more, but they were usually brought up to be domesticated so that they could make good marriages.

Children of professional men like lawyers, and also of merchants or master craftsmen, would likewise learn the elementary 'three Rs' at home, if it was possible. Then they could go on to one or other of the grammar schools which were sprouting up in England from the time of Henry I. The Norman schools were often good, some so good that they even attracted pupils from abroad.

There was one other way to get to school and that was to be picked as a choir boy for a church or monastery. Many of these foundations had what were called song schools, where you learned to chant the psalms and hymns. Quite often boys were picked if they were heard singing in the fields. At song school they were given some lessons in reading, but for the most part they had to memorize long verses of hymns or anthems in Latin—a language that meant nothing to them. If they were clever enough, or had enough family money to see them on to a grammar school, they would learn there what the language meant. They would acquire a vocabulary, be able to parse words, and even learn to discuss things or make speeches in Latin. In those days medieval Latin was the language spoken by the church throughout Christendom, although there were numerous dialects, and the only way to understand it was to learn classical Latin.

In the Castle Museum at Norwich there is a fine medieval book of Latin hymns, with both words and music, and it is illuminated with bright coloured capitals. It is called the Sarum Antiphoner, and it belonged to the church at Ranworth near Norwich from about 1400, when it was compiled up to the 1530s. It was lost during the upheavals of Henry VIII's dissolution of the monasteries. It was discovered at a second-hand shop in London early this century, bought and returned to Ranworth Parish which lent it to the Museum.

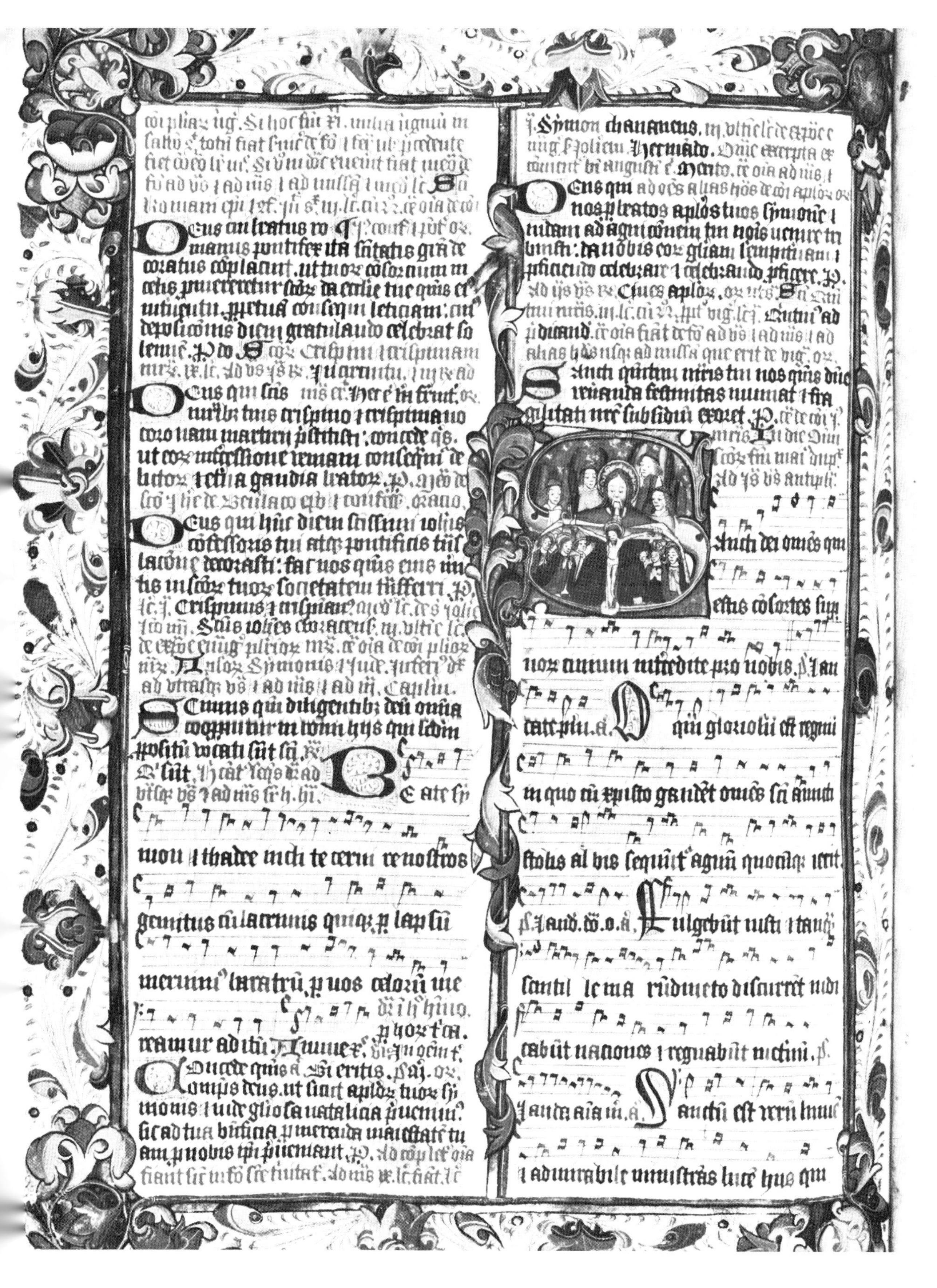

Above: Here is a picture from the Middle Ages of a monk illuminating a manuscript. It was probably drawn by another monk.

Below: Roger Bacon (*c* 1214–94), the English friar and scholar who discovered the explosive power of gunpowder. The Chinese had invented it centuries before, but only used it for fireworks. Bacon was a distinguished scientist who did valuable work in many fields, including optics, chemistry and physics.

Scholars who shone at Latin and wanted to go on to further studies could take up mathematics, astronomy and music. Many did go on to study theology and become priests. But quite a few branched out to read church law (canon law) or civil law.

For some time, on the Continent, centres had been growing, where educated people came together to increase their knowledge and learning, corporations of teachers and students, as it were. These were the origins of the universities. There was one at Bologna in Italy which specialized in law, and another in Paris where more general subjects were studied. Young men went there to attach themselves to the teachers. There was nowhere for them to live in, and they had to fend for themselves. Many took menial jobs as servants to earn their keep. This idea spread to England at the beginning of the 13th century, and the first place where such a corporation or university sprang up was Oxford. This sleepy town, lying amid the north Berkshire hills near the Thames and about eighty kilometres (fifty miles) from London, seemed a fine site for such an institution. Added to that in the later years of the 12th century, it had housed the schools of several scholars of international reputation, by chance all at more or less the same time. In John's reign the schools at Oxford were brought under the control of the Bishop of Lincoln who appointed a chancellor to run the university.

In the next generation, Franciscan and Dominican friars came to Oxford to open up more schools. One teacher was Robert Grosseteste, who became Bishop of Lincoln, and another, who began as Grosseteste's pupil, was Roger Bacon, the man who discovered the explosive properties of gunpowder and who was one of the leading scientific thinkers of the century.

At first, students had no colleges in which to live. They found their own lodgings, attended lectures and demonstrations more or less as they pleased, and if they felt like it obtained their degrees after the required number of years' study. In most cases this was several years, seven or more, so as a student usually began at about 12 or 13, he spent his entire adolescence there.

The first colleges at Oxford—and it was the same at Cambridge

Sir Thomas More (1478–1535). This wonderful English scholar and statesman was made Lord Chancellor by Henry VIII after the death of Cardinal Wolsey. At first things went well, but by 1534 when the king commanded all men to recognize him as Supreme Head of the Church, relations deteriorated. More refused this order, and he was tried, found guilty and executed.

in the 15th century—were halls of residence for young men who had acquired degrees and wanted to go on to what we would today call post-graduate research. There, professors and graduates enjoyed a semi-monastic life, were not allowed to marry, grew their own vines, and occasionally allowed students to join them for study in return for doing the housework and waiting on them at table. One of the first Oxford colleges was Merton, and an early one at Cambridge was Peterhouse.

By the end of the 15th century there were several such colleges, and the first students were being admitted to live in with the graduates and professors. Among the most famous figures of the 16th century, who were students at Oxford in the last years of the 15th century, were Cardinal Wolsey and Sir Thomas More. Archbishop Cranmer studied at Cambridge early in the 16th century.

The importance of towns

One of the most important features of the Middle Ages in England, as in other European countries, was the development of towns. By 1100 there were over a hundred in England, although at that time a town was little more than a large village with a stone wall or earth rampart surrounding it. In many cases it belonged to a feudal lord, and there was continual quarrelling between the lord

Left: A model of part of London in the 16th century, showing the area around the Fleet river, much of which runs under today's Fleet Street. In the background you can see old St Paul's Cathedral as it was before the Great Fire of 1666.

Below: A model of London Bridge as it was in the Middle Ages. It was the only bridge in the capital across the Thames. It had been started in the time of Henry II, but it was his youngest son, John (1199–1216), who saw to it that it was completed, during his reign.

and the citizens over privileges and duties. Some had a castle on the outskirts where the lord kept an eye on the activities going on inside. But as towns became more prosperous, usually through giving permission to have a regular market within the walls, the townspeople demanded more privileges for which they were quite willing to pay. Eventually, they were able to buy charters from the king or from feudal lords, granting them freedom to manage their own affairs, through their own elected officials. Thus arose the idea of mayor and council. In those days they had their own courts as well.

By the end of the 13th century nearly every town of any size had its own charter. Today, many of these towns are proud to advertise the year when their charters were won—such as Wallingford, in Berkshire, in 1153. These charters were hard to come by before the time of Richard I, for the kings and lords, bishops and abbots, who were the landlords, regarded the towns as good, reliable sources of income every year through the various taxes. But when Richard became king in 1189 and determined to help organize and finance the Third Crusade to wrest the Holy Land from the Saracens, he had urgent need of large sums of ready money. What better way than to sell charters? Many were sold and by the end of his reign the practice of selling them was well established. His brother, John, who was often short of money, and who, it should be said, appreciated the value of giving freedom to towns, to trade in the interests of the national economy, also sold many charters. Lancaster bought one, and so did Liverpool. In the latter case, John was quick to see the value of the town as a port, standing as it does at the mouth of the Mersey.

These towns were very small by our standards. London, by far the biggest, was about a third of the size of Venice as it was then. There was nothing else like it in England. The next largest were Norwich, Bristol and York. In 1066 Norwich had 1,300 houses, but even as late as 1400 no more than a handful of towns had more than 1,000, which means the average population was probably under 5,000. But if they were small, they played a vital part in the country's economic well-being. Most of them were situated at a river mouth, ford crossing or a road junction. They were natural communication centres and obvious places for such institutions as law courts, schools, coin mints, markets and in many cases cathedrals. They had, outside their walls, their own fields where every citizen had a strip or two to cultivate. There was also town pasture land for cattle-grazing, sheep-rearing, and pig-raising, which all citizens shared. Port Meadow outside Oxford was one example. Another was the common at Hungerford on which townsfolk today have common rights of grazing.

Townspeople understood all about the countryside, which is hardly the case today. They had gardens and orchards within the walls, and their homes were not squashed up together in soul-less rows of like frontage such as those to be seen in the industrial cities up and down England. Their harvests outside provided nearly all the food they needed. In London in Henry II's time, for example, people kept hounds which they used for chasing hares and other animals for food.

By the 14th century most towns had several churches, a guildhall, perhaps a monastery, and a market hall not unlike the Roman forum of early Romano–British times. There is a fine market hall, or tolsey, at Chipping Campden in Gloucestershire. But while these public or church buildings were often built of stone, most of the houses were not. Wealthy traders could afford stone-built homes of two storeys, but the average house was mainly of timber beams and plasterwork. Here and there one or two might have a lower storey of stone or, in the 15th century, of brick. Usually the windows were not glazed, and you could only keep the cold out with shutters.

While the medieval town was fairly well planned from the point of view of lay-out of buildings, and was provided with some amenities, the roads and streets were terrible. The surfaces were nothing like the old Roman roads. In summer they were rutted, dusty and full of pot holes. In winter they became slushy, muddy quagmires, and woe betide anyone who was walking along the edge when a horse and cart came by at speed! If he was lucky he

How a medieval artist saw a state carriage, with horses. The people looking out of the ends and the windows in the middle are members of the royal family. This picture is from the Luttrell Psalter, now in the British Museum.

could step on to a sort of pavement which at least protected the soles of his shoes, but these pavements were rare.

The reason for bad roads seems to have been largely an unwillingness on the part of the mayor and council—or anybody else, for that matter—to spend money on them. The town bridges fared no better. These were seldom maintained and there were never enough of them. In London there was only one until the middle of the 18th century. This was the stone-built London Bridge put up between 1176 and 1206. Even if a lord did put up a bridge the locals let it deteriorate.

Townspeople did their best to avoid walking, and they rode on horseback wherever they could. This was as true of women who sat astride like men. Here and there carriages were used. Peasants used small carts on two wheels, and you can imagine the clatter on market days as rows and rows of these noisy vehicles converged on the main market hall and the trade and craft streets.

Townspeople were very proud of their charters and jealous of their rights. They constantly sought more independence, and in the earlier centuries regarded their towns, however small, as self-governing dominions. The great historian G. M. Trevelyan said that they formed commercial treaties between each other and Norwich spoke to Southampton in much the same way that England spoke to France. Let us look at how they protected these rights.

The magnificent guildhall of Hereford, as it appeared to an engraver of the 18th century. This massive timber-framed structure was built in the late 16th century and, sad to relate, demolished in the 19th century.

Merchant and craft guilds

Burgesses (or citizens) of towns were traders, property owners, craftsmen or just residents. They had the right to vote in local elections, and they owned a share of the commercial property of the town. No stranger was allowed to sell his wares in the town unless he did so in the market place or tolsey, and then only on market days. Even then he had to pay a fee to the borough. Trade in the town was strictly controlled by the leading traders (who doubtless proved their position by means of their accumulated money and perhaps property investments), who got together to form merchant guilds. These guilds, the earliest of which was formed in the time of William II, monopolized all trade except food. This was endorsed in a charter of Henry III granted to Liverpool, which says that no one who is not of the guild shall transact any merchandise unless by consent of the burgesses.

Monopolies are generally disapproved of, but it should be noted that many guilds did a lot for their towns. They saw that they were kept clean, they built fine guild halls, gave money to the church and financed schools. They took care of the sick and the elderly and even brought some relief to the poor. Naturally, therefore, the local council would be made up very largely of members of the guild. Here and there a guild was corrupt because the majority of its members acted only in their own selfish interests.

The guilds provided excellent control of the quality of goods on sale in the towns. If any craftsmen wanted to be members or to trade in town streets, or from a house, they were obliged to get the agreement of the guild as to prices, and the guild also reserved the right to forbid the selling of some commodity which was not up to standard. In those days it was not difficult to enforce these rules as the whole spirit of the Middle Ages was against underselling or sharp profit-making. 'A fair exchange is no robbery' was the maxim by which traders and craftsmen worked. The guilds also tried to get the different craftsmen to occupy one street for each skill. This is reflected in common surviving street names like Sadlergate (street of saddlers), Smithfield, Wheelergate, and so on.

At first, the craftsmen were in a minority and therefore content to abide by guild rules. But as the populations of towns expanded and the demands for craft skills and goods grew—rapidly for some of the time—the craftsmen began to feel the need for representation of their own interests. There were more and more branches of the crafts developing. Once, the blacksmith had handled every demand for metalwork. Now, specialists in each of the metals began to emerge—ironsmiths, goldsmiths, silversmiths, and coppersmiths. This also happened with other materials like leather. It was clear that each craft ought to have its own guild, and by the 13th century these were being formed. Each skill had its own association to control prices, standards of fabrication, and terms of entry into the craft. These associations or guilds began to look like the merchant guilds, and before long master craftsmen were being elected to the town councils. The guilds became powerful and edged the merchant guilds into second place. By the middle of the 14th century the merchant guilds had all but disappeared.

The craft guilds embraced a huge range of skills. They had sets of regulations for membership as well as for standards and prices. No-one could hope to practise unless he was accepted as a member of a guild. He had to be elected by the masters of the skill after serving an apprenticeship and then a further period as a journeyman, or wage-earner. Even the number of apprentices and journeymen a master employed was regulated, and so was the way he was to behave to them and what wages to pay them.

This is a woodcut picture of a late medieval blacksmith at work. It was printed by William Caxton in one of his early books.

The guilds were also clubs. Members met for recreation, feasts, and other social activities. The guild came into all its glory on Corpus Christi Day, when the town's pageant was usually staged. Then, the guild officials wore their decorous ceremonial dress, and some fascinating displays of the crafts were staged. But it was expensive to be a member of a guild, and many journeymen could not afford the fees. This meant they could not practise the craft for which they were trained, and often they could only work as hired hands in a menial capacity. Among the rebels in the Peasants' Revolt of 1381 were many journeymen who wanted to break the stranglehold the officials and master craftsmen had on their crafts, and to gain the right just to be allowed to work with dignity.

Language

When the Conqueror looked down on the lifeless body of Harold at Hastings in 1066, he probably felt and stated that Harold had brought his end on himself. Any of Harold's Anglo–Saxon bodyguards still alive, who may have been lying on the ground pretending to be dead, would not have understood, for William spoke Norman–French, a language made up of French and Viking, and unintelligible to any Anglo–Saxons except scholars.

A marvellous medieval picture of a weaving loom, of the 15th century. The woman, wearing a coronet, is holding a shuttle. See how that compares with the shuttles of John Kay in Chapter 9

For the next two centuries at least, the Normans in England spoke their own language, or Latin if they were connected with the church, while the conquered English continued with their Anglo–Saxon in one dialect or another, depending on what part of the country they were from. Gradually, however, some mingling took place, but even as late as the battle of Créçy in 1346, the archers spoke English while the knights hailed each other in French, the language spoken by their enemies.

Then the Black Death removed, among other victims, many of the clergy who were the teachers in the schools, colleges and villages. A new type of priest had to take their place, often straight from a humble English-speaking home, and this led to the more general adoption of English as a national language. In 1362 Edward III made it compulsory to use English in the law courts. And the first really great poet of England, Geoffrey Chaucer, (around 1340–1400) wrote his wonderful *Canterbury Tales* in English, using occasional longer Norman–French words. Thereafter, even if lawyers and clergy used Latin, classical or medieval, and courtiers Norman–French, English became the national language, and has remained so.

These *Canterbury Tales* are important in our social history. They are a series of stories told by various members of a party of pilgrims on the way to the shrine of St Thomas Becket at Canterbury.

Two of the pilgrims from Chaucer's famous *Canterbury Tales*, the Miller (left) from a Caxton printed copy of the book, and the Merchant (right) from a facsimile of the Ellesmere manuscript of the book. In the book both miller and merchant told their tales to the other pilgrims.

Thomas Becket, Archbishop of Canterbury in Henry II's reign, was murdered in his cathedral at Canterbury, in 1170. The picture shows the spot where he is said to have been cut down. It was a place of pilgrimage for centuries.

They give a lively picture of every class of person whom one might meet on such a pilgrimage, from a knight to a humble ploughman. Pilgrimages themselves were classless, and everyone was as good as his neighbour. They were also regular features of English life. The stories show how members of the church did not always practise what they preached—in other words, they lived rather too well and neglected their duties while urging others to live simply and be God-fearing. The tales also tell us a great deal about the everyday life of all classes, what they wore, ate, and even talked about. Chaucer himself, apart from being a poet, was a government servant who moved in high circles. He was married to the sister of John of Gaunt's wife, and John was the fourth son of Edward III. Chaucer received pensions from both Edward and his grandson Richard II. But he was an acute observer of human nature and he had a rumbustuous sense of humour as well as a marvellous gift of language.

Food

In Chaucer's day, as in the centuries before and after, the diet of the classes varied enormously. The ploughman on the pilgrimage in the *Canterbury Tales* and the journeyman who joined so heartily in the Peasants' Revolt, lived on bread, ale, some meat, cheese and vegetables. Some may have kept poultry and eaten eggs. They grew peas, beans, worts, kept a cow or a pig, and occasionally shared in an ox slaughtered at Christmastide. One of their main dishes was bacon, boiled, smoked or roasted. But if that was not variety enough, the peasant class loved poaching on the lord's estate, and could not resist a rabbit or hare, or a trout from a stream or pond. Higher up the social scale, more exciting dishes were relished—the professors and graduates at one Cambridge college are said to have eaten several thousand doves in one

Two more drawings from the Luttrell Psalter—above, gathering in the harvest, taking it by horses and cart up a hill; below, a scene from a lord's kitchen, showing medieval cooking implements.

academic year. Partridge was also enjoyed, and smaller birds like thrushes were a great delicacy.

Mixed fortunes

The 15th century had not been a happy one for England. It had started off badly and, with the exception of one or two illuminating features like the great victory at Agincourt in 1415, the rise and fall of the wonderful Richard Neville, Earl of Warwick, and at the end the accession to the throne of Henry Tudor as Henry VII, it had continued as a sorry catalogue of disasters. Richard II had been deposed in 1399, and in 1402 it was given out that he had died of self-inflicted starvation. Henry IV, egged on by the church, had allowed the disgraceful statute, *De Heretico Comburendo* (On the Burning of Heretics) to be passed, and hundreds of followers of John Wycliffe, who in the previous century had questioned the state of the church and campaigned for fundamental reforms, had been cruelly burned.

In France, after Henry V died in 1422, his brother John, Duke of Bedford, had valiantly struggled to hold on to the possessions

Another drawing from the Luttrell Psalter—enjoying the sport of hawking.

won at Agincourt. But France found a leader in Joan of Arc whose career injected some much-needed vigour and desire for unity into the French people, and less than 20 years after her death in 1431 the whole country, except for a few towns on the coast, had been recaptured from the English.

Then at home the most devastating civil war broke out between the supporters of the king, Henry VI (a saintly and harmless man) representing the royal house of Lancaster, and his cousin, Richard Plantagenet, leader of the royal house of York, who considered Henry unfit to rule. This lasted on and off for thirty years (1455–1485), the worst being the first six, and it was accompanied by the most brutal cruelties. The chivalry which both sides had shown in the French wars of Edward III had gone. Father turned on son, brother against brother. Men broke their word, betrayed their friends and fellow soldiers, and the victors of battles indulged nearly every time in an orgy of execution of the leading losers if they survived, or the rest of their families if they did not.

Finally, the gloom was relieved by the short but interesting reign of Richard III (1483–85) who in two years introduced more legislation than any monarch before him, and who had the laws of England written down in English, and the longer and more rewarding times of Henry VII (1485–1509) the first king to understand accountancy and leave more cash in the royal treasury when he died than he found when he acceded.

It was the century in which the Portuguese discovered the route round the Cape of Good Hope to India, when Columbus discovered America, and Cabral discovered Brazil. It was the century in which Leonardo da Vinci began to paint, draw and invent, in which Michelangelo began to sculpt, paint and build and Savonarola began to question the teachings of the church. It was the age of the Renaissance in Europe. England was to play its part in the exciting changes in the next century.

6 How the Tudors lived

Some time in the later Middle Ages, some scholars began to look at learning from a new angle. We do not know exactly when, for it is always difficult to date this sort of movement precisely. It seems to have coincided with a number of events, like the fall of Constantinople in 1453, the opening up of the sea routes round west Africa, the decline of the authority of the popes as spiritual lords into mere temporal rulers, and the introduction of printing. It also coincided with a growing interest in ancient Greek and Latin language, literature, sculpture, building design, ideas about government and so forth.

This movement, known as the Renaissance, affected all of Europe and Britain, and it reached out into many fields, including art, literature, architecture, scientific experiment, and religious teaching and practice. It began in Italy, the land from which the popes had for centuries ruled over the spiritual and sometimes the more earthly life of Christendom. It manifested itself in the glories of Renaissance art and architecture, over which towered people like Leonardo da Vinci and Michelangelo, and many others of hardly less stature.

In more northern parts of Europe, it showed itself in the desire of many scholars to search out what was true, especially in matters of religion. The revival of interest in classical Greek and Latin led men to study the New Testament in its original Greek form, and in 1516 Erasmus, a Dutch-born scholar of exceptional brilliance even in an age of dazzling minds, published a complete edition of the Greek text along with a new Latin translation. In this he corrected what he thought were mistakes, and he made a lot of notes about various passages, with no punches pulled. For example, the phrase 'On this rock I will build my church' he believed did not refer just to the pope but to all Christians. This was heresy indeed, but there was more to come.

The following year, another scholar, Martin Luther, a German monk who had given up his monastery, began to question the doctrines of the church, and he published a long list of his views and nailed them on the door of Wittenburg cathedral. This was the signal for a movement among peoples and countries to reform

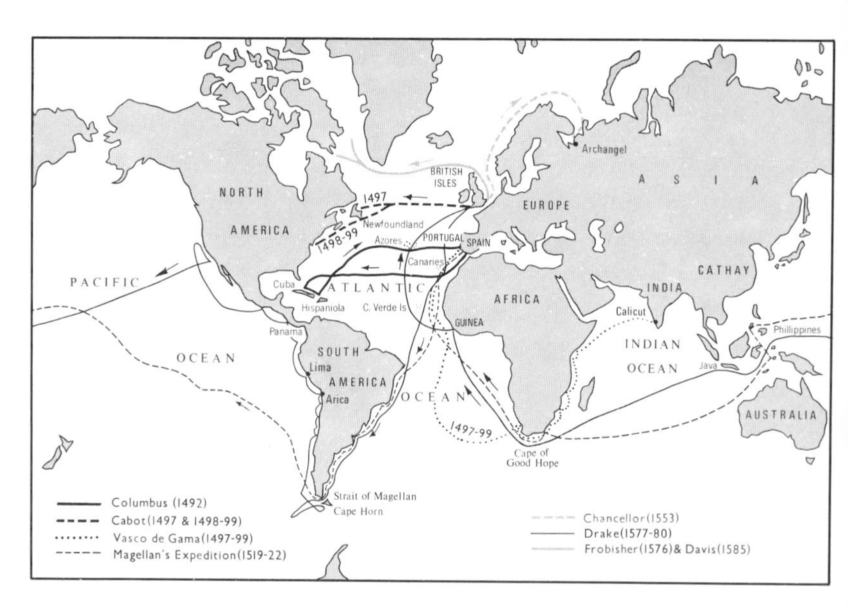

Routes followed by the great discoverers of the 15th and 16th centuries. These brave men and their gallant crews set out in small ships in search of sea routes to India and the Far East, to find a cheaper way to buy spices and other things. Previously Europeans had to buy them after they had been brought across land by caravan, increasing in price every time they crossed a frontier.

the church. Within a generation or so several nations had taken matters into their own hands, broken away from Rome and founded their own reformed churches. One of these was England.

The work of the reformers was enormously helped by the invention and development of printing. When William Tyndale tried to smuggle copies of his English translation of the Bible into England, all but a few of the 5,000 copies, which had been printed secretly abroad, were confiscated.

Printing – the great innovation

The Chinese had been using moveable type for printing since about AD 600, and it is strange that the idea never came to Europe. It is thought this may have been because the Chinese alphabet was so utterly unlike western European letters that it never occurred to anyone that our smaller and simpler lettering could be treated in the same way. In about 1430 Gutenburg invented a printing press in Germany. Over the next generation several more presses were made, and one of these, at Cologne, was seen by William Caxton, a rich English silk merchant who was travelling about Europe on holiday. In 1476 he brought a press to England, after he had tried one out in Germany and had even printed some books. He set it up at Westminster. It was the first in the country and it created great interest. Edward IV is said to have visited Caxton one afternoon to see how it worked. Caxton demonstrated the press, and on that day dedicated one of his publications to the king.

Until this time, books in England had been laboriously copied out by hand on expensive rolls or sheets of parchment or vellum. None but the very wealthy could afford them, and even the best libraries, like Duke Humphrey's at Oxford (now part of the Bodleian) had no more than fifty or so, and these would often be chained to the table so that they could not be stolen. Caxton changed all that.

At about the same time, paper made from linen and cotton rags began to be made on a mass scale, so that many copies of a book could be run off. The first mill producing paper for Caxton was at Stevenage in Hertfordshire, and towards the end of the 15th century it supplied enough for his first edition of Chaucer's works. Caxton printed over eighty books in his lifetime.

It would be difficult to over-estimate the importance of this revolutionary introduction in Europe and Britain. It was the most marvellous tool in the spread of knowledge which was the mainspring of the Revival of Learning. More and more people longed to learn about a multitude of things, and all the presses in Britain were kept extremely busy for a long time to come. This printing was of course invaluable to schools and colleges.

This woodcut of about 1500 is one of the earliest surviving drawings of a printing press in Europe.

Colleges and schools

You will remember that in the Middle Ages there were grammar schools, song schools and universities. Towards the end of the age the first schools like Winchester and Eton were founded. But learning on a wider scale did not come to England until the Tudor Age. The Revival of Learning had been under way for a century or more in Europe, but it was slow to reach England. This was largely because of the French wars and then the awful Wars of the Roses, both of which arrested the nation's progress.

So far as England was concerned, Tudor times were on the whole quieter and less troubled by war. It was not the same in Scotland or Ireland. Great strides were made in education. Oxford and Cambridge universities had been going for some time, and now some new colleges were added. Scotland already had St Andrews and Glasgow universities. New schools were founded. Dean Colet founded St Paul's in London. Edward VI sponsored some new grammar schools, like Shrewsbury, King Edward's,

Dean Colet, the famous Oxford scholar, founded St Paul's School in London, near the old cathedral. When that was burnt down in the Great Fire of 1666 the school went too. This picture is an 18th-century engraving of the new school.

Birmingham, and in Elizabeth's reign, Harrow, Rugby and Uppingham were begun. Some of these became boarding schools later and thus acquired the status of public schools.

Latin and Greek became compulsory, and there was greater scope for the study of the sciences and geography.

Buildings and gardens

In the Tudor age, house-building entered an exciting new phase. The kings had control of gunpowder supplies. Rich men felt safer as the danger of civil war receded, and no longer sought to live in huge, dark, dank, ill-lit castles or even fortified manor houses (like Stokesay in Shropshire), where the window space was only a fraction of the wall area. They could, and did, build splendid

An example of a late medieval half-timbered house, Little Moreton Hall, in Cheshire.

A 16th-century oak chest, with the Tudor rose motif carved on the front. This is in the Victoria & Albert Museum in London.

mansions; the size and the elaboration of the decoration depended on their wealth. They could concentrate on having homes of comfort and beauty. And up and down the country hundreds of such houses were built during the 16th century. Many of them are still standing today.

Large mansions were built of stone or brick, and in the later part of the century the influences of the architecture of the Renaissance in Europe can be seen. The buildings were symmetrical; one end balanced with the other and the centre with both. They were also profusely glazed, that is, the window area was a substantial part of the whole walling. Inside, they featured new rooms like a large drawing room (taking the place of the old solar) and a long gallery (on the upper floor and often overlooking the garden). Rooms were much more spacious and the walls were often panelled with oak. Ceilings were covered with decorative plaster-work, often of a most intricate design. In Tudor times, for example, a popular motif was the Tudor rose. Some of the rooms were festooned with hanging tapestries on the walls, and for the first time oil paintings began to be hung. In Britain it was the age of portrait painting, and celebrated painters from Europe spent long periods carrying out commissions for wealthy men. The example had been set by Henry VIII and Wolsey who had given work to Holbein, a leading German painter.

Another major feature of great Tudor houses was the main staircase. No longer a cold, twisting stone affair, it had become a craftsman's dream. Wide wooden steps, deep and shining, were enclosed in a framework of carved wooden posts and balustrades. Each flight was broken by a square landing, and the whole encircled an open well.

Smaller houses were of course less elaborate, but they had great individuality and style. Built usually of brick and timber, or timber and plaster-covered rubble, the upper storey or storeys, under a sharp gable roof, stuck out beyond the lower storey. Windows were often bay type, with side glass frames as well as the main frame. Occasionally, the walls were hung with tiles like the roofs. An enormous number of these houses have survived,

This is the Great Bed of Ware. Constructed of oak in the time of Queen Elizabeth I, who is believed to have spent a night in it, it is 2·7 metres (8 ft 9 ins) high, 3·3 metres (10 ft $8\frac{1}{2}$ ins) wide and 3·4 metres (11 ft) long! It is big enough for a giant, and much too big for the queen who was a short and slim person.

A Venetian glass jug of the 16th century.

and in some cases the original title deeds exist to prove their age. They can be seen in many counties, but Essex and Suffolk seem to have an exceptionally large number of them in good repair.

Out of the top of the roof, at either end or both, or in the middle, chimney stacks reached up into the sky. The 16th century ones are generally of brickwork. They had become essential by the 17th century when coal burning was done on a wide scale. Some of the stacks were composites of several chimneys, decorated in spiral twists or hexagonal or quatrefoil shapes. On the tops were pottery chimney pots, often decorated with flower motifs.

It was in Elizabethan times that house furniture first began to be more than just an assortment of functional and not at all graceful pieces. Until the 14th century, in England at all events, the single moveable chair was practically unknown, though they had had them in Wales since at least the 12th century. Medieval kings had often granted audiences to ambassadors or members of foreign royal houses sitting on one end of the bed, their guests precariously perched on the other. Now, great houses boasted a range of pieces, many finely carved and elaborately decorated. The four-poster bed, the hall settle, the high-back, curving-arm chair with squiggly 'barley-sugar' legs and stretchers, the long bulb-leg refectory or dining table—all can be seen in many homes of the period.

On the dining tables families would eat a rapidly growing variety of dishes, as more and more exotic delights came into the

In the 16th century many rich people adorned their gardens with hedge mazes. This one, still preserved at Hampton Court, was planted in Tudor times.

country from the East and the Americas, following the discoveries of the sea routes. These would be served in plates and bowls made of glazed earthenware of coloured design, of pewter, even of gold or silver. They would drink from cups or goblets of glass which might be the new Venetian coloured type or just the duller, less clear English kind. Utensils were of silver or pewter, or polished iron, and knives generally had bone, horn or ivory handles.

And for the first time people began to sit down comfortably. Chairs had cushions, sofas and day beds were equipped with padded mattresses and quantities of luxuriously covered and embroidered silk or velvet cushions of many sizes. Benches were upholstered, and there was no need to be stiff from hours on a hard seat.

Outside the houses of the rich were laid out the most wonderful gardens. The Tudors loved flowers and they had rows of flower beds, often arranged in geometrical patterns, interspersed with grass or with paving stones, also in geometrical patterns. Sometimes they liked red brick paths laid in straight lines or in what is called 'herring bone' pattern. One interesting garden design was the knot garden, a number of small flower beds cut in formal patterns and edged with low hedging or shrubbery, made to look like a symmetrical series of knots. Some gardens had mazes, and a famous one was at Hampton Court, where you can still see it, along with a knot garden.

Above left: The garden at Hampton Court Palace.

Above right: A 16th-century engraving of a formal garden of Elizabeth I's time.

Gardens were not confined to great mansions or large town houses. Small businessmen, farmers and master craftsmen had them too. They were not unlike the average garden of today, except of course they could not have been so tidily kept as there were not the garden tools available. If there was any grass patch – you could not call it a lawn – it may have been kept close cut by scythe, or perhaps a sheep or two. Flowers were sometimes laid out in beds round it, and while there were several kinds of roses available, you certainly could not get the many hundreds of kinds you can today. These gardens were often larger than the eighth to half-acre average size today. They also contained herb patches, in an age which preserved its food in herbs and spices and cooked with them.

And even the smaller gardens had orchards of fruit trees alongside. Apples were the most prolific fruit, from which you could make your own cider and get your guests rolling drunk.

Inns

A particular kind of building, the inn, rapidly became a feature of both towns and countryside in Tudor times. Inns first appeared in England in the 14th century and were chiefly intended to provide food and rest for pilgrims. But by the 16th century the inn had become a kind of institution. Much care was lavished by the owner on keeping it warm, inviting and well-stocked.

An inn was built round three, or sometimes four, sides of a yard which might be cobble-stoned. Stables were provided for horses and one side might be a long open-sided shed for the various carts which travellers and merchants were taking to and from towns or ports or big private houses. A good inn had a staff of servants under a cheerful, rotund landlord who ordered

This is a picture of the Old Tabard Inn in Southwark, London. It was a good example of an Elizabethan inn, with the first floor gallery round the courtyard.

them about in a genial manner. The ostler took care of your horse, the chamberlain (or perhaps a pretty chambermaid, daughter of a local farm labourer) showed you to your quarters. There was no bar as we know it now, but more than one room was given over to drinking, and the drinks were brought in on trays by serving wenches or lads. There was a tap room which had a barrel or two of local ale or wine, cider or mead, and the drinking would be more prolonged, soon to be advertised by shouting and singing and banging of cups or pewter tankards on the heavy wooden tables.

You could also eat meals at these inns – good, homely, country cooking, the meat quite possibly from freshly slaughtered beasts. A beef joint, or a whole carcase would perhaps be turning slowly on a spit over a fire, guided by a lad or girl pulling on saw-edged crane and chains.

Inns were not peculiar to England, or to Britain, but it was often said that the English inns were the best in the world. This is an interesting comment because today the British public house still has no counterpart anywhere else, and is one of the biggest attractions to tourists. In Tudor times most good inns already had their own individual signs, and many took the form of silhouette illustrations, to bring in customers. Knocked out by the local blacksmith, they would sometimes advertise that they catered for a particular type of customer – for example, a large cross indicated that the inn catered for pilgrims.

The one feature that outweighed all others in English inns was the spirit of welcome pervading the whole staff. It is rare enough to find this today.

Enclosures and the people

What had been happening to the land, to the villages and to the manor farms? We have seen that the great shortage of labourers for the land which followed the terrible Black Death of 1348–49 led to labourers being able to state their own terms for hire. The government's attempts to check this were harsh. The landlords sometimes found their own answer. Many of them decided to turn their land over to sheep-raising, for English wool and the cloth it made were still in enormous demand. They could afford to pay good wages to shepherds. One man could care for a large flock over an area of land that it would take several men to cultivate. So, the need for the villein and the labourer began to die out. Their services were not required on so wide a scale, and by 1500 there were few of them left in England. The income from sheep-farming enabled a lord to buy his corn from farmers who worked large farms, or he could buy it from merchants. But if the need for the villein had gone, the class from which he was drawn remained and was growing in size. This brought widespread unemployment and all its attendant miseries, for there were no welfare allowances in those days, and little was done by the state to help.

This conversion of land from corn-growing to sheep-rearing was accompanied by a new and very ugly feature – the enclosure. It was not a new thing in the 16th century, but the practice began to grow rapidly. This was due to a steady rise in the population of the country and to the demands of the cloth industry for more wool.

The population of England in the days just before the Black Death is calculated to have been about 4,000,000 (at the Domesday Book survey in 1085 it was about 1,500,000). The dreaded scourge cut that down to about 2,500,000, which may have risen to 2,750,000 by about 1400. By 1500 it had risen to 3,500,000 and by the end of the 16th century it was about 4,500,000. So the rate was rising as well as the actual numbers. These people had to be fed.

The practice of enclosing land had begun at the end of the 14th century. Country landlords, as well as many in towns, began to buy up estates and turn the arable land into enclosed areas for sheep-rearing. Notable among the sellers of land were the monasteries and abbeys. The practice accelerated throughout the 15th century, and by about the middle of the 16th century, nearly one tenth of the arable land of England was fenced off. This is not a bad overall figure, but the fencing off was not done evenly. About a third of all arable land in the Midlands, for example, was enclosed, and this brought a lot of unemployment and misery there. We shall see that the practice continued for another two or more centuries: so did the misery.

Enclosures did not hit the big landowners, for it was largely they who were doing it. But the smaller farmer suffered greatly. It threw many men out of work more or less permanently, and created a pool of beggars and vagabonds, who tried desperately to fight off death from starvation by begging and stealing. If they were caught stealing they could expect no mercy under the law and would finish up dangling from a gallows, erected probably by a crossroads on a hill, as a lesson to others.

The government did little, until the very beginning of the 17th century, when the Poor Law Act of 1601 was passed. This put the responsibility for relieving the poor on the parish. Justices of the peace had to see that each parish collected a poor

A woodcut from Holinshed's History, showing an Elizabethan execution scene.

rate, and got children of the poor apprenticed to craftsmen and tradesmen. Some years earlier beggars, who were quite able to get jobs but did not try, were discouraged by an act which made them liable to be flogged if caught once, and hanged if caught a third time.

Recreation and leisure

A great many of the leisure activities we enjoy today were not available to our 16th-century ancestors. But there were perhaps surprisingly many forms of recreation for the individual or groups. The Tudors certainly believed in getting as much out of life as they could, in work and in play. Richer people had their grand homes, and they derived enormous pleasure from furnishing and decorating them with the latest designs and expensive cloth. Many spent a year or two in Europe, perhaps in Italy, Germany or France, learning the language and visiting friends in their big homes or attending foreign courts. They would get all sorts of ideas from these for the design and decorating of their own homes and gardens. They met a great many interesting people – poets, musicians, artists, lawyers, historians, and as they had a lot of time on their hands, they might dabble in art or poetry themselves.

When they came home again, they could create their own circle of friends with similar tastes. Dressing in doublet and hose (like jacket and breeches), with a ruff high round the neck and sporting a beret-type cap with a feather, they would caper about the drawing-room of their mansion reciting some of the latest verses of one or other of the great poets. Or they might have written some of their own verse. Perhaps these verses were accompanied by music, for Tudor Englishmen were fond of music. Henry VIII had composed several short works which are now highly rated, and his daughter Elizabeth I played the virginal better than most people in the land.

There were other musical instruments, such as the lute, which was like a mandolin, and the viol, an ancestor of the violin. The lute was especially fashionable. Not only did it accompany singing in a great house. If you went to an ordinary barber's shop you would often hear one played by another customer waiting his turn for a trim.

If you were a guest at a great house, and you did not like music, you could probably spend the evening in the library. Most rich men had volumes of books bound in leather, with the titles etched in gilt lettering on the spine. They collected these on their European tours, or bought them in one or other of the growing number of bookshops springing up in London, Norwich, Bristol, Exeter, Oxford, Cambridge and other towns. The printing press was now commonplace, and the quantity of literature of all kinds printed and published was enormous. At first most books were huge and heavy, and the print face was almost as large as modern newspaper headlines, but then an Italian printer introduced the octavo-sized book and you could in many cases slip this into a pocket.

If you were not rich, you would probably not be taught to read or write. And you would possibly be living in one of the simpler half-timbered houses. What entertainments were there for you? There was no cricket, but some kind of football was

Morris dancers in Elizabethan times. Teams of Morris dancers travelled about the countryside at about the end of April every year to celebrate May Day (May 1). They dressed in all their finery, with caps and bells on their feet and legs, wearing scarves and ribbons. It was an excuse also for a tremendous round of parties. This is still carried on in East Anglia today.

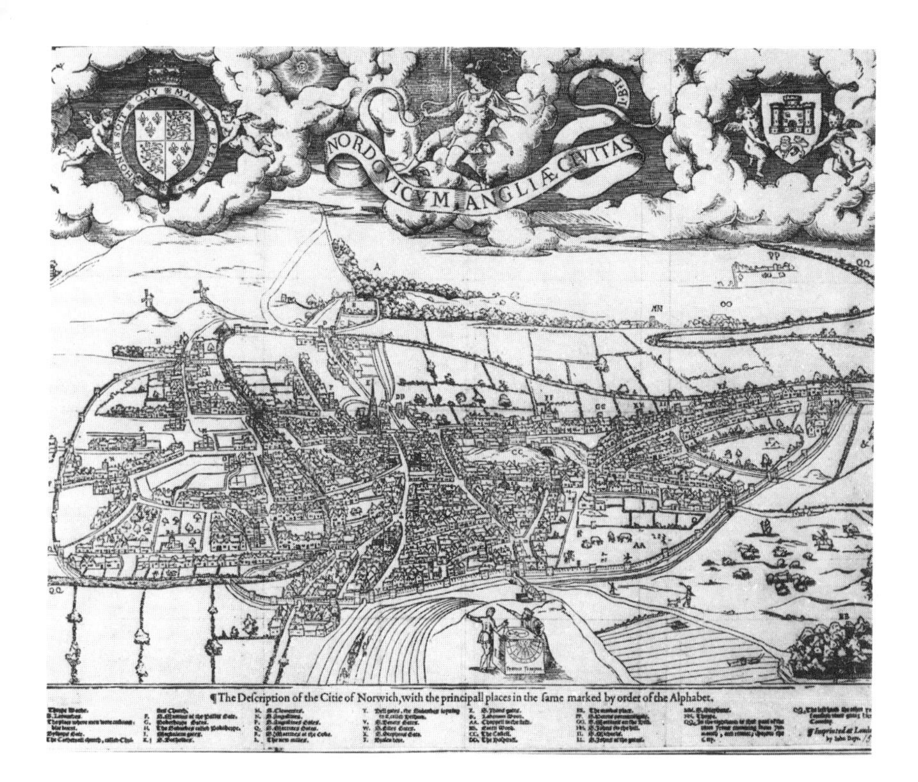

Left: This is a map of Norwich in 1558. Norwich was the second city in England for several centuries, up to the Industrial Revolution. By Elizabeth's time it was still immensely rich, with far more houses and other buildings than other towns, except for London. The only town of similar size was Bristol.

Above: An engraving of a picnic scene in a wood, from the 16th century. It shows Elizabeth I under the tree at the top (left). The same picture was altered in the next reign, and the figure of James I was drawn in Elizabeth's place.

known. There was cock-fighting. This was a disgusting pastime where specially trained cocks, with steel spurs fitted to their claws, fought to the death in a confined space known as the cockpit. Bets were placed on which would be the last of a group to die. In the next century the Puritans rightly tried to ban cock-fighting, but it was not officially prohibited until the time of Queen Victoria (1837–1901) and even now you can, here and there in the north of England, and illegally, see a cockfight.

Another awful pastime was bear-baiting. A bear was tied to a post by a chain in the middle of a pit, and a pack of mastiffs was let loose against it. The bear usually gave a good account of itself, and bets were placed on which dog could survive for longest. Sometimes, however, the bear would be worn down, and that was the occasion for prolonged cheers. This, too, was banned by the Puritans, but was revived in the time of Charles II (1660–1685).

Other games you might play in your town included bowls (Drake is said to have been playing at Plymouth when the Spanish Armada was sighted coming up the Channel in 1588), marbles, skittles, darts (the targets were often the ends of wooden ale casks), billiards (played with a flat-topped mace) and of course archery which, though the bow and arrow was no longer used in war after about the 1560s, was very popular.

One kind of entertainment enjoyed by everybody, irrespective of class, was the theatre. Elizabethans seemed to love the stage

Above: This drawing is from an old view of London published in 1579. It shows the famous Globe Theatre on the Bank Side in London, where Shakespeare acted when a young man, before turning to become the greatest playwright in the English – possibly any – language.

Above right: A woodcut of 1588 showing the *Ark Royal*, a royal ship. She was Lord Howard of Effingham's flagship in the fight against the Spanish Armada. She weighed about 800 tons, carried over 50 guns, and the upper hull was probably painted in the Tudor colours of green and white.

more than anything. By that we do not necessarily mean the putting on of a play, with costumes and props on a stage in a building, so much as the actual business of acting. The courtyards of inns, surrounded as they often were by three or four two-storeyed sides with covered galleries, were natural places for ad hoc performances of plays. It might be a company of wandering actors, known as strollers, who came to the 'Lamb and Flag' in Oxford. They would be wearing ordinary travelling clothes and would act out some well known play by, say, Marlowe, without any scenery. Or they fooled around, acting a composition of one of their own number, which might be a daring attack on the church or the Queen and her men friends.

In London and in some other towns, towards the end of the period, real theatres were built. One was the Globe, on the south bank of the Thames. It was made of wood, octagonal in plan, with its top open to the elements. The stage was a platform running more or less centrally through the space inside, except that one side of the space was shuttered off with curtains or screens for dressing rooms. Around the inner walls were covered seats in tiers, like the boxes at many London theatres today, or the galleried boxes at the great Albert Hall, only much smaller. If it rained, the spectators were all right, but the actors got wet, unless someone remembered to pull the thin muslin veil across the top to keep out the worst of it. The Globe had been built in 1591 by the actor Richard Burbage, who was to appear in many of Shakespeare's plays as they were written. It was destroyed by fire in 1613 and then rebuilt.

Above: Queen Elizabeth I, from a portrait now in the National Portrait Gallery, London.

Above: If you visit the Tower of London, you can still be shown the execution block and an axe for removing an offender's head. The block probably accommodated the necks of such famous victims as Lady Jane Grey, Sir Walter Raleigh and Sir Thomas More. The axe may not be as old as that.

Opposite above: One of the shipyards of the East India Company, on the Thames, as it was in the middle of the 17th century. The striped flags indicate that the ships are ocean-going merchantmen and not royal ships.

Major changes in England

The Reformation of the Christian religion had not been achieved painlessly in England. Henry VIII forced his subjects to acknowledge him as Supreme Head of the English Church, thus forbidding them to recognize the authority of the Pope in Rome. At the same time he compelled them to continue accepting many of the Roman doctrines. Edward VI's reign saw a marked swing away from Rome and the publication of a new Prayer Book in English, which to some extent ironed out this dilemma. Then Mary I (1553–1558), the embittered, humiliated Roman Catholic daughter of Henry VIII, succeeded and at once set out to restore England to the orthodox Roman faith. She did so with great violence and cruelty. Hundreds of people who refused to accept the change back were burned at the stake, including an archbishop of Canterbury (Cranmer, who had written the New Prayer Book), and some bishops.

Then came Elizabeth I (1558–1603) who wisely decided to steer a moderate middle-of-the-road course. The settlement she and her splendid chief minister, William Cecil, worked out has lasted more or less to the present.

This was one of the major developments of the age. Others included the strengthening of the power of the monarchy at the expense of the feudal baronage, which found itself increasingly isolated. The Tudor kings' policy was to employ in the highest government positions men noted for their ability and not their social background – which, in the most brilliant of them, Cecil, Walsingham, Hatton and Bacon, was middle class. The danger of war with France receded as that country sank into a long and gloomy period of civil war over religion. A new enemy emerged Spain, with all its wealth from the rich colonies in North and South America and elsewhere. But the amazing boldness of England's privateers and sea captains, the prudence of the Queen and her ministers, coupled with the astonishing forbearance of Philip II of Spain (1556–1598) resulted in only one major confrontation, the attempted invasion of England by the Spanish

Armada in 1588. This ended in catastrophe for the Spaniards. When that danger passed, all England breathed an immense sigh of relief. And the last 15 years of the old Queen's reign were packed with interest.

English literature blossomed marvellously into its finest period, with prolific and peerless work by Marlowe, Spenser, and the incomparable Shakespeare, to name but a few. English music entered a new vital stage and William Byrd became one of the best composers in Europe. English art began to get off the ground and Nicholas Hilliard, the miniaturist, was in great demand. We have seen it was an era of grand building, and Renaissance-style houses began to shoot up all over the land, in town and country. There was considerably more money about. Trade increased. The East India Company was founded. So was the Merchant Adventurers' Company. Both were repositories of enormous wealth. England began to found colonies in North America, the West Indies and elsewhere.

But beneath all this ran undercurrents of political unrest. Elizabeth's last Parliaments were angry ones. They did not like her absolutism, nor did they see it as necessary. They wanted more say in the running of the country, especially over financial affairs. And already the religious settlement was in danger, for on one side was ranged the expanding Puritan movement and on the other the growing tendency of some of the established church hierarchy to revert to more authoritarian doctrines better associated with Rome. These were the major conflicts of the next century.

Above: An engraving of Elizabeth opening Parliament one day towards the end of her reign. She is on the throne at the top of the picture, with her Lords Temporal (peers) and Spiritual (bishops) in rows in front of her. At the forefront is the Speaker of the House of Commons (he has his hand up), and he is accompanied by MPs.

The Rise of the Celtic nations

In Chapter One we saw what Celtic society was like before the coming of the Romans. In Chapter Two we looked at the impact of Roman civilization on Britain. What was happening to the Celtic peoples in Britain in the centuries following the collapse of Roman administration, when the Jutes, Angles and Saxons invaded and ultimately conquered what is now England?

In Scotland, Gaelic Celts, kinsmen of the Brythonic Celts who had driven them into the highlands and islands several centuries earlier, emerged slowly into a state of civilization, although they remained preoccupied with war. As late as AD 449 they were still conducting raids into southern Britain. They were certainly interested in the material benefits of Roman civilization, such as jewellery, expensive clothes and weaponry. Nothing justified a raid more, in their eyes, than a series of wagon-loads of Romano–British treasure like brooches, belts, robes, helmets, swords and sc on. These Celts remained warlike, disunited and pagan for twc centuries longer.

In Ireland, the Gaelic Celts had been in occupation since abou 500 BC, or perhaps earlier. They had mixed with the more primitive people they found there. They, too, were practically unaffected by Roman civilization. The nearest the Romans go to invading Ireland was talking about it round the table at the house of the governor of Britain, Julius Agricola, in the 80s AD. I is true that Roman merchants traded with the Irish Celts through out the centuries of Roman occupation of Britain, but that was all. The Irish developed their own civilization and adopted thos aspects of Roman culture which they wanted. They wer imaginative and gifted people, and by combining their nativ talents with the inventive genius of the Romans, they shon brightly in a Europe otherwise dark and gloomy after the collaps of the western Roman Empire.

In Wales, although the Romans had strongholds of some siz and importance, at places like Caerleon-on-Usk, Caernarvon Caersws (Montgomeryshire), Carmarthen, and Neath, these wer a very long way apart. In the spaces between, most of whic were mountainous and in the winter treacherous, Brythoni

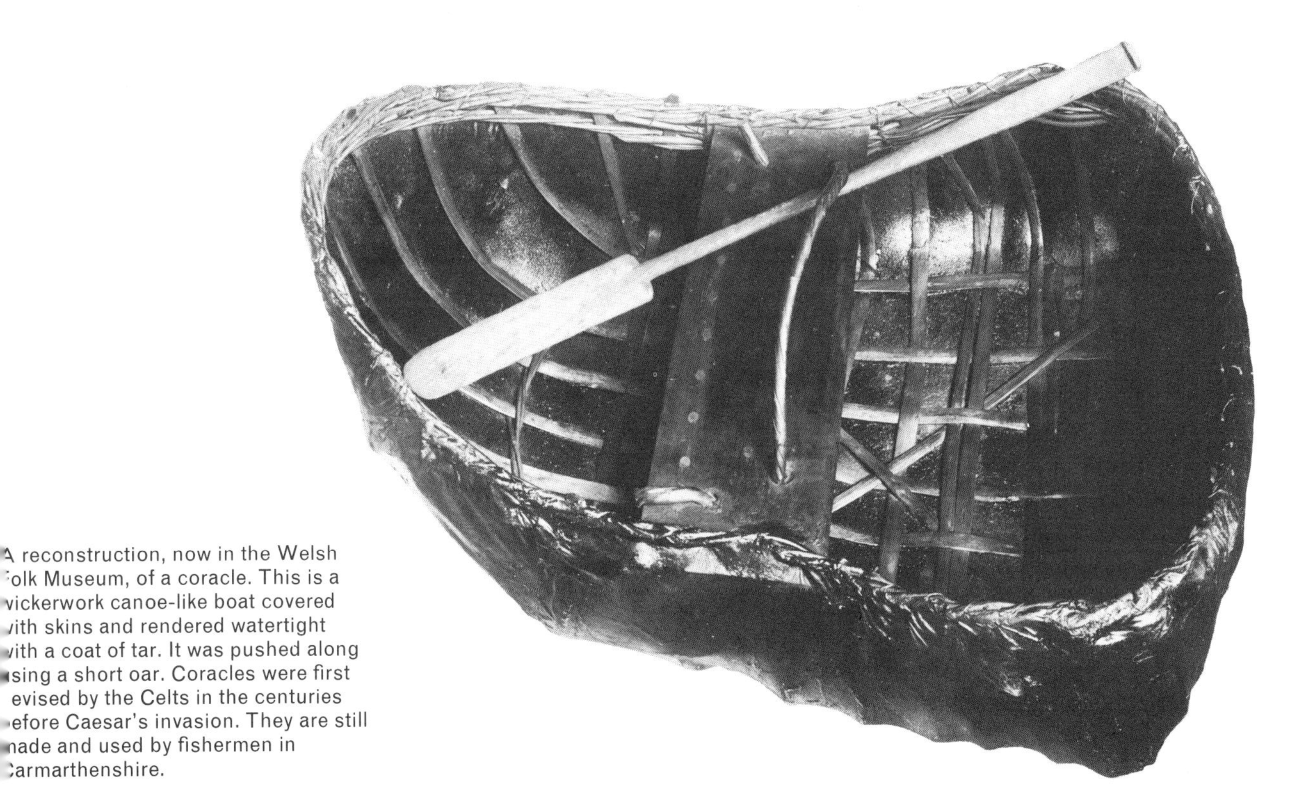

A reconstruction, now in the Welsh 'olk Museum, of a coracle. This is a vickerwork canoe-like boat covered vith skins and rendered watertight vith a coat of tar. It was pushed along ısing a short oar. Coracles were first evised by the Celts in the centuries efore Caesar's invasion. They are still nade and used by fishermen in Carmarthenshire.

(or British) Celts carried on their tribal lives much as before – fighting, celebrating, idling away the hours, sheep- and cattle-rustling, and so on. There is little evidence of Roman settlement, and there are very few remains of villas or towns.

When the Anglo–Saxon invaders came across the sea and landed in southern Britain, the British Celts put up considerable resistance here and there in the Gloucester-Somerset-Devon-Cornwall arc. Notable among the resisters was Arthur, a Romano–Celt cavalry leader whose stand against the English was so spectacular that a whole canon of legend grew up around his career and associates. When they were finally pushed out of England, however, they went in three main directions – north to Strathclyde, west to Wales, and south-west to Cornwall, there to join their kinsmen. Some, perhaps, also went to the Isle of Man.

Wales

One of the most interesting things about Wales is the language. Today it is the oldest spoken language in Europe, and over half a million people in Wales are fluent in it. It has not altered much in more than two thousand years. In Roman times they persisted in speaking it, adding from Latin only engineering, building and

This is a drawing of the inside of a Welsh farmhouse of the 12th century. It appeared in *Archaeologia Cambrensis* in 1899, a famous Welsh archaeological journal that is still published regularly.

scientific terms which they did not have themselves. Window i Latin is *fenestra* and in Welsh it became *ffenestr*. This languag was not written down in pre-Roman times, but everyone under stood it, and it was kept alive by the bards (or poets) who san ballads and songs in it, at the courts of the several princes o in the tribal gatherings. The language had – and still has – severa dialects in the different areas of Wales in which it is spoken.

In Chapter One, we mentioned the kindred or clan as a integral part of Celtic society in the years before the Roman oc cupation. Long after the Romans had gone, when the Anglo-Saxon had a grip on England, the kindred continued to be the basis of Wels society. It was known as the *cenedl*, and you could only inheri membership through men – in other words, your father, uncl brother, or close male cousin. The head of the *cenedl* was calle the *pencenedl* and he officiated at ceremonies admitting ne members.

In Wales, anyone who owned land, or who was heir to lan was a member of a *cenedl*. Whatever his class of society, he ha certain legal rights, whether he was a freeman or a villein lan holder (called a *taeog*), like the English villein who had to do servic on the lord's demesne for a certain number of days in every yea The *taeog's* lot was a hard one, however, for he could not hun nor was he allowed to leave the land to seek a better job in on of the crafts, like ironsmithing. He could not leave the communit in which he lived without forfeiting all his possessions. More ofte than not, he was part of a community, in a hamlet or villag which was devoted to working the land. This community, or *tre* functioned on a work-sharing basis. *Taeogs* were formed in plough teams, and they had to see that a fixed area of land w ploughed within a certain time limit.

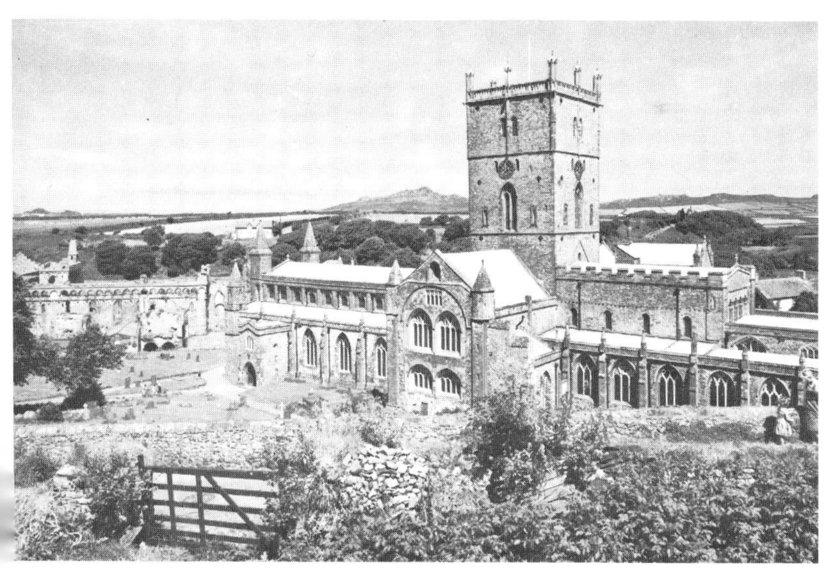

St David's Cathedral, Pembrokeshire, in Wales. St David, first organizer of the Christian Church in Wales, created the see and died there in about 600. The cathedral in the picture, however, is of a much later date, and was begun in about 1180.

But Wales was very largely pastoral – that is, most of it was given over to sheep- or cattle-farming. This was partly due to the physical nature of the land – mainly mountainous and hilly with poor soil. But it was also due to the character of the Celt, who was essentially a man with an idle nature. Pasturage or hunting were less arduous than tilling the soil, and meat was more attractive than grain products.

The *cenedlau* were close-knit units which were jealous of their achievements, kindred history and position in the land. They supported each other in quarrels with *cenedlau* of other districts. They intermarried, keeping the kindred connected by blood, which of course led to the development of large families. As there was no law stating that only sons born in wedlock could inherit land, the distribution of a man's property, when he died, could be more widespread.

Wales was for centuries divided into a number of principalities. These never retained the same borders for very long, for the princes constantly squabbled over who owned what. The main principalities were Gwynedd, Powys, Dyfed, Morgannwg, Deheubarth and Ceredigion. Gwynedd, which incorporated Anglesey, Caernarvonshire and Meirionethshire, was from about 850 regarded as the most important principality, and its rulers regarded themselves as princes of all Wales. Some, like Rhodri Mawr (844–878), Owain Gwynedd (1137–1170) and Llywelyn Fawr (1194–1240) certainly dominated Wales in their time.

These principalities were divided into regions called *cantrefs* – largish administrative units, perhaps like some of the new district councils created by the Local Government Act of 1972. A *cantref* might be further divided into two or three *commotes*, and each *commote* had its own law court. A *commote* would be made up of a number of the small, individual communities called *trefau*.

Christianity came to Wales early in the fourth century AD, and it never died. All through the dark years, after the departure of the Romans in the fifth century, churches in Wales remained bastions of the faith among a people who were frightened by the raids of the Anglo–Saxon peoples. And when the Romano–British fled to Wales, they found comfort in the fact that God did not seem to have deserted Wales. It was a British scholar from Wales, Patricius, who was to go to Ireland in the fifth century, after many adventures and many years of training in a religious community in France, to bring the faith to Gaelic Ireland.

In the sixth century, another Welsh religious leader, David, regenerated the Welsh church. He founded some monasteries in Wales, and organized regular meetings of church leaders. These early Welsh monasteries were not like those, say, at Fountains. The Celtic monks were not confined to cloistered quadrangle buildings, but were free – indeed encouraged – to go out on preaching expeditions, for there were pockets of the Welsh countryside where Christianity had not taken root. The monastery was much more than a home for monks. It was a religious centre for the whole district. It was open to everyone who wanted to come in and enjoy what facilities it had, such as a school or shop or meeting place. It was supported largely by the lands surrounding it, which the monks and their servants tilled.

The monastery was ruled firmly by an abbot who, generally, passed his post on to a son or nephew. He kept the monks to a work schedule. Much of their day was spent in the fields, and they had only one main meal, supper, which consisted occasionally of meat but more generally of dairy products like eggs, cheese and butter, with vegetables. They could have ale, but drunkenness was regarded as a serious offence. After supper they spent some time studying the scriptures and learned works of the early doctrines of the church. Some of the monks had writing lessons. On Sundays and Saints' Days they took holy communion, did less work in the fields and could have a more interesting supper. In many ways their lives were not unlike those in the monasteries of England, such as at Jarrow where Bede lived and wrote.

Welsh monks were encouraged to go out and found new religious houses, particularly on the islands off the coast, where they could find peace and isolation in which to lead lives of self-denial. Some of these foundations became famous, such as on Bardsey Island, off the Meirionethshire coast, and Priestholm off Anglesey. The Welsh monks were not allowed to marry, but although at first the clergy were also discouraged, after the 9th century marriage was allowed. As a result sons often followed their fathers in church livings. At some island monasteries, however, women of any kind were strictly forbidden, as at Priestholm.

After the Norman conquest of England in the 11th century, when parts of south and east Wales were occupied by Norman Marcher lords, there was a spate of religious-house building. Splendid abbeys, as good as anything in England, went up at Strata Florida, Tintern, Aberconway and Valle Crucis. These were among the earliest church buildings in stone. Before then, buildings were of timber and wattle. There were hundreds of churches, called *llans*, and many are perpetuated in place names

Below right: Here is a famous Celtic Cross, at Margam in south Wales. It is from the 8th–9th century, and is known as the great cross of Conbelin. The figures on the shaft are of St John and the Virgin Mary.

Below left: In the Welsh Folk Museum is a reconstructed kitchen as it would have been in a 17th-century castle. Many of the utensils are of those times, and they were not unlike those used in earlier times.

today, centuries after the buildings have gone, such as Llanfairfechan in Caernarvonshire, Llangefni in Anglesey, and Llandeilo in Caermarthenshire.

Among the stone buildings were two cathedrals, on a smaller scale than those in England. These were St David's in Pembrokeshire (the largest religious building in Wales) and St Asaph, a tiny cathedral of local red sandstone in Flintshire, first begun in the 13th century.

It was in the 13th century, too, that the Welsh began to build their own stone castles. Three that were interesting were Dolbadarn, on the northern end of the Pass of Llanberis in Caernarvonshire, Dolwyddelan near Betws-y-Coed also in Caernarvonshire, and

Dolbadarn Castle, Caernarvonshire. The round tower of this Welsh-built castle, near the pass of Llanberis, was put up in the early 13th century during the reign of the splendid ruler, Llywelyn Fawr (1194–1240) who was Prince of all Wales.

Pembroke, almost certainly started by the Normans. Dolbadarn is a cylindrical great tower inside a curtain wall flanked by smaller rectangular towers. It was built by Llywelyn Fawr (Llywelyn the Great), prince of all Wales (1194–1240). Dolwyddelan is a rectangular great tower, with a hexagonal curtain wall. Prince Llywelyn Fawr is said to have been born here. Pembroke is a huge cylindrical great tower within a thick curtain wall with flanking towers. The cylinder was nearly 30 metres (100 feet) tall, well over 15 metres (50 feet) in diameter, with walls 6 metres (20 feet) thick at the bottom end.

Apart from these cathedrals, churches and castles, Welsh buildings were generally of timber, right up to the conquest by Edward I. But if the houses remained of wood, they did begin to have gardens in the 12th century. Some even had fruit trees, though these were chiefly confined to the counties bordering with England, like Monmouthshire, Radnorshire and Montgomeryshire. Even today a big garden is a comparative rarity in Wales, and so is a fruit orchard, compared with Worcestershire or Kent.

The Welsh had for centuries been poets and songsters, though they did not often record their verses in writing. They handed them down from generation to generation. The 12th century, however, which witnessed the fight back against Norman dominion, particularly under Llywelyn ap Seisyll and Owain Gwynedd, was an age of literary revival, so often a feature of great patriotic movements. One of the works which emerged was the *Historia Brittonum*, written in Latin by the historian-monk Geoffrey of Monmouth. Geoffrey was probably not Welsh, but more likely Breton (from Brittany in France). He rebuilt the legend of King Arthur, a long-standing Celtic hero, and doubtless the princes of Wales who in this century scored so many successes against their Anglo–Norman neighbours believed themselves to be, in some way, reincarnations of Arthur who had held the original Saxon invaders at bay at the end of the 5th century.

Poetry, story-telling, and reciting flourished, and it was a great age for bards, who entertained the prince's court and the gatherings of the Welsh nobility. Bards indeed were given special privileges.

A page from a medieval volume containing the laws of Hywel Dda, Prince of all Wales in the early 10th century (*c* 916–950). Hywel Dda (Howell the Good) was famous for codifying Welsh laws. Among his new ideas was to abolish the death penalty, more than 1,000 years before the British government at Westminster did so!

When Edward I came to conquer Wales in the 1280s, the country was still largely pastoral in its agriculture, and society was still tribal. Perhaps the tribal hangover was in part responsible for the quick collapse of Welsh resistance to the English king, for Llywelyn the Last should certainly have received much more support than he did in his great stand of 1282. The national economy was still based on flocks of sheep and herds of cattle, and a ploughed field was an unusual feature. Welshmen ate a lot of meat, cheese and butter, but had little bread. Anglesey, a low-lying area and known for centuries as the granary of Wales, was the exception, and its fields were rich with corn. When King John invaded north Wales in the early part of the 13th century, his army was unable to live off the land it conquered. The Welsh took all their livestock into the hills with them and the fields had no corn. His men had to buy eggs at a $1\frac{1}{2}$d each, over 50p in today's money.

How this intelligent, poetic, sad, impulsive, unreliable race settled down under the dominion of England we shall see in Chapter Ten.

Scotland

It would be wrong to think that the people of Scotland were brute savages when the Romans came to Britain in the first century AD. They had already learned how to build towns, they had developed a strain of the Celtic language, they knew how to farm, had bronze and iron sickles, and used carts pulled by horses on their farms. They wore tunics and breeches of gaily coloured cloths woven either in their own land or across the Tweed in northern England. They had been visited by Greek mariners centuries before, and they were in close touch with their kinsmen in Gaul and Belgium. They used money, chiefly Roman coinage, and archaeologists have been interested in the quantities of Roman coins dating from before Julius Caesar that have been found all over Scotland.

They built in stone as well as in wood and plaster. Perhaps their biggest structures were the brochs. These were round towers,

Mousa broch, in the Shetland Islands, was built about 2,000 years ago by the ancient Picts (Gaelic Celts in north Scotland) as a refuge against raiders who came from Rome in search of slaves for the idle Roman upper and middle classes. There were many brochs built by the Celts, but Mousa is probably the best example to survive.

many as high as 20 metres (60 feet) or so, and 10–12 metres (30–40 feet) in diameter. The walls were very thick, with no outside windows. In the wall thickness were rooms, connected at different levels by staircases. Some even had galleries. The walls also had passages all round them. The light was provided by the open space inside the building. To be able to see much required strong sunshine especially at the lower levels. One such broch, which has survived in good condition for 2,000 years, is Mousa Broch, in Shetland. This has one small entrance at ground level. Its wall is about 5 metres (15 feet) thick, and the rooms are joined at the various levels by spiral staircases.

Brochs were usually built close to the sea. They were probably refuges for the Celts or Picts against Roman slave trading vessels which used to ply the North Sea and the coast of Britain in search of human beings who could be enchained, taken to the slave markets in Rome or elsewhere in Italy, and sold for good money. These brochs probably came into use again when the Scottish coasts were invaded in the 9th century by the Vikings. Mousa is actually mentioned in a Viking saga.

The story of Scotland in the one and a half centuries from the departure of the Romans to the start of the 7th century is almost unknown. During these tempestuous days the Picts continued to raid southwards, and they fought incessantly with each other. Then, at some time, hosts of Gaelic Celts from northern Ireland, called Scots, came over to the west coast of Scotland, set up the kingdom of Dalriada (approximately Argyllshire and its islands) and stayed there. Then Scotland was divided into four distinct areas, which later became kingdoms. They were Dalriada, the Pictish kingdom (north-east Scotland down to the Forth river),

Above: A picture from a medieval manuscript showing a Scottish monk working in a library.

Top right: St Columba, who came to Iona, off west Scotland, from northern Ireland in the 560s, set up his headquarters on the island and sent out missionaries to spread Christianity to the Picts on the mainland. His building has disappeared, but the place became a shrine, and in the 800s another monastery and chapel were built there. In 1074 Queen Margaret, the wife of Malcolm III, built St Oran's chapel (at right) and it is said that over 40 Scottish kings were buried there. The chapel was restored in 1958

Above right: Jedburgh Abbey, one of the four splendid abbeys founded by David I in the counties near England. The other three were Kelso, Melrose and Dryburgh, and the remains of all are still there.

Strathclyde (south-west Scotland and including Cumberland and Westmoreland) and Bernicia (the northern part of England's Northumbria), which later came to be called Lothian. The divisions were not in fact as clear cut as this, but they give a rough idea.

In the middle of the 6th century, Columba, an Irish Christian missionary, brought a team of followers to Scotland. He settled on the island of Iona, where he built a monastery and began to organize Christianity on a working basis for introduction to the hitherto pagan people of Scotland. The conversion of the country was relatively swift, and soon all over the land there were monasteries, Celtic crosses, Christian communities, craft workshops, studies in which manuscripts were laboriously written out, and smithies where iron, gold, silver, copper and tin were worked to produce a great variety of ornaments, tools, boxes, jewellery and so on.

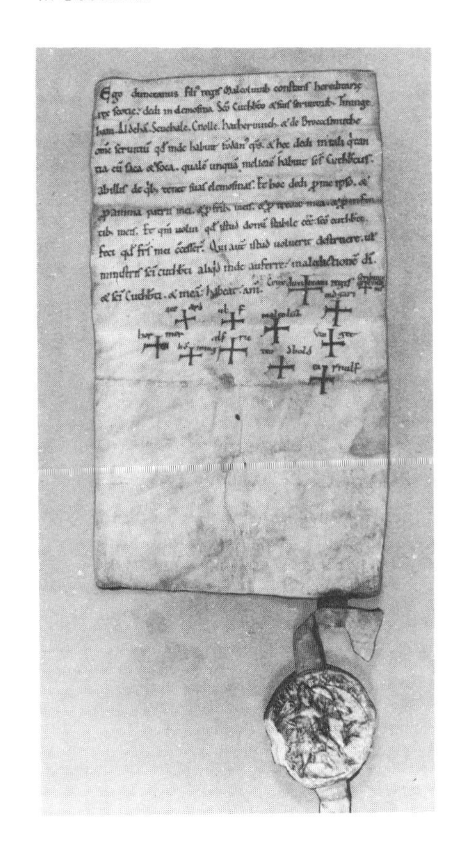

This is a charter of 1094 granting lands in East Lothian to the monks of Durham. It was marked with a cross by King Duncan II, and is one of the very oldest royal documents to survive in Scotland.

The monasteries in Scotland were more like those in Wales and less like those in England. Monks did not have to take vows of chastity and they were often married. They had their own houses inside the monastery grounds, in most cases a small wooden hut. There was an organization of some kind, but a great deal of independence seems to have been accorded to monasteries. Perhaps it was impossible to enforce any uniformity of discipline. The country was divided into dioceses which in turn were split up into parishes. But not until the Normans came to southern Scotland did this mean much. The Normans had been invited by some Scottish kings who preferred the Anglo–Norman way of doing things. When they came they pulled the earlier wooden churches of the Celts down and put up stone ones, as they had been doing in England.

It is difficult to date the earliest towns of Scotland. There were very few which began as Roman towns, decayed after the departure of the Romans, and then were re-built, as had happened in England. Most of the early towns grew up around monasteries which did not begin to appear, apart from St Columba's in Iona, until the 7th century. They were also sited near good natural harbours, for even in those days the inhabitants of the coastline of Scotland were busy traders. And they welcomed the many foreign traders who liked to come to Scottish ports. Very swiftly a merchant class grew up which bought goods from traders and sold them again at a profit. These merchants also bought from the craftsmen in the towns.

Many of these towns, or 'burghs', had considerable freedom to run their own affairs. They could make their own laws, hold courts to settle local disputes, and sentence wrong-doers. Some of them had trading monopolies granted by the kings. Dundee, for example, had the right to make every foreign trading ship coming up the estuary of the Tay put in at its harbour, whereupon the town traders had first option on the ship's goods.

In the 12th and 13th centuries, Dundee consisted of groups of small houses on both sides of a wide main street. Behind the houses were gardens which backed on to cornfields and common

Above: This is a medieval portrait of Robert Bruce, King of Scotland from 1306 to 1329. It is not at all like him, and does little justice to the greatest of Scotland's heroes, but it is probably the earliest surviving portrait.

Above right: Dundee, one of the principal towns of Scotland. It has flourished since the 1100s. The church in this picture is said to be 14th-century in parts, and the photograph of it was taken in 1893!

pasture land. The houses were very small and cramped, low, with thatched roofs, timber-built. The guildhalls were built of stone. One church still standing in Dundee is of this early period.

Ireland

Ireland used at one time to be filled with forests in the centre parts, and so the earliest settlements were on the coastline or beside lakes and rivers where there were fewer trees. The early Gaelic Celts used to live in small groups of houses, very simple structures made of wattle and daub, roofed in thatch, or if there was a supply not too far away, they would be built partly of stone. Some of the houses were surrounded by a circular ditch and bank of earth, or perhaps a stone wall. The houses were often built as lean-to's against a wall, to provide shelter. They were not big, unless they belonged to kings or chiefs, in which case they might be as much as 16 metres (50 feet) across.

They cannot have been very comfortable inside. They had no chimneys and the smoke from the hearth fire in the middle of the floor spiralled up and out through a hole in the roof. If it was windy and wet, the smoke was blown back down again, and you had to live in a thick smoky atmosphere, which made your eyes smart.

Outside the housing groups, there was some kind of field system, but it was not clearly arranged. In the summer and autumn months (May to November), cattle and sheep were taken to special summer pasture fields. They were often herded by specially trained sheep dogs which also acted as guards at night. If you killed one of these guard dogs, by the way, the penalty was to replace it with one of the same breed, and also to pay five cows and restore whatever may have been taken by the wild animals which had not been staved off by the dog. This may seem odd but it was more humane than the punishment for a comparable crime in England.

The Irish economy, such as it was, depended largely on cattle. Indeed, the ownership of cattle determined one's social status. And you could pay for things with cattle, though such things as lawyers' services, crafts goods, and so on, could be repaid in kind. There was, certainly, in the earlier centuries, more than enough to eat for everyone, and everyone was able to eat meat. Animals were usually left out during the winter months and killed when required. Meat thus became a winter diet, and in the summer people turned to dairy products.

Eventually, the Irish began to cultivate their fine soil, probably through the influence of the many monasteries, and soon were growing enough to ensure they were all well fed. This happy situation did not last, however, as we see in Chapter Ten. Apart from farming, the early Irish did not do much else in the way of constructive work. There was little trading, for people grew, or stole, what they wanted and bought their other needs from craftsmen. They spent a great deal of time in the pursuit of leisure, hunting or trapping or even cattle-rustling. They played games like chess, they recited legends and heroic poems, especially about their great heroes Conchobar and his son Cuchullain. Hardly a single Irish peasant did not know some of his national verse, and everyone knew by heart the epic of Cuchullain.

Like England, Scotland and Wales, Ireland was attacked by Viking raiders from the 9th century onwards, and in Ireland's case the raids were very severe. Vikings actually made settlements in and around Dublin, and even established a small kingdom there. These early Vikings went for the monasteries and we may never know how much damage they did to Irish art and craftsmanship, for every monastery had been a repository of culture. The Viking settlement in Dublin was an important one. Founded in about 840 and called Dublin, or Black Pond, it remained in the

Centuries before Jesus Christ, some Gaelic Celts in Ireland lived in crannogs, or lake dwellings. These were artificial islands built in lakes, with wooden buildings, thatch-roofed, surrounded by wooden palisading. Crannogs continued to be built right up to the Middle Ages.

From the Book of Armagh, now at Trinity College, Dublin, this is an entry about the greatest of the kings of all Ireland, Brian Boru (1001–1014). Brian achieved the almost impossible: he united Ireland for about 12 years.

hands of a member of the Norwegian royal family for over a century. A town was built, largely of mud and wattle, with some stone buildings. There, many merchants opened up business houses and traded with the mainland of England and Wales and with European lands. The first coinage in Ireland was used in Dublin by the Vikings.

At first, the Irish and the Vikings kept apart from each other, but by about the 900s the two races were being drawn together and there was a lot of intermarriage in the Dublin area. This brought the Vikings to Christianity. They also settled in other parts, on the east coast, like Wexford, Arklow, Wicklow and Waterford, and by the end of the 10th century they were quite a powerful group of people in Ireland. The native kings did not like them, but until 980 there was not much they could do. In that year, Maelsechlainn II, king of Meath, defeated them in a great battle at Tara, and then called himself king of all Ireland. Twenty years later, Brian Boru, king of Munster, who had conquered Leinster and subjected part of Connaught, declared himself king of all Ireland, and Maelsechlainn conceded this to him. For about twelve years Brian was the real and effective ruler of all Ireland, except for the Viking part round Dublin.

In 1014, Brian fought and beat the Vikings at one of the greatest battles of all Irish history, at Clontarf. But, to the grievous sadness of Irishmen everywhere, Brian himself was slain after the battle was over. This meant that his dominion did not last, and for the next century, first one, then another king asserted himself as king of all Ireland.

In the 1160s, Dermot, king of Leinster, quarrelled with Roderic O'Connor, king of Connaught who also claimed to be king of all Ireland. Dermot called in the help of a Norman lord from south

Wales, Richard de Clare, known to history as Strongbow. O'Connor was defeated, Dermot died soon afterwards, and Strongbow, having married Dermot's daughter, became king of Leinster. He also thought he would be king of Ireland, but England's Henry II was not going to allow this build up of power by one of his vassal lords, and in 1171 he set out to invade Ireland. He conquered it, and it remained in English hands for the next seven hundred and fifty years.

When considering Ireland in the earlier centuries, we should never forget the unique rôle the country played as the cultural and artistic home of Europe in the dark centuries that followed the collapse of the western Roman Empire in the late 5th century.

Historians rightly describe those years, from about 500 to about 800, as the Golden Age of Ireland. When St Patrick had converted the Irish to Christianity in the 5th century, monasteries began to spring up everywhere. They became the homes of scholars as well as monks, and they also became workshops of artists and craftsmen. By the 6th century there were more than sixty of them, and the biggest and best, like Clonmacnois, Armagh and Clonard, were like universities. There, all the intellectual people of the day, not only those born in Ireland but also from other lands, gathered, as there were no other centres of learning.

In these and many other places in Ireland great works of art and craftsmanship were executed. The jewellery of the time is world famous. There were many experts in enamel work. Stained glass of the highest quality was made. Craftsmen wrought iron and carved in stone. They cultivated calligraphy, that is, the art of handwriting, and the writing schools of the monasteries were accorded special privileges. Out of these came a flood of illuminated manuscripts such as the world had not seen, and which even now bear comparison with any. As there was no printing known to western Europe (although it was practised in China), books and papers had to be done by hand. Here the Irish excelled themselves. The Book of Kells, which is an illuminated manuscript of the Gospels from the New Testament, is often

The Ardagh Chalice is a triumph of the metalworker's art in Ireland. It was executed in the 8th century and is regarded as one of the most beautiful artefacts of that century anywhere in Europe.

The Book of Kells is one of the most richly illuminated manuscripts produced in 8th-century Ireland.

called the most beautiful book in the world. There were many others of the same kind of skill. The Irish wrote not only religious books, they also wrote their own history and legend.

Not content with glorifying God and themselves in their artistic and intellectual works, the Irish started to go out to all kinds of places in Europe to teach, to keep alive the flickering flames of knowledge which might otherwise have died after the collapse of the Roman Empire. They spread Christianity, they taught manuscript illumination, they schooled craftsmen in stained glass and so forth. And willing pupils in Europe came over to Ireland to learn as well. Three thousand people are said to have gathered at Clonard for lessons under St Finnian. Armagh was so crowded with Anglo–Saxon students that it opened a special department for Saxons. Royalty and men of high birth came as well, and Dagobert I of the Franks (629–639) is believed to have been educated at Slane. The Abbot of Aghadoc was teaching his pupils that the earth was round, in an age which still believed it was flat and continued to believe it for centuries more.

This great work was in large measure responsible for the minor renaissance, or revival of learning, which spread across western Europe in the time of the Emperor Charlemagne, from about 800. The great theologian John Scotus taught for a quarter of a century in France under Charles the Bald, and he was an Irish scholar of the first rank. Little wonder that Ireland was called the land of saints and scholars.

17th-century England

The seventeenth century was very important indeed in the development of English politics. In Elizabeth I's time the continual danger from Spain had made absolute rule by the queen and her ministers necessary, and Englishmen were, on the whole, content to accept it. But when James I became king, the Spanish danger was over, England was on good terms with France, and there was nothing to fear from abroad. The need for absolutism was therefore gone. But both James and his son, Charles I, got it into their heads that they ruled by divine right and were answerable to no man but only to God. The need for absolutism was something they would determine without the advice of ministers or parliament.

Charles was to reign for eleven years with no parliament at all. His conduct of affairs led to a situation in which neither he nor the parliament he finally summoned in 1640 could agree on any major issue. Civil war had to come, and while it was not attended by the frightfulness experienced in the Wars of the Roses two centuries before, it did change England a lot. Parliament won the battles; it also won its point. Kings are in the long run answerable to Parliament.

The execution of the king led eventually to the assumption by Cromwell of the title Lord Protector. He was compelled to create a dictatorship of the very kind the war had been fought to avoid. He proved, nevertheless, to be the greatest ruler England ever had.

Charles II, restored to the throne in 1660, behaved with much more discretion than either his father or grandfather. He was aware of the pressure building up for Parliament to have an even greater say in the running of the country, and he relieved some of it by governing through able but usually unscrupulous ministers who generally took the blame for unpopular or clumsy acts. His brother, James II, however, reverted to his father's line and in three years so angered everybody by his absolutism that he was forced to flee the kingdom.

His successors were his daughter Mary and her able but morose husband William III. They were invited by Parliament to rule but had first to agree to the Bill of Rights which set out

clearly how far they could go. They accepted, and it was at last established that Parliament ruled through the king, and not the other way round.

The 17th century was dominated by the struggle between the kings and Parliament over the government of the country. When civil war broke out in 1642 between Charles I and Parliament his supporters were called Royalists. They were generally portrayed (left) as gay, colourful people with long hair and fine clothes. The other side, called Roundheads because they kept their hair cropped short, were usually drawn serious and gloomy (right). Neither picture is accurate. Cromwell, contrary to belief, enjoyed games, music and sport; the Royalists, on the other hand, soon found they had little to be gay about, for they lost the war.

Reclaiming the land

You will remember that the sad business of enclosing land for pasturing sheep had gone ahead by leaps and bounds in the 16th century. This slowed down in the 17th century, though it is not easy to say exactly why. In the land that remained open – and it was the greater part of the land of England – there had been little change since the time of the Conqueror. The three big fields round the village were still split up into a number of strips. They were still farmed in just the same way, and the crops were no different. True, Thomas Hariot had introduced the potato in 1586, but potatoes were not grown in open fields just yet, nor indeed did the average yeoman eat them, except perhaps as a luxury. The farmer's life just had not changed.

The growing population increased the demand for home-grown food. It was not normal practice to buy staple-diet items from abroad, except, of course, spices and salt and tropical fruits. But there was a reluctance to encroach on the village pasture land which nourished their pigs and cattle, sheep and hens. And so fresh land had to be found. One area, where for centuries Englishmen had lived a special kind of life peculiar to their surroundings, was the flat, marshy Fens of East Anglia and Lincolnshire. These Fens were dry enough in a good, warm summer, but in winter the waters of the North Sea rose up in every river or stream and flooded the land, so that it resembled a sea itself. Here and there a farmhouse and a few acres around it stood clear of the water level. And wonderful Ely cathedral, magnificent to look at from any angle, reared up, towering over the landscape for miles. This Fenland was, when not submerged, very fertile, its grass rich and green, and its reeds splendid for thatch roofing. So when the English Parliament of the 1590s heard of the Dutch reclaiming land from the waters of the North Sea, they naturally welcomed similar projects brought to them for discussion.

Oliver Cromwell (1599–1658) was the greatest ruler of England after Alfred. He commanded armies of Parliament in the later part of the Civil War with spectacular success. Then, after the execution of the king, Charles I, and following a few years of indecisive government by committee, Cromwell was chosen Lord Protector. He governed with strength and wisdom for five years. In that time he laid the foundations for the development of British democratic government as we know it today.

Astonishingly, the Fenland men bitterly resented this. They wanted no change in their waterlogged life. They had worked out an economy and manner of living of their own. They had organized fishing and fowling to a high degree, and the proposal to drain the Fens seemed to threaten their livelihood. Luckily for them, there was not enough money available for the government to arrange any significant scheme. But the draining of the Fens could not be put off forever. The family of the Earls of Bedford were the principal promotors of a reclaiming scheme in the 17th century, and they put a lot of their money into it. Huge canals were cut, one of which is still there, called Old Bedford Level, and the drained lands were swiftly converted to pasture.

The scheme did not go ahead without hitches. Angry Fenmen cut the dykes and reflooded the fields at night. Much reclaimed land thus returned to its bog-like state. Cromwell, himself a Fenman by birth, approved the reclamation work, and during his Protectorate did much to help the authorities protect the dykes.

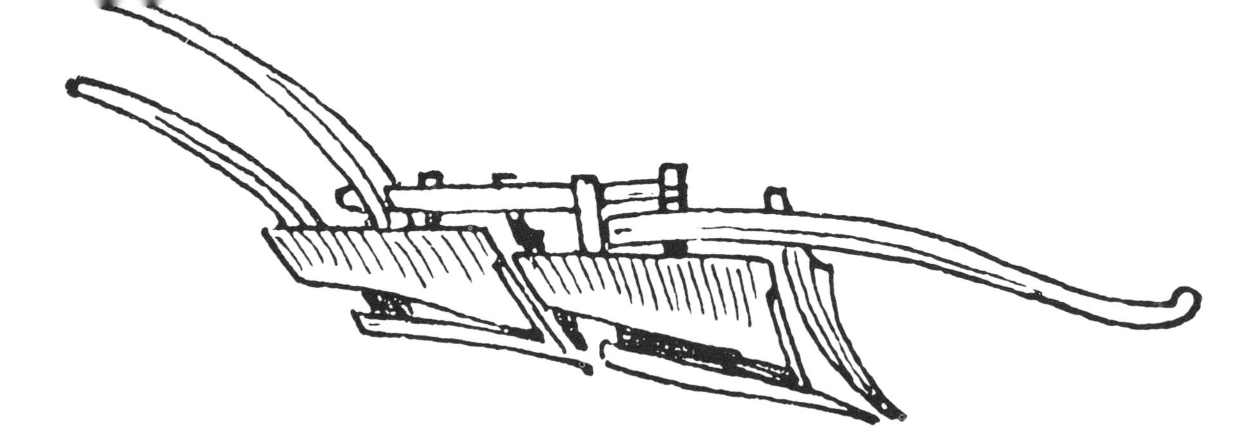

Above: Here is a drawing of what a double plough looked like.

Left: There has been a windmill of one kind or another at Saxtead Green, near Framlingham in Suffolk, since the 13th century. The mill you can see is not as old. It is a wooden post-mill with sails and a brick roundhouse, and it was used for grinding grain. Much restoration was done a century ago, and today it is cared for by the Department of the Environment.

But in time the new canals were unable to empty the waters into the sea, because the river estuaries got silted up. Worse, the reclaimed land itself began to sink, leaving the canals with their banks elevated several feet above it. You can see this sort of thing in the Fenlands today. How then could they possibly drain off the water from the land? The answer was the windmill to pump the water up, and East Anglia soon became festooned with these attractive structures which had already been a feature of the Dutch landscape for some time.

Windmills were introduced in England in the 12th century for providing power to grind corn into flour. One very early mill was the post mill at Bury St Edmunds in Suffolk. The post mill was the original kind. It had a wooden frame and covered body perched on a massive post. In the 17th century a new type was devised, the smock-mill, which had its sails and windshaft attached to a revolving dome-like cap. The body could therefore be a fixture. There is one at Lacey Green in Buckinghamshire, dated about 1650. The East Anglian mills will have been of both kinds, but how far they were successful we do not know.

But in the 19th century the problem was clearly still there, for massive pumping operations were carried out by steam-engine-driven pumps.

Whatever the difficulties, the reclamation scheme should be regarded as a success. Trevelyan said that 'a new, rich province, eighty miles long and ten to thirty miles broad, was added to the farmland of the kingdom.' Today this area is the richest farm land in the country.

The 17th century also saw the introduction of new agricultural implements, though they were not used on a wide scale. John Evelyn the diarist mentions a machine from Spain which could plough, sow and harrow the ground all at the same time. There were also a number of new types of plough. One was a double plough which cut two furrows at once, and reduced the time taken to plough a field by about a third. It could not do so by half, for the effort required to drag or push a double plough was greater than for a single plough.

Misuse of churches

Significant changes in agricultural methods did not come until the 18th century, and we shall look at three in the next chapter. The village, meanwhile, did not change much in a hundred years. Among the most noticeable differences was the appearance of the churches after the middle of the period. Some of the Puritan religious sects, like the Independents, did not like stained glass, with its beautiful pictorial representations of Biblical scenes or of famous saints. Nor did they like statues of the Virgin Mary, or even of Jesus Christ. They thought it was idolatrous – that is, like worshipping idols. They harked back to the first Commandment, 'Thou shalt have no other god but me', and they considered that statues represented people as being on the same level as God. So they smashed the windows, and because it was cold in winter filled the holes with clear, whitish glass. They also pulled down the statues – a practice which had begun the century before.

On top of this, Parliamentarian armies often used churches as stables (like Saffron Walden church in Essex), or as garrisons for troops brought in to keep down areas just won in battle. Many an English church today boasts its history of suffering at the hands of Parliament and the New Model Army. It is said that troops damaged many wonderful brass rubbings, pilfered the church's plate, and even took the gold thread out of gilt-embroidered cushions, robes and curtains.

Architecture and building

In the 16th century, Englishmen had begun to build for themselves fine stately mansions of brick or stone, with spacious windows, overlooking wonderful gardens laid out in geometrical patterns. But it was not until the 17th century that architecture really came into its own in England. The prime exponent was Inigo Jones, a designer of court masques and play sets who had spent some years in Italy studying under the great architect, Palladio. Jones was commissioned by James I (1603–1625) to build the famous

The inside of Inigo Jones' marvellous Banqueting Hall in London's Whitehall. It was built in 1619–22 in part of the Old Palace of Whitehall. The ceiling was painted by Rubens. Charles I stepped from a window on the first floor to the scaffold, in 1649.

Banqueting Hall in Whitehall, which survived the fire of London (1666), the bombs of the Second World War (1939–1945), and which has been lovingly cleaned and restored by the Department of the Environment. You can see this grand structure today.

The Banqueting Hall is not a house. But it is a fine example of revived classical architecture based on designs used by the ancient Romans. It heralded a new era of building in England. Indeed it was an important feature of the Renaissance which reached its height in England during the century.

England was very fortunate in having Inigo Jones, not least because he lived to the ripe old age of 88, and was still designing parts of great houses a year or two before his death in 1652. This meant a whole generation was influenced by his ideas, and that gave them time to take root. He also had brilliant pupils, one of whom, Webb, his cousin, built houses.

Houses began to change shape. They were more square, with one side, the front elevation as it is called, given over largely to an impressive entrance, reached by a flight of steps, through a grand pair of doors under a triangular pediment. Once inside the doors you were in a huge hall, the height of the whole house, sometimes with a glazed dome roof and black and white marble squared floor. In front of you was a huge staircase of marble, stone or wood. Along the sides of the hall were doors opening into the rooms. These rooms were now as a rule single-storeyed. The tall, raftered ceilings with a gallery had given way to lower rooms, but with elaborately decorated ceilings of plaster, some carried out by the leading sculptors and plasterers of the day.

And in these rooms the decorations were magnificent. Oil paintings, often with many of them filling the walls, oak panelling, tapestries, these were the wall coverings over smooth plaster work. Carpets appeared in place of rushes or rush-matting, and these were woven in many wonderful colours to intricate patterns, or they might be of leather, carefully put together so that the lines of the joins were not easy to see. The carpets may have come from Turkey, now still a rich empire in the Near East, marketing many products, especially their carpets for which they had become famous. Occasionally, a hand-woven carpet was made in England, but carpet-making died out in the course of this century. It did not return as an industry for more than a hundred years.

Outside, the gardens had if anything become even more formal, with straight paths and close-cut grass patches, the larger ones beginning to look like the kind of lawn we can produce today. Shrubs and small trees were popular. Box hedges became as common a garden feature as brick walls, and these were sometimes clipped into extraordinary shapes, like birds and animals. This practice is still carried on in many parts of England today.

What of the lower class building? The half-timbered house of Elizabeth's time continued to be erected right through the 17th

In 1653, Oliver Cromwell, the foremost general in the country, got tired of the indecisive government of the committees of Parliamentarians, and he took a troop of men down to the Commons, expelled the Speaker, along with other members, and closed the chamber for the time being. The Clerk of the Commons entered in the Commons Journal the fact that "This day His Excellency the Lord General dissolved this Parliament." (20th April 1653). The entry is under the ink scratching-out, and that was done after Cromwell's death. Evidently, some people did not want to remember the event, necessary though it had been for the good governance of England.

century – in some counties through the 18th century, too. The roof of a typical small town house was usually thatched, for in those days tiling was a luxury. Today, by the way, it is about as expensive to thatch a roof as it is to tile it with old tiles.

Furniture

In the Tudor age, Englishmen had begun to make furniture or to import it, and had also started to make it comfortable, especially if it was a chair or bench or day bed. Furniture-making came into its own in the mid-17th century. Then, rich exiles, who during their years abroad, out of reach of Cromwell and Parliament, had made themselves familiar with trends in European art and craftsmanship, came home and commissioned work for the houses they were going to have built or rebuilt. It was the age of walnut.

A model of how Charing Cross, London looked in about 1620. It is very different today.

This lovely golden-brown wood has a natural beauty of grain. It even gets richer in colour over the years. You can cut four veneers or slices of a tree or branch, very very thin, and square them off, put them together to make a bigger square producing a marvellous effect. This is called figuring, if the pattern is the same, which it should be if you cut all four sheets next to one another at one point on the trunk. A lot of furniture was made with walnut veneering as a surface. Nearly as much was made of solid walnut. And from about 1660 to about 1710 a host of pieces were produced in this wood. These included chairs, flap-top desks, chests of drawers, tall-boys, dressing tables, and long case clocks (known as grandfathers).

One idea new in England at the time was the skill of marquetry. This is where you cut a plain sheet of wood with a kind of pattern, such as flowers or a Greek vase, and fill your design with different woods or ivory, either in natural or in dyed colours. In 1709 a severe disease attacked and destroyed thousands of walnut trees in north-west Europe, making the wood scarce.

Towns

Even by the 1600s the English town had not developed much beyond the stage it had reached in 1485. In most towns the buildings looked the same – the half-timbered first or second storeys projecting over the ground floor, with lattice windows. The streets were just as narrow, uncleaned, smelly and cluttered with rubbish, carts, animals and so forth. The size of towns had barely altered. While London had, probably, 400,000 or so people by 1600, no other town could boast more than about 25,000 (the approximate populations of Bristol and Norwich, still the two largest towns after London). As for the others, the older ones like Exeter, Southampton, Lincoln, Oxford, Hereford and Salisbury hardly had more than 8,000 people each, while the newer ones like Liverpool and Manchester had appreciably fewer. The average Englishman still lived and worked in the countryside; the drift to the towns had not yet begun.

Roads and travel

In the Middle Ages, roads were very bad in England. They had hardly improved at all by the 17th century, and many people wrote about them, either privately, in their diaries or letters, or more vociferously in books and pamphlets. What it must have been likc for armies like Cromwell's New Model Army, or Monck's Coldstream Guards, to march down such roads is hard to imagine. The state of the roads was largely responsible for towns and villages remaining isolated. Why go all the way from Northampton to Leicester in a coach if the journey was so arduous that it took most of the day to cover only 40 kilometres (25 miles)? You could walk faster than that. Carriages, such as they were, ran the risk of being submerged in mud, or overturning in the ruts. So they were often drawn by six horses when on better roads two would have been enough.

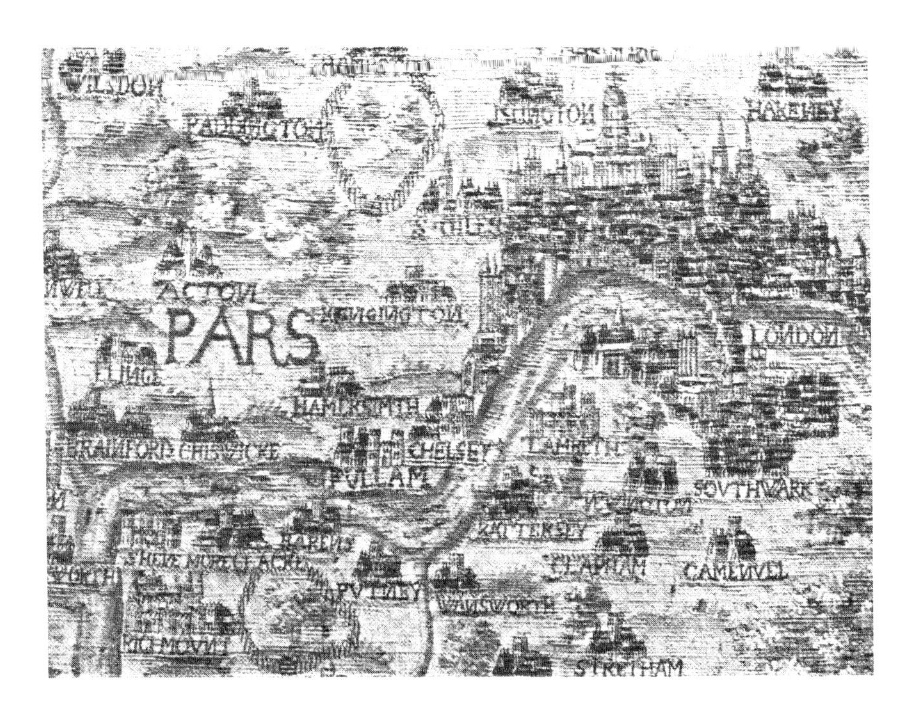

A section of a 17th-century tapestry map of part of England. This is London as the craftsman (or craftswoman) saw it. Some of the famous districts are still called by the same names today.

You will not be surprised to know that people as a rule did not bother to make long trips. It was enough in a simple country workman's lifetime to go occasionally from his village to the nearest sizeable town and back. Nothing seems to have been done about the roads. Stage coaches took as long to travel from London to Edinburgh, 640 kilometres (400 miles), at the end of the century as they had at the beginning (six days). And they were extremely uncomfortable – springs were not introduced until the 1780s. People preferred to travel by horse and to send luggage or goods by pack horse. It was quicker and, as in those days there was not the urgency of today, one could stay en route at one or other of the many inns which flourished along the highways.

Large four-wheeled coaches with covered compartments for travellers were introduced in England in the middle of the 16th century. Walter Rippon, a wheelwright, made one for Elizabeth I in the 1560s, and this had curtains. It set a fashion which was adopted by the nobility. These early coaches were ornate. They had a timbered bottom half lined inside with bench seats on which were thick cushions. The top half was open, but at each corner was a post. Around the top of the posts was a canopy of embroidered cloth or silk, and curtains could be pulled across each of the four sides. Some had extra decoration at the top, like a dome of cloth or a plume. The body sat on the wheel frame, and so had no insulation from the bumps of the bad roads. Elizabeth presumably was transported at very slow speed by the pair of horses in front. Perhaps she used her coach to pay her visit to English troops at Tilbury at the time of the Spanish Armada, where she spoke to them in such stirring terms. The, word coach, by the way, derives from the Hungarian town of Kotze where they were first thought of in the 1400s.

Early in the 17th century the first four-wheeled Hackney coach or carriage, pulled by two horses, appeared. It could carry six people and it waited outside London's principal inns and taverns hoping to pick up fares. Strangely it was many years before there was any sizeable number of these obvious benefits in the city. They were of course very noisy because of the roads, and sometimes in Charles I's time laws were passed keeping carriages outside the city limits. Samuel Pepys, the great diarist and Secretary to the Navy, who flourished in the time of Charles II, said he did not like to be seen in a Hackney, and ordered his own smaller coach to be made for him. Evidently he was delighted with this, for he talks about it a lot in his pages, relishing the decorations of silver, the window frames in gilt and so on. Windows were introduced into coaches in 1667, made of plate glass, a technique invented by Venetian glassmakers in the 1630s.

By 1700 there were several hundred Hackneys in London. The maximum allowed by law was 700. By that time, too, the stage coach had been running for about fifty years.

Commerce and industry

By the 17th century England had become a commercial nation, this is to say, a sizeable proportion of her people worked not on the land but in some sophisticated industry. The country had begun to trade with others, was becoming increasingly less self-supporting, and had entered the world of empire-building.

What sort of industries were flourishing? The wool and the cloth industries of course continued to prosper. Amazingly, English cloth was still enormously in demand abroad. It was still woven, for the most part, in the homes of master weavers, who still took in a few local lads or girls as labourers and taught them the skill. Clothmaking was organized by what some social historians call the domestic system. Merchants bought the wool from sheep farmers and placed it with the master weavers for spinning and weaving into cloth, or had it made into cloth in small cottage factories of their own. The cloth was then sold. This system applied also to trades like ironsmithing and leatherworking, for the old guilds had disappeared.

In the 17th century, the wool industry, once the monopoly of London and East Anglia, now spread to the Cotswolds (Gloucestershire, Oxfordshire and Wiltshire) and also to Yorkshire and Lancashire. Here, unlike flat East Anglia, there were moors

A 17th-century iron founder. He is pouring molten metal into a mould.

and hills, long ranges of them, on which the sheep, which provided the wool, grazed. This eliminated the transport costs, which were high because of the state of the roads. And so other parts o England began to acquire a prosperity which is today illustrate by the fine buildings and picturesque towns that flourished, like Witney in Oxfordshire, still the best known town in Europe fo woollen blankets, and Halifax in Yorkshire.

Iron smelting, which up to the middle of the 18th century depended on charcoal burning, grew enormously in importance It had been centred for generations in the Forest of Dean in th West Country and in the Weald of Kent and Sussex, because o the quantity of timber there. Charcoal was produced by cuttin down trees, chopping the trunks into logs and building these int huge piles or pyramids, setting them alight in the middle an covering them with earth to produce long slow burning.

Coal production

The Romans knew about coal and burnt it in their villas, bath and public places. Then it went out of use, like so many thing

A coal mine in Germany, in 1619. This would have been very much like a coal mine of the same time in England.

in Anglo–Saxon times. It was used again in the 13th century, when it was known in London as 'sea coal' as it was brought by ship from Tyneside. Coal had an acrid smell and its fumes choked people, and so for a long time it was not widely used. It was quarried from outcrops and sea cliffs, until the 14th century when it was dug from pits. Deeper mining did not begin until later.

The coal mined in the 17th century was used for many manufacturing purposes. It had by then also come to be burned in homes up and down the country, at places not far from sea ports, where it could be delivered reasonably easily. But the Midlands were also rich in coal, especially in Lancashire, Derbyshire, Nottinghamshire, Warwickshire and Leicestershire. Estimates have been made of the amount of coal produced in England. At the start of Elizabeth's reign, it was about 150,000 tons in a year. By the 1680s the amount had risen to nearly 3,000,000 tons, and by the 1780s it was 10,000,000.

The coal industry, however, had its uglier aspects. As the coal pits got deeper, and digging became more like mining, the dangers to workers increased. The pit owners seemed quite indifferent to this, and to the sufferings of the women and children whom they employed as lifters. The number of pit accidents was alarming. Nothing was done for the miners and their families for a long time.

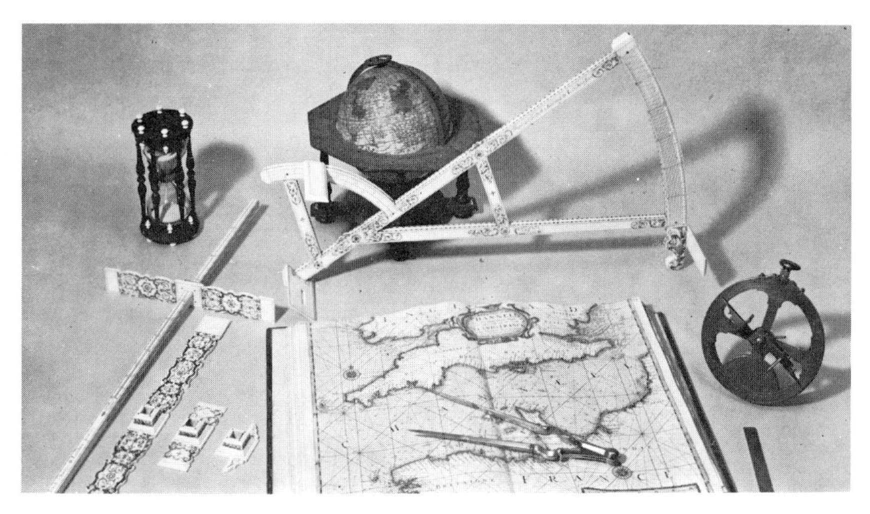

Top: Some navigation instruments of the 17th and 18th centuries. These are in the National Maritime Museum at Greenwich.

Above: This is an early 17th-century drawing of a man smoking a pipe. The pipe is very long. It is not unlike those white clay pipes whose bowls can still be found in the garden or in the fields almost anywhere in England.

Foreign trade

While home manufacturing proceeded to grow steadily, English traders overseas expanded their activities dramatically. This trade was largely in the hands of a few private enterprise companies, like the East India Company, the Merchant Adventurers (trading with German states), the African Company (trading with the Guinea coast) the Levant Company (operating in the eastern Mediterranean) and the Eastland Company (Baltic states). The directors and shareholders became extremely rich, but in time the wealth accumulated and spent in England began to filter outwards. If a merchant adventurer built a huge Palladian-style house and employed Inigo Jones to supervise the construction, there was work for many masons, carpenters, bricklayers, tilers, ironsmiths, glassmakers and decorators.

The East India Company, one of the earliest, made a significant contribution to the wealth of England throughout the first century of its existence (it was founded in 1600). It brought rich silk, spices and saltpetre to London in such quantities that even before the death of James I in 1625 the company's private merchant fleet was bigger than that of England. What is more, its ships, marvellously built of English oak, lasted for half a century or more, with relatively little maintenance costs. Trevelyan says that in 1621 the company exported to the East £100,000 in gold bullion, a commodity greatly in demand there, and this had purchased goods worth five times as much, of which 75 per cent were promptly resold in Europe, at great profit.

In the 1660s, tea from China was introduced into England from Holland. It cost about £6 a pound, which was extremely expensive. The East India Company had a monopoly of this trade, which added to its wealth, for tea quickly became a popular drink among the upper classes who enjoyed sipping it in coffee houses and inns

Smoking and tobacco

Another taste which people began to enjoy in the 17th century was smoking tobacco. The tobacco plant had been brought to England in Elizabeth's reign by Sir John Hawkins. Sir Walter Raleigh was one of the first people to smoke in public, thereby introducing a craze that became a national, and is now an international, habit. It was at first thought to be beneficial to the health, possibly because of the robust health of the American Indians who used to enjoy smoking. Men smoked short clay pipes, which can still be found in diggings all over the country. Elizabeth I did not like the habit, however, and even introduced a ban in 1584. But it survived, and in time the government, seeing it could probably not stop it, decided to cash in on it. An excise duty was put on tobacco of six shillings per pound weight in James I's reign. This prompted illegal trading, and the inlets of Cornwall bustled regularly with small French and English boats smuggling in quantities brought over from the American colonies.

James I attacked the habit of smoking in his 'A Counterblast to Tobacco', which he called a custom 'loathsome to the eye, harmful to the brain, dangerous to the lungs, . . .' In this he was over 300 years ahead of the Royal College of Physicians which only recently, after many years of enquiry, proved him right and led the government to start a campaign against it.

Newspapers

While some men smoked, they might have read a newspaper or two. The 17th century witnessed the introduction of many new ideas, and newspapers were among them. The earliest were not daily, or even regular. They were news-sheets, issued by publishers as and when they had enough to fill a page or two. Sometimes they included reports of what was going on in foreign countries, or even in the countryside. News-sheets appeared during the Civil War, on both sides, but they contained more propaganda than facts. When Charles II became king in 1660 there were still

Numb. 78. Worcester-Arms

[THE

Worcester Post-Man:

Containing the Heads of all the remarkable Occurrences both Foreign and Domestick.

Semper Eadem

From *Friday* December 8, to *Friday*, December 16. 1710.

Saturday's and Monday's Post.

From Dyer's *Letter, and other Intelligence.*

A Holland *Mail brings us the following Advices.*

LEtters from Paris of the 8th say, That a Courier was arriv'd at Court, with Letters of the 29th past from Vittoria, which bring, That King Charles fearing the ill Consequences of the D. de Noailes entring with his Army into Catalonia, had quitted his Army on the 22d, and was gone to Sarragossa, under a Guard of 2000 Horse, to be near at hand to give his Order; and that the rest of his Troops being about 10000 Men, were following after towards Arragon and the Kingdom of Valence, having past the Zerunna, which fall into the Tagus, breaking all their Bridges after them, and sinking the Barges to retard the March of 4000 Horse, which K. Phillip had sent in pursuit of 'em. 'Tis said they have also drawn out of Toledo all the Provisions and Ammunitions which they had laid up there, having only left a few Troops and some other Posts to conceal their Retreat. But had discharg'd all the Ladies which they had brought thither Prisoners from Madrid, whose Husbands are with K. Phillip.

Those from Vienna of the 29th past say, That the Lower Hungary was all free from Malecontents: That the Officers and Hussars having demanded the Emperors Protection, which being granted 'em, above [illegible] came in and surrendred themselves: And they assure, That the Rebels have but 5 Regiments together in their main Body, and that Prince Ragotzi has again by his Minister at Constantinople, offer'd to put himself under the Protection of the Port, but it has refused to grant him the same as before, and the Grand Signior will not intermeddle in the Troubles of Hungary; so that there is great Hopes that the same will suddenly come to an end, which will be well for the Common Cause. The Turks (also according to Letters of the 17th past from Constantinople) shew not the least Inclination to make a Rupture with the Czar of Muscovy and Poland, and their Ministers disown the Promise (as twas pretended by the King of Sweden) of convoying him home thro' Poland with a great Army of Turks and Tartars; so that there is no appearance of any Fresh Trouble in the North.

Zurich, Nov. 30.

Letters from Venice say, the Overflowing of the Rivers in Lombardy have done incredible Damage to several Provinces and particularly to the Brescian. They have Advice from Turkey that the Town of Mecca in Arabia is almost intirely destroy'd by an Earthquake.

They write from the Hague of the 12th, that the main drift of the Conferences that have been held there with the Princes of Savoy and Marlborough, has been about the Succours from Italy to Spain, and that no time may be lost for their Imbarkation. 'Tis still assur'd that the Troops which the Emperor is to send Consists in 5 Regiments of Dragoons of Vaubone and another of Hussars, & it may be some Cavalry besides, and on the part of England and Holland instead of the Troops of Sax Gotha which are in their pay in Italy (which they had thoughts to send to Spain) will be sent the 4000 men that are Imbarked at Spithead, with 2500 from Ireland, and 4 or 5 Regiments of Walloons from the Netherlands. This [illegible] to discontent the D. of Savoy, by making further Detachments of Troops from Italy, and the Minister of the said Prince residing at the Hague, having understood that it was under consideration the sending from thence a good number of Troops for Spain, signified to the Grand Pensionary, That if the Allies had a mind that his Royal Highness should Command the Confederate Army next Summer in Italy, it would be necessary to let the same remain entire as it is, and that the design of the Allies be signified to his Royal highness in time, that he may take such Measures and make such Dispositions against the ensuing Campaign as to render it more successful than some past. As to what the Imperial Generals signified that it was impossible for them to Act with success in the Mountains, his Royal Highness was of another Opinion: however if the Allies are resolv'd to Act only on the Defensive on that side, his Royal Highness hop'd that they would leave a sufficient number of Troops there to Guard his Frontiers

Brussels, Dec. 12.

Some Letters from Germany and Italy import that there has been another Battle in Spain near the River Guaya, in which K. Phillips Army was entirely defeated, and the D. of Vendome with the Counts d' Aguilar and las Torres kill'd; but this meets with no great Credit.

Dublin, Nov 30. On Saturday last Mr. Patrick Campbell a Rigid Presbiterian Bookseller of this place was taken into Custody by a Warrant from my Lord chief Justice Brodrick for publishing several scandalous and seditious Pamphlets, many of which were seiz'd in his Shop, and on Monday the Grand Jury found a Bill of Indictment against against him for High Crimes and Misdemeanours, on which he is to be try'd next Term at the Queen's Bench Bar In the mean time he has given 1500 l. Bail for his appearance.

Falmouth, Decemb 2 We have an Account from Mount's-bay, That last Thursday a Ship lost all her Masts and was stranded. She carried 30 Guns, but we cannot learn her Name. 'Tis fear'd we shall hear of a great many more Losses by Sea, occasion'd by the late stormy Weather.

London Decemb 7. On Tuesday last the Sons of the Clergy had their Annual Meeting or Feast at Merchant-Taylors-Hall, having first heard the Reverend Mr Sherlock, Master of the Temple preach a most excellent Sermon to them at St. Pauls upon that Occasion. And the Money collected for Charitable Uses in putting out poor Children, amounted to 185 l. Yesterday morning the Convocation met at Westminster, and the youngest Bishop of the Province of Canterbury having said Prayers in the Upper-House, in Henry VII. Chappel, the Lower House was sent for to present their Prolocutor, Dr. Atterbury, Dean of Carlisle, which accordingly the Reverend Dr Smallridge, did in a Latin Speech, after which the Dean himself made a Speech also in Latin, both which were answer'd by his Grace, the Archbishop of Canterbury, approving and confirming their Choice. Then the Lower House return'd to their House and adjourn'd to that Day-sevenight. Yesterday upon the Motion of Mr. Wortley Mountague, seconded by Mr. Downing, Mr. Thomas Onslow, Son to the late Speaker, the House gave Leave to bring in a Bill for limiting the number of Officers in the House of Commons; and the said Gentlemen with some others were order'd to prepare and bring

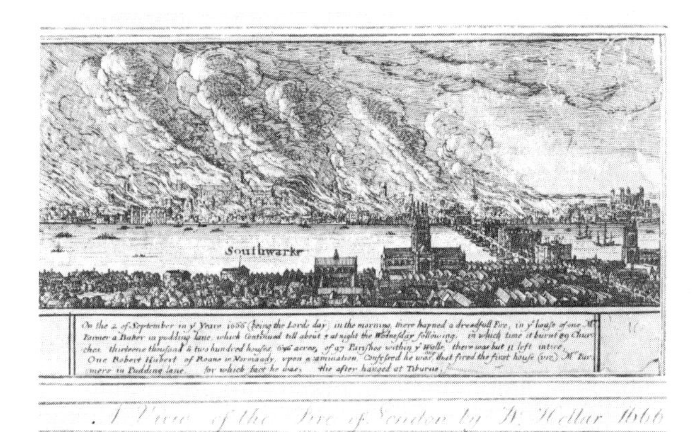

Above left: Wenceslaus Hollar, a Bohemian (Czech) engraver, drew this picture of London as it was during the Great Fire in 1666. ". . . . . . . it burnt 89 churches, thirteene thousand & two hundred houses . . . . . ."

Above right: Here is a page from Berrow's Worcester Journal, dated 1710. It is very nice to record that Berrow's Worcester Journal is still going strong, after 286 years.

many people who objected to the Stuarts, even to monarchy itself, and these people sometimes took to circulating scurrilous broadsheets about the new king and his government. In 1663, the government retaliated with a Licensing Act which prohibited such works, and for the next 25 years or so the legislation had to be renewed.

But one of the terms which William III was expected to accept when he became king was a promise to be more liberal over printed matter. By the end of the century one could more or less print and publish what one liked, though one could be sued in the courts for libel. Regular newspapers began to appear fairly soon after this. Berrow's Worcester Journal (still going strong) which appeared in 1690, became a weekly in 1709. The first daily was the Daily Courant, in 1702.

The Parliament of William III was made up very largely of aristocrats and of landowners of not such high birth but with plenty of money. In this respect it represented its own interests as much as those of England. When the two clashed it was usually personal interests which prevailed. Consequently, Parliament was unwilling, possibly unable, to do anything about the build up of abuses which were to emerge during the progress of the Industrial Revolution.

The Industrial Revolution

No one really knows what started the two great revolutions of the 18th century in Britain—the Agrarian and the Industrial Revolutions. They did not, as you will see, happen overnight. Jethro Tull's seed drill took a generation or more to be adoped on a wide scale, and so revolutionize crop farming. And James Watt took years to get his steam engine working effectively, and more years to get any appreciable number of them into production and use in factories. But whatever the causes, the face of England in 1800 was quite different from that in 1700. The changes were far more profound than in any previous century.

The reason why these changes took place in Britain and not elsewhere is probably that, after the Treaty of Utrecht in 1713, Britain was not involved in any major war for forty years or so, until the Seven Years War of 1756–63. This gave the country more than a generation of comparative peace in which to progress, when other lands in Europe, whose technical brilliance was every bit as promising as ours, were heavily involved in one crisis after another. There was something more. Democratic government had advanced much further in England than it had anywhere else. In France for example, the leading artistic and cultural nation of the world, society outside Paris was still feudal.

New farming methods

Farming methods had not altered much over the centuries. Men still cultivated their one-acre strips on the common fields. But the 18th century saw a revolution in agricultural methods. It began very quickly. Jethro Tull, a Berkshire-born lawyer practising in London, gave up his job because of ill health, and returned to the country to study farming. He was struck by the noticeable wastage of cornseed as farmers took handfuls of it from a sack or basket slung in front of them and scattered it around the ploughed field at sowing time. He also saw how very difficult it was to do a good tidy job weeding between the shoots when they emerged through the earth because of the haphazard way in which they were sown.

An 18th-century drawing of Jethro Tull's drill, which Tull said "makes the channels, sows the seeds into them, and covers them at the same time, with great exactness and precision."

Mowing grass in the 18th century. Scythesmen used to be able to get grass looking quite like a modern lawn, if they worked at it.

So he sat down and designed a special machine for sowing seeds in tidy, straight lines with little wastage. This was his famous drill. The first practical demonstration of Tull's drill was in 1701, but he himself did not write about it for about thirty years, and so the idea was slow to catch on. All the same it was a startling improvement. It was a kind of box slung between two wheels, which was pulled along the field up and down in tidy rows. Out of the bottom of the box some tubes projected, and the tips of these tubes cut small troughs in the earth. As they did so, seeds dropped out through them into the troughs. These were then raked over afterwards. When the shoots came up, it was possible to take a hoe down the line and weed between them. The drill and the hoe made fields very much more productive.

Root crops

The new process coincided with the introduction of root-crop growing—that is, planting vegetables like turnips and potatoes in fields that under the old system would have lain fallow for one year in three. This was called the rotation of crops. Corn would be sown one year, turnips or other roots the next, and corn again on the third. This was possible because root seeds have to be sown much deeper than corn seeds. And at this time men had begun to understand the value of manuring their fields systematically. The growing of turnips was additionally useful as it provided a food for the cattle during the winter, which would previously have been slaughtered in the autumn because there would be nothing for them to eat after, say, October. The carcases were salted and spiced for preservation during the winter months. Keeping the cattle alive meant a greater supply of manure, which was vital to the fields.

Land drainage

Another new process at this time, which helped the development of agriculture, was land drainage. We saw how the Fens were drained in the 17th century to produce some of the richest arable land in Britain. Now, with the expansion of the practice of enclosing land, whole fields could be fenced off and drained. Ditches were dug along the edges of the fields, generally near the hedging. The bottom was covered with stones, and the water drained away to a nearby stream, gully or pond. This practice was employed widely on land that had hitherto been regarded as barren or not worth ploughing, and for the first time vast areas became available for crops.

Livestock breeding

One more development was the systematic breeding of livestock, which grew at just the time that farmers had grasped the value of growing turnips and so on for winter food. Robert Bakewell (1725–1795), a Derbyshire breeder, introduced the longhorn, a cow which gave a high milk yield, and so was much in demand. It is said that people from all over Europe came to visit him and buy his cattle. John Ellman (1753—1832) introduced a new breed of sheep, the Southdown, which fattened in about half the time that other sheep took.

Now, these changes did not all happen at once—indeed they were spread over the best part of a century. But they met the demands for food of a growing population, which jumped from 5,500,000 in 1700 to 6,000,000 in 1750, and leaped to 10,000,000 by 1800. This last increase brought its own peculiar problems. It was at a time of prolonged warfare between Britain and France, and Britain and the American colonists.

The new farming methods were, generally, pioneered by the richer country gentleman-farmers. They were encouraged by George III himself, known to many as Farmer George, who at Windsor kept his own model farm that was an example to many. There he bred merino sheep, among many other animals. Another pioneer was Thomas Coke, Earl of Leicester (1752–1842), who practically converted north-west Norfolk from a rye-growing to a wheat-growing district.

Enclosing the land

These progressive farmers met strenuous opposition, however, from their smaller tenant farmers and poor freeholders. Some of the resistance arose merely because the ideas were new, and they did not like change. But there was more substance to the opposition when the bigger landlords began to extend enclosures. They hedged or dry-stone-walled around the village land and parcelled it out to tenants. The process was done by private members' bills

his cartoon of George III is an ffectionate reference to his great iterest in all things concerned with irming and the countryside. It is as 'ell to remember that, even though the ng was markedly peculiar in ehaviour towards the end of his life, e was extremely popular among rdinary people.

in Parliament, and commissioners were appointed to divide the land.

But there were many hardships in train for the poorer. The hired labourer, who had a cow or two on common land, no longer had anywhere to put them. So he had to sell. And his job itself was endangered. New methods necessitated less labour, and he had to take lower wages or go out of work altogether. If he poached or stole to make ends meet, he ended up on the gallows or in the hull of a ship going to Australia for a life sentence in a convict settlement. The smaller freeholder likewise could not pasture his animals. His farm would have to be fenced, and at his own expense. If he could not afford this, there was always a greedy agent for a bigger farmer waiting to buy his land at a knock-down price. In time he became a landless labourer, or joined the growing ranks of the unemployed. Nothing much was done to help him.

Near Newbury in Berkshire, the magistrates of Speenhamland met in 1795 and introduced a scheme of poor relief to supplement the aid men like these could get from the ordinary poor rate. The scheme spread throughout the country and did alleviate suffering here and there. But in time it produced a change in the peasantry of England. They ceased to be the tough backbone of the country. Instead, they became listless and demoralized.

The enclosures were probably necessary, and the better farm productivity certainly enabled England to support itself in food during the Napoleonic wars and the blockade imposed on goods coming to England from European ports. But these were unhappy times in the countryside. Later, we shall see that things were no better in the towns.

The Industrial Revolution

The Agrarian Revolution was not the only change in 18th-century English life. From about the middle of the century there were vast developments in methods of production of goods, so rapid indeed after the many centuries of doing things in much the same way by hand, that they are rightly lumped under the title, the Industrial Revolution. This embraced the invention of machines to do the work of many men in a fraction of the time, the discovery of steam power to operate these machines, the use of coal to produce iron (thus increasing its output enormously), the development of road surfaces, the expansion of road networks, the cutting of canals, the improvement of transport. and in the 1800s the introduction of railways. Let us look at a few of the more revolutionary innovations. There were so many that we can only pick out the more important.

John Kay's invention was quite revolutionary, and it ought to have brought him wealth. But it did not, and some time after his death his family was discovered living in very poor circumstances indeed. A number of people thereupon drew up and signed a 'Memorial' (a petition) to Parliament to get the government to do something to relieve the family's distress.

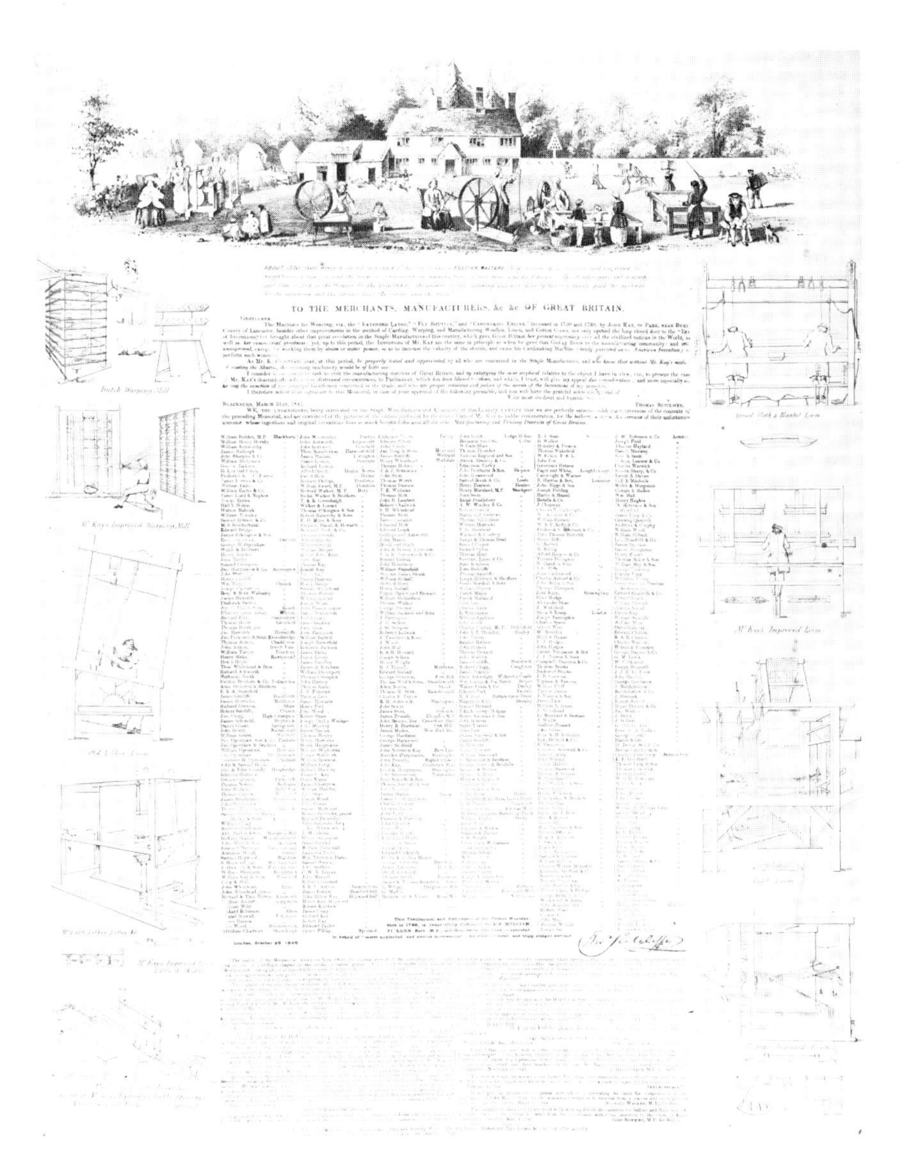

TO THE MERCHANTS, MANUFACTURERS, &c &c OF GREAT BRITAIN.

Gentlemen,

Thomas Sutcliffe.

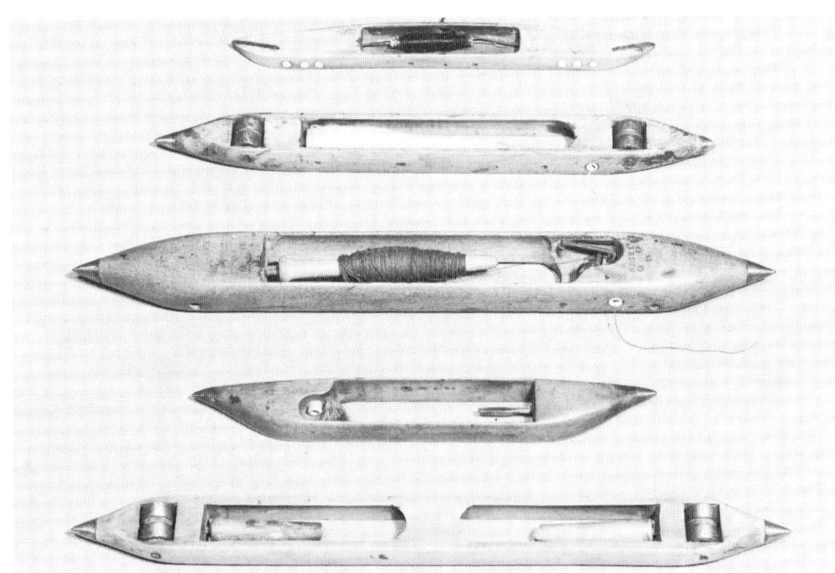

Some spinning shuttles used by John Kay, the inventor of the flying shuttle which greatly increased the rate at which cloth could be woven on a loom.

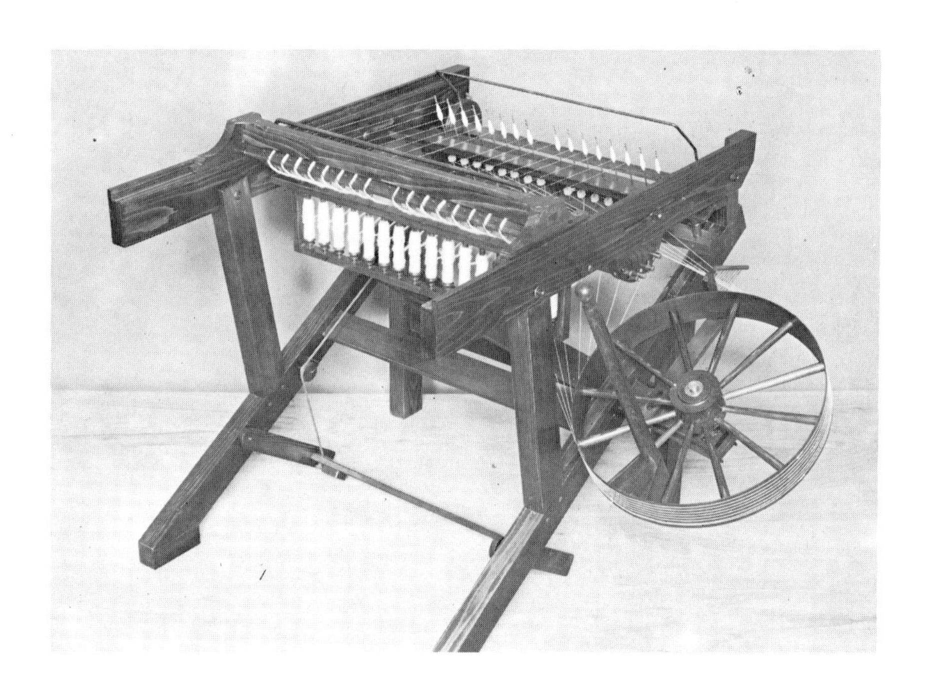

Above: Richard Arkwright invented the spinning frame driven by water power, in 1769. This was even better than Hargreaves' 'jenny', and Arkwright made a lot of money out of it, earning a knighthood towards the end of his days.

James Hargreaves invented a spinning 'jenny', or engine by which one person could operate several spinning wheels at one time.

Weaving inventions

The industry into which new machinery was widely introduced was the textile industry—that is, woollens and cottons. Most of the wool, which went into making an enormous amount and variety of clothing, tapestry and carpeting, bought by countries all over Europe, was spun with wool thread by wives and daughters in their homes, and the yarn produced was woven into cloth by men in their cottages or in those of their employers, using handlooms.

In 1733, John Kay, a Lancashire clockmaker, invented a 'flying shuttle'. He had a woollen factory at Coggeshall in Essex, a town famous for its weaving, and now still well-known for its beautiful period houses. This shuttle enabled the loom operator to work twice as fast as before, and also to make cloth of twice the width. He could make broadcloth two metres (six feet) wide.

Thirty years later, James Hargreaves, an uneducated weaver from Blackburn in Lancashire, invented his 'spinning jenny' to increase the output of yarn. Up to then, a single spinning wheel had been used, operated by a foot pedal or treadle. Hargreaves' machine was a spinning frame with eight revolving spindles worked by one man. This naturally saved a lot of time, but it also meant that employers did not need as many men to work for them. You will not be surprised to hear that Hargreaves' fellow workers hardly welcomed his invention, and in 1768 they broke into his house and smashed it. He had to leave the area, and went to live in Nottingham.

Above: A spinning wheel, such as was in general use before the invention of the new machines shown opposite.

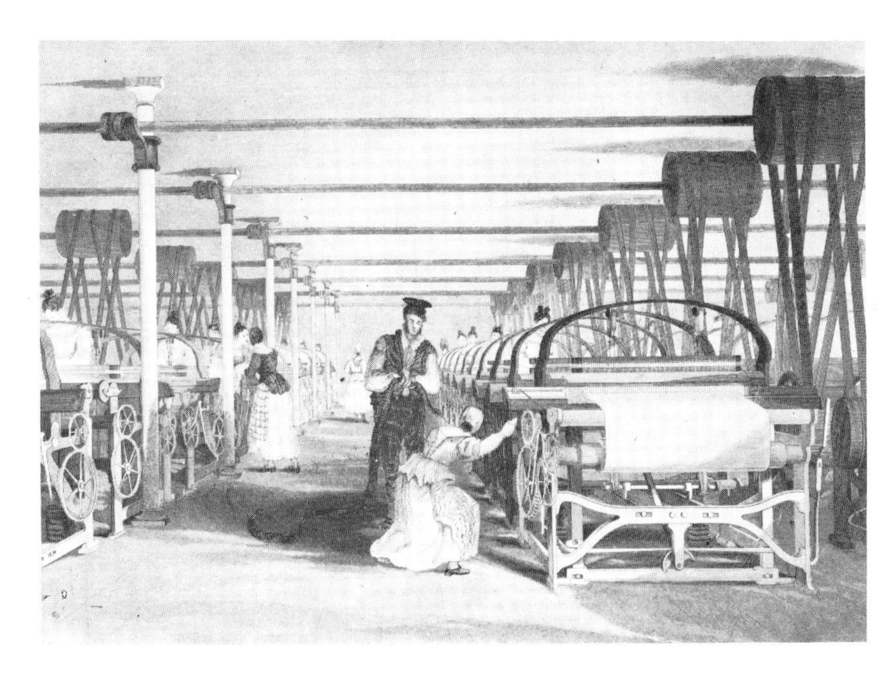

Right: A power loom of the 1830s. It is quite a sophisticated looking machine.

A year later, Richard Arkwright, a barber from Bolton in Lancashire, invented the spinning frame which was worked by water power. This effectively doubled the speed at which Hargreaves' 'jenny' worked. Arkwright, too, incurred the anger of fellow workers, who threatened to damage his machine, and he also fled to Nottingham. But he was more fortunate than Kay or Hargreaves, who both died in obscurity and poverty. Arkwright had applied his machine to the spinning of cotton, and he set up mills in Derbyshire and Lancashire. There he produced cotton in enormous quantities, once more stirring up opposition. Several of his machines were smashed, some weavers stole his idea and made their own machines without paying him any fees for copying it. The government, however, recognized the great contribution he was making to industrialization in England, and Arkwright was knighted in 1780. He died extremely rich.

Meanwhile, in 1779 Samuel Crompton, yet another Lancashire weaver, invented a spinning mule, which could operate by means of water or steam power and which would spin fine yarns like muslin. It was a great success, but so many people wanted to steal his idea that he had to stay indoors to protect it. Someone then offered him a lot of money, and he parted with the secret. But he was cheated and all he got in the end was about £60.

These great inventions—and many others like them, which were often modifications—led to a huge upsurge in wool and cotton spinning. Cotton was spun largely in Lancashire because the countryside has a wet atmosphere and the cotton yarn lasts better on machines in such conditions. Before long, one or two

Above: James Watt (1736–1819), the Scottish engineer who greatly improved the steam engine to make it an effective power unit for operating machinery in factories. The steam engine had been thought of by other people before Watt, but he noticed the wastage of condensed steam once the boiler had produced it for power use, devised a method of collecting it for re-use and constructed engines in which the whole process was compressed into an engine unit. The steam engine was perhaps the greatest individual contribution to the progress of the Industrial Revolution.

Above right: A model of one of Watt's steam engines, at the Science Museum in London.

bright wool-spinning mill-owners appreciated that a water driven mill could also be harnessed to grinding corn, and so two industries could be driven off one water-powered machine.

The production of so much wool and cotton, however, had its disadvantages. To begin with, the weaving looms could not cope with the pressure of wool supplies. So in 1785 the Nottinghamshire born clergyman, Edmund Cartwright, invented a powered loom. The first model, worked by a beast of burden, was a clumsy machine, but the weaving industry was quite enthusiastic about its development. By the mid-1800s powered looms were being worked up and down England using steam power. Let us look at this steam power.

The steam engine

In 1698, Thomas Savery, an English military engineer who had invented a gadget for polishing glass, constructed a machine that would pump water out of coal mine pits, using steam power. The water was lifted up by the power of a vacuum created through condensing steam in an enclosed vessel. By all accounts it was not very successful. Then in the next years, Thomas Newcomen, a Devonshire-born mining engineer who had worked with Savery, developed some improvements. This was the atmospheric steam engine. Steam was injected into a cylinder, condensed to make a vacuum so that the pressure of the atmosphere forced the piston down, and then another injection of steam pushed it up again. The upright piston was fixed by leverage to a pivoted beam, the other end of which was connected with a pump.

These Newcomen engines worked after a fashion, but no one seemed to get them to function for any length of time or with any reliability. Their effectiveness was limited until 1765. Then

A steam-powered carriage, designed and built by W. H. James, a civil engineer, in about 1828. It weighed two tons, developed 15–20 horse-power and could travel at about 20 km.p.h. (12 mph), maximum speed. Six passengers could be carried inside and twelve more outside.

James Watt (1736–1819), a brilliant Scottish engineer who at fourteen had already drawn on paper how he was going to make a Newcomen engine work properly, got hold of an engine for repair. At the time he was instrument maker to the University of Glasgow. Watt got it to work and studied it very closely. He was amazed at how much of the steam generated was utterly wasted. The steam was condensed by directing jets of cold water under the piston in the cylinder. At once you had to refill the cylinder with more steam. Watt tried an experiment. He connected the cylinder by means of a pipe to an extra tank, in which the steam could be condensed. This relatively simple idea worked extremely well, and after several further experiments he was able to show not only a substantial increase in engine speed, but also a considerable saving in coal fuel for water heating. Simple enough, yes, but it proved to be the greatest discovery of the century. Later on, he connected the piston to a crank shaft and cogwheel, providing rotary movement, and in 1782 he added another refinement when he enabled the steam to enter each side of the piston alternately, a double-acting engine.

Watt's principal obstacle was getting his steam engines built accurately. He teamed up with Matthew Boulton, a Birmingham engineer, and after nearly twenty years of diligent and patient work they managed to produce steam engines for a variety of uses over and above pumping water out of coal mine pits. It is said that some 500 of them were working in ironworks, mills, factories and mines by 1800.

At the turn of the century Richard Trevithick, a Cornish mining engineer, invented a high pressure steam engine with which he propelled a steam road carriage at about 6 km.p.h. (4 m.p.h.). This was the first powered road vehicle ever to be run. He also introduced his new type of engines into mines.

Richard Trevithick, a Cornish engineer, devised a steam engine that drove a vehicle. This one was called the 'Catch me who can'.

This is the first bridge to be built of iron. It was erected over the river Severn, at Ironbridge, near Shrewsbury, in 1779, and it is still there.

Steam engines were made of iron. To work efficiently the moving parts had to be accurately made. This was one of the problems encountered by the Watt and Boulton partnership. What was the state of the iron industry in the 18th century?

The iron industry

We saw in Chapter Seven that iron was still being smelted by charcoal. No-one had got around to using coal, but in the early years of the 18th century, several ironsmiths were trying to use coke made from coal to heat their furnaces. In about 1735, Abraham Darby, who lived (appropriately) at Coalbrookdale in Shropshire, and his son, succeeded in creating enough air draught to get coke to burn and heat up iron for smelting. This father-and-son partnership—the grandson built the world's first iron bridge over the river Severn at Coalbrookdale—set off the search for

The steam hammer in the picture was invented by James Nasmyth, a Scottish engineer, in 1839. It was devised to help forge iron castings fo[r] one of Brunel's ocean-going ships, the *Great Britain*.

better ways to produce the air blast required. In the 1760s, the Carron Iron Works in Stirlingshire, Scotland, used water power to create the air blast with success, and from then on the basic problem seems to have been solved. The industry was in fact revolutionized. Iron production rose from about 17,000 tons in 1740 to 120,000 tons at the end of the century and to nearly 750,000 tons by 1830. What is more, ironworks no longer had to be sited by forests. They were better placed near coal sources, such as in Staffordshire, Yorkshire, and the midlands of Scotland.

Iron production increases affected the whole of industry. They made all kinds of machines possible. They enabled Britain to make more and bigger cannons for ships and for the field of battle. Iron railings could be made in quantity for whole streets of houses in towns. The lovely Nash houses in Regent's Park, in London, could have iron balconies, railings, doors, gates and furniture.

In 1784, Henry Cort introduced a special kind of furnace which got rid of the impurities from the iron, and produced stronger wrought iron. This was called 'puddling'. In 1829, James Neilson, a Scottish engineer, developed the idea of using hot air in an iron furnace, thus saving fuel. And James Nasmyth, another Scottish engineer, invented the steam hammer in 1839 for forging wrought iron on a large scale.

Transport and communications

These revolutionary changes in the way men made the things they needed would have been greatly inhibited if at the same time there had not been some marked improvements in the country's communications which were then, like everywhere else in the world, remarkably bad. Indeed, it may largely be put down to this factor that the inventions we have looked at above took so long to get into general use. What was the good, for example, of increasing the output of a coal mine in Northumberland only to find that it took weeks to get the coal to the ironworks in Sheffield? How could you hope to make much profit on your bales of cotton in Manchester if they hung about in your mills waiting to be carried to London on a cart, probably only a dozen or so bales at a time, and at great cost? So men turned their minds to improving their lines of communication.

Roads

Hardly anything had been done about the roads of England since Roman days, thirteen hundred or more years before. We have seen in earlier chapters how bad roads and bridges were. They were so bad in the 18th century that many drivers, on long distances, preferred to cross the open fields. Even in the towns the streets were bad. George II was overturned in his carriage in Chelsea one day in 1739.

Then, in the middle of the century, the 'turnpike' system, originated in the time of Elizabeth I (1558–1603), was expanded to meet the demand for better roads and to pay for them. Turnpike means a frame that turns on a pivot like a turnstile, with spikes to stop people getting through. They could go through only on

No 14, Park Village East, Regent's Park Estate, London, a fine early 19th-century house designed by John Nash. Note the use of iron for railings and balcony.

A painting of the turnpike at Tottenham Court Road in London.

The Sedan chair was a portable, covered-in chair for one traveller. It was generally carried by two men using poles. Introduced in the reign of James I, it had become quite popular by 1634 when Sir Sanders Duncombe was given a licence to operate a fleet of fifty such chairs on a hire basis, like taxis.

payment of a fee. You have probably seen these at fairs and exhibition grounds, and they are being used now in some London Transport Underground stations. These turnpikes were placed at each end of certain stretches of the road, and a toll or fee collected from each traveller or merchant. The money was supposed to be used to keep the road concerned under repair. In 1663 an Act of Parliament enabled local magistrates in several counties to erect new turnpikes on suitable stretches of road, and early in the 18th century local companies were given the same powers.

In the 1750s the turnpikes spread rapidly, and by 1770 nearly 1,000 such turnpike companies controlled some 32,000 kilometres (20,000 miles) of road in Britain. The toll levy was very unpopular, but there seemed no other way to get the money to repair the roads, unless the government provided it, something they would do now but which was not expected of them then. By the end of the 18th century most of the industrial towns were connected by at least one road maintained through this turnpike system. Then, in the early years of the 19th century, John Macadam, a Scottish merchant who had made a fortune and settled in Ayrshire, determined to do something about road surfaces. He invented a new way to put them down. In 1816 he had been appointed surveyor to the Bristol Turnpike Trust, and he resurfaced the roads in its area. Big stones were broken down into smaller ones, laid down, covered with sand and water, more big stones broken down into smaller ones on top of that, and rolled upon. The surface improved as it was used by traffic whose wheels hardened the mass. He also introduced the camber, that is, the crown of the road was slightly higher than the two edges,

The 'Penny-farthing' was a bicycle, emerging in the 1870s, which had a front wheel about 2 metres (6 feet) high, and a rear wheel only 30 cm (1 foot) or so high. This enabled the machine to go quite fast but it was both uncomfortable and dangerous to ride. The name arises from the difference in size between the old penny piece and the old farthing, two coins that were in use up to a few years ago.

to allow rain and snow to drain away into guttering or ditching along the sides. He insisted on the use of very small stones—no stone should be used which was not small enough to go into a man's mouth. After the Bristol experiment, his services were sought all over the country, and he is said to have surveyed over 48,000 kilometres (30,000 miles) of roads, supervising the adoption of his techniques.

These new road surfaces greatly increased the speed and reliability of transport, and goods began to move much more quickly between the sources of supply and their outlets. Journeys also became more comfortable when iron springing was introduced.

Canals

The Romans had cut canals in their time, but most had fallen into disuse and were covered over. One, the Fossdyke between Lincoln and the Trent, was cleaned out and used again in the reign of Henry I (1100–1135), but this was an exception. The first completely artificial canal cut in England was the Duke of Bridgewater's canal from Worsley to Manchester. He wanted it to carry coal from his mines at Worsley. Up to then it had been laboriously carted in baskets on horseback. He engaged James

Brindley, the son of a Derbyshire farmer, who in 1752 had invented a water engine for draining coal pits. This extraordinary man, who to his death remained illiterate, used no drawings. When he was faced with an engineering problem he just went to bed to think about it, and the solution occurred to him. Between 1760 and 1772 the canal was dug and completed, and it proved a great success. Coal was shifted from Worsley to Manchester in great quantities, enabling the price to be halved. Brindley was called upon to supervise other canal projects, and by the time of his death he had built over 550 kilometres (360 miles) of artificial inland waterway. By the end of the century most of the industrial areas were linked by canals. The cost of water transport worked out at about a quarter of the charge for land transport, and the mania for canal building went on, right up to the 1830s, by which time over 6,400 kilometres (4,000 miles) of canals crisscrossed the face of England, and appeared here and there in Wales and Scotland, too.

Canal building was a vast engineering undertaking, involving the labour of many men. The canals were usually referred to as inland navigation, and Brindley himself used to call the workers 'navvygators' (as he could not spell properly). From this came the word 'navvies', to describe this special breed of men, tough, hard-working, hard-drinking and violent in their leisure hours, who cut them with their hands or hand-operated tools. This same type of men also built many of the railways.

Railways

The roads were improved and new ones built. Thomas Telford, the great Scottish engineer, built the A5 from London to Holyhead in Anglesey, giving it a wonderful suspension bridge across the Menai Straits at Menai, in 1826. The canals took an increasing amount of goods from one part of the country to the other.

But the volume of production in the factories, the ironworks, and the mines outstripped these transport facilities. New means had to be devised. More material was moved from port to port by sea or

Inside an early 19th century shop.

ship or barge, but there was room for another method. And it was not long in coming.

In 1808, Richard Trevithick set up a ring of railway track in a London field, and demonstrated his high-pressure steam engine in a locomotive pulling a carriage of passengers, for a shilling a ride. Unfortunately the cast iron rails kept breaking, and no one took much notice of his pioneering work which was to be triumphantly emulated seventeen years later by George Stephenson, when he demonstrated his first passenger train.

Stephenson was a poor colliery worker's son living near Newcastle-upon-Tyne. When he was fifteen, he worked alongside his father for many hours during the day, and at night, by candlelight, he taught himself to read and write. Stephenson noticed the heavy work required by many people to pull the trucks of mined coal along a railway from the pithead to the assembly point. So he thought of ways to make the burden lighter. In about 1814 he built a locomotive, modelled on Trevithick's, and tried it out pulling coal carts on iron wheels along a track. It was a success, and he developed it at another colliery where his rail track was several miles long. This, too, was successful.

Soon, Stephenson thought of conveying people in carriages

No 1 engine of the original Stockton and Darlington Railway, started in 1825 by George Stephenson. This is on a pedestal at Darlington Station.

Left: This is Paddington Station inside, in the 1850s. The overall scheme was designed by Brunel and the detail by Matthew Wyatt.

along a track, and in 1823, with his brother, he set up a railway works at Newcastle. Before long he got the job of superintending a new railway planned to run between Stockton-on-Tees and Darlington. In 1825 it was completed, and when it was opened a team of horses pulled a line of carriages gently along the track. Then he tried a steam driven locomotive and the speed was about 24 km.p.h. (15 m.p.h.). The age of the railways had arrived.

The first railway line of national interest was that from Manchester to Liverpool. Here, in 1830, the opening was attended by all sorts of high personages, including the great Duke of Wellington, and William Huskisson, once President of the Board of Trade. Huskisson was knocked down by an engine and died from his injuries. It was the first major railway accident.

From the 1830s on, there was a spate of railway building throughout the country. Many brilliant men made their names, none more so than the incomparable Isambard Kingdom Brunel (1806–1859), who conceived a comprehensive journey from London (Paddington Station, which he built) by rail to Bristol (Temple Meads Station, which he built), via Maidenhead Bridge (which he built) and thence to the United States of America in one or two of his great steam-powered ships, the *Great Western* and the *Great Britain* (both of which he built), which left the great west country port of Bristol from a harbour (which he built).

Below left: Engraving of a photograph of Isambard Kingdom Brunel (1806–1859), the brilliant engineer and innovator whose genius and achievements were said by Lord Clark to be worthy of comparison with those of the greatest men of the Renaissance. Brunel designed and built railways, bridges, tunnels, ships, harbours, a village of houses, a portable hospital complex, the water towers at the Crystal Palace, and a host of other things.

Two kinds of railway line gap, called a gauge, were used at first, the 143-centimetre (4 feet $8\frac{1}{2}$ inches) gauge determined by Stephenson from the gauge of a farm cart on his own farm, and the wider 213-centimetre (7-foot) gauge called the broad gauge, which Brunel devised and favoured for safety and comfort. A fierce argument developed, as railways of different gauges were built and so could not join up conveniently. Eventually, Parliament settled for the narrower gauge, which has remained to this day.

A room furnished with Regency style pieces, at the Geffrye Museum in London. Regency furniture was made in the period *c* 1800 to *c* 1830, a longer time than the years of the actual regency of Prince George, eldest son of George III.

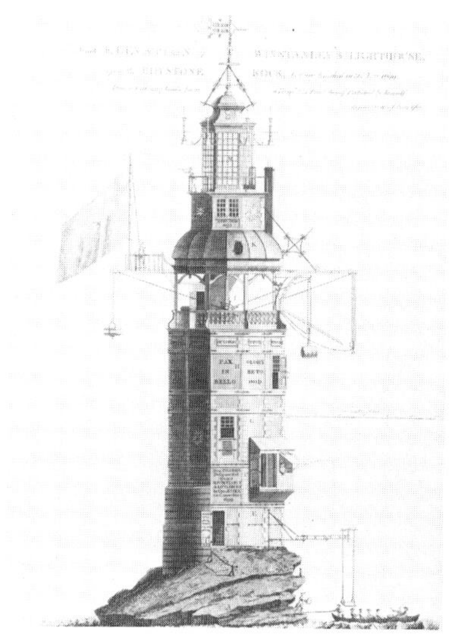

Above: This is an engraving of the first Eddystone Lighthouse, built at the very end of the 17th century.

Above right: One of the first people to introduce gas lighting in England was a German professor, Albrecht Winzer who changed his name to Frederick Winsor. Here, he demonstrates various gas lights to an audience at the Lyceum Theatre in London, in about 1804.

It has not been possible to give a full picture of all the changes that took place in these feverish years of industrialization. They must have been exciting, wonderful and perhaps alarming in some cases. What is sad to record is that these marvels were not produced without human suffering on a very big scale. The Victorians reaped the benefits of the brilliance of their predecessors. They did little to improve the lot of the millions of men, women and children who made these benefits possible. That was the tragedy of the Industrial Revolution.

10

Wales, Scotland and Ireland : 13th–17th centuries

In 1282, Edward I of England invaded north Wales to deal with Prince Llywelyn the Last, who had refused to swear fealty to him and had attacked English garrisons. The campaign was a swift one. Llywelyn was driven into the Snowdon mountains. He fled towards Brecknockshire to rouse the men of mid-Wales but was spotted by an English soldier, Adam Frankton, and killed. His head was sent to Edward who ordered it to be taken to London and mounted on a spike at London Bridge.

Wales

To keep his new dominion subservient to England, Edward filled the land of Wales with English administrative officers, and ensured that they operated from a position of strength. Their residences and places of work were, for a start, to be impressive, attack-proof and strategically sited. Thus began the programme of castle-building in Wales, the glories of which are still to be seen today as at Caernarvon, Conway, Harlech and Beaumaris.

But it was not possible to hold the Welsh down all the time by castles, brute force, foreign laws or troops of men. The first two centuries of English rule were filled with revolt of one kind or another, the biggest and longest-lasting being the struggle of Owain Glyndŵr, early in the fifteenth century, who actually managed to take Harlech Castle and set up a parliament.

The Welsh lived very much in these first centuries as they had before. The country was still more or less divided into *cantrefs* and *commotes*, and these *commotes* were not like the English manors. This was largely because the Welsh enjoyed the freedom of livestock farms of huge acreage on the slopes of their native hills and mountains. The geography of Wales with slopes, streams, crags and dingles, was against the creation of villages as they were known in England.

A typical *commote* may have looked like a scattering of small, single-storey houses at the bottom of a valley, in which several streams were running. Some houses had haphazard areas under cultivation, more of them had none. All over the slopes were the

livestock, for the land was usually regarded as common pasturage ground. In among the houses was a small church, probably with its own cultivated strips to provide food for the priest.

The Welsh were quite different from the English in many other ways. They did not speak English for they had their own language. Their legal system was different in many respects, too. It had been codified by the prince of all Wales, Hywel Dda (916–950), and there was, for example, no death penalty.

There was little class structure in Wales. Indeed, it has been said that the system was not unlike a communist one. Property was regarded not so much as an individual's possession, but something to be shared and enjoyed by everybody. Welshmen, for example, did not leave their property or money to the eldest son, but to each member of the family equally. This was known as *gavelkind*, and the practice persisted in Welsh law until the time of Henry VIII.

But this was really not very satisfactory. What happened was that land was divided up into smaller and smaller units as the years went by, and quite often a holding was so small that it was not worth having at all. In this case, an inheritor would probably sell it to a brother, or to someone else, so increasing that person's holding. But the inheritor then had no property at all. He could either get himself a job on someone else's land, or go off to join the wars, probably on the English side, in France.

The preference of Welshmen for livestock stood many of them

Top and above left: Two drawings, from 13th-century manuscripts, of Welsh soldiers.

Left: Harlech Castle, Meirionethshire, is a concentric-type castle built in the time of Edward I who conquered Wales in the 1280s. This castle has a huge gatehouse.

At the end of the Talyllyn narrow gauge railway, in Wales, is the mountain-ringed village of Abergynolwyn. In medieval Wales, villages lay just like this one in mountain-surrounded valleys, and farmers reared sheep on the grassy sides of the hills.

in good stead in the Middle Ages, when the wool trade in England was developed and when British wool was valued so much in all parts of Europe. When the Normans occupied areas of south and east Wales, they introduced sheep farming on a big scale. The abbey at Neath, for example, is said to have had over 4,000 sheep, and the abbey at Strata Florida, a similar number. Before long, native Welshmen caught on to the idea, and by the 1300s, although they were a conquered people, they had become in many instances rich because of their sheep farming. The Welsh sheep farmer also taught himself to spin and weave the wool which was sheared every year off the backs of his flock. This is why, throughout the centuries, there has been a strong traditional weaving industry in Wales. There were regulations about the industry, then in its beginnings, in Hywel Dda's laws.

Wool was moving quickly and in great quantities in Wales in the 14th century. Caermarthen was a staple town and was shipping bulk loads to Europe and Ireland. Inland, wool was being taken by cart to distribution points like Hereford and Shrewsbury.

The industry grew up among the country people, as it did in England. Once it was sheared, the wool was washed and then spun by hand on oak or elm spinning-wheels in the lowland farmhouses by wives and daughters of the shepherds. Then it was woven by men in sheds on hand looms. Even the different

Above: A portrait of Henry VII from the National Portrait Gallery. Henry Tudor was the son of a Welsh noble. As king of England and Wales (1485–1509) he brought the two countries out of the Middle Ages and into the new age of the Renaissance, the Discoveries and the Revival of Learning. He crushed the power of the nobility whose wars had been crippling development for decades. He organized tax collection in such a way as to leave his treasury filled with money when he died. Cold, shifty and mean, he was nonetheless one of the best kings of England and Wales.

districts of Wales produced different kinds of cloth. In the south, the weavers specialized in heavy cloth, like tweeds, as indeed they still do today. In the middle of Wales, they produced what we call flannel, a word which came from the Welsh *gwlan*, which means wool.

In 1485, a Welshman, Henry Tudor, son of Margaret Beaufort who was a direct descendant of John of Gaunt, Edward III's fourth son, won the battle of Bosworth and became king of England as Henry VII. His supporters in Wales fancied that he had fulfilled a prophecy made at the time when their last prince, Llywelyn, was killed at Builth Wells in 1282 – namely, that one day a Welshman would indeed wear the crown of England.

Henry was a sound businessman, with a good head for figures. When he came to the throne, he had many Welsh advisers around him, but he was realistic enough to know that the population of England was very much bigger than that of Wales, and that it would not do to overfill the court with his own countrymen. His son, Henry VIII, decided in 1536 to join England and Wales together by the Statute of Wales. The old areas were made into counties, and each county was able to send members to Parliament in London. But he also stipulated that English was to be the official language of Wales, and that Welsh should be 'extirped', that is, rooted out. The English Justices of the Peace system was also extended throughout Wales which came to be known as the Principality, following the creation of the eldest son of Edward I as Prince of Wales.

Valle Crucis Abbey was a Cistercian foundation, built in the time of Llywelyn the Great. It is near Llangollen in Denbighshire.

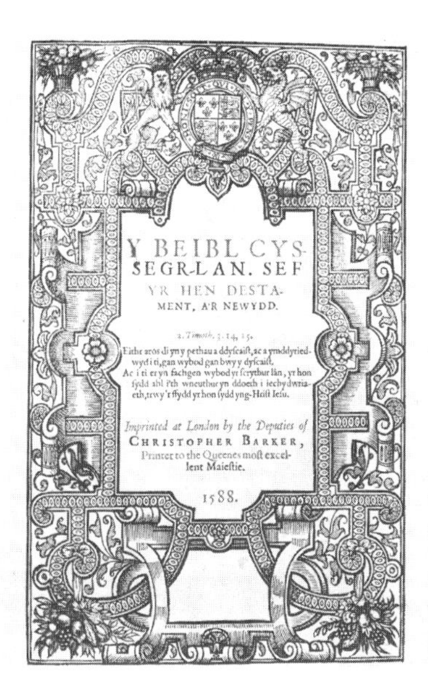

Y BEIBL CYS-
SEGR-LAN. SEF
YR HEN DESTA-
MENT, A'R NEWYDD.

2. Timoth. 3. 14, 15.

Eithr aros di yn y pethau a ddyscaist, ac a ymddyriedwyd i ti, gan wybod gan bwy y dyscaist.
Ac i ti er yn fachgen wybod yr scrythur lân, yr hon sydd abl i'th wneuthur yn ddoeth i iechydwriaeth, trwy'r ffydd yr hon sydd yng-Hrist Iesu.

Imprinted at London by the Deputies of
CHRISTOPHER BARKER,
Printer to the Queenes most excellent Maiestie.

1588.

Title page of Bishop Morgan's translation of the Bible into Welsh, 1588. This great project did a lot to save the Welsh language from dying out.

One of the adverse effects of the Statute of Wales was the fact that when Henry VIII, short of money, had dissolved the monasteries in England, between 1536 and 1540, his expropriations reached into Wales. Among those which suffered at his hands were Strata Florida, Aberconway, Valle Crucis and St David's.

The Act of Union did not benefit Wales very much at all. Perhaps it was not meant to, for Henry VIII hardly ever had anything to do with the land of his father's people. Those Welshmen, who did represent the counties in Parliament at Westminster, protected their own individual interests and did little to stand up for the views of the people of Wales. Indeed, these views were hardly ever asked for. And many of the seats in Wales were held by Englishmen who had acquired, by one means or another, large estates in Wales and kept them running by using native Welshmen in conditions that were little better than slavery. This was to persist right through to the present century.

Henry VIII's daughter Elizabeth I did do something for Wales. The English version of the Bible had been issued in the reign of Henry VIII. But this was of no use to many Welshmen who did not understand the language beyond the kind of words needed for passing the time of day. Elizabeth ordered the Welsh bishops to get together and translate the Bible into Welsh. The man who did most of the work was Gwilym Morgan, a Welsh priest, and in 1588, the very year in which the Spanish Armada made its vainglorious attempt against England, the book was produced. This had some important results. One was that it saved the Welsh language from extinction. And this language is still strong today.

The Bible, or *Y Beibl* as it is called in Welsh, was not published in any large quantity to begin with, for it had taken a long time to get it done and it was expensive. After a while, a cheaper leather-bound copy was made available for five shillings. This was more than the average worker earned in a week, but it did mean that every parish – and there were many of these throughout Wales – could have a copy for the parishioners to come and hear read, or read themselves. Richer men like farmers also bought copies. This publishing event had another result. It converted

One of the craftsman-made objects peculiar to Wales is the love-spoon. They have been made there for centuries. Here is one dated 1667. It is a token of love from the carver to the girl he was courting. Lovespoons were usually carved out of a single piece of wood, no matter how intricate the design.

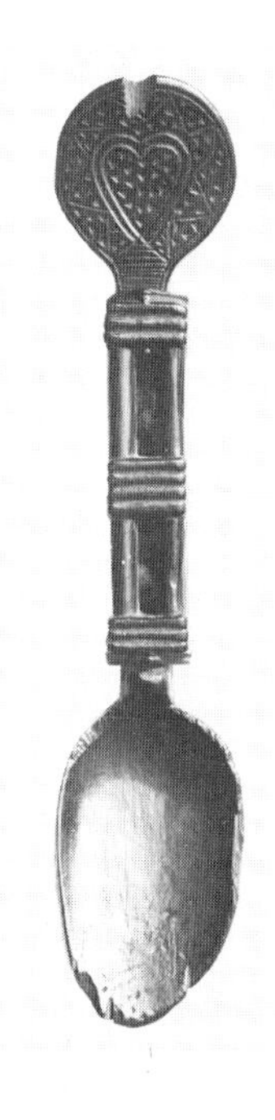

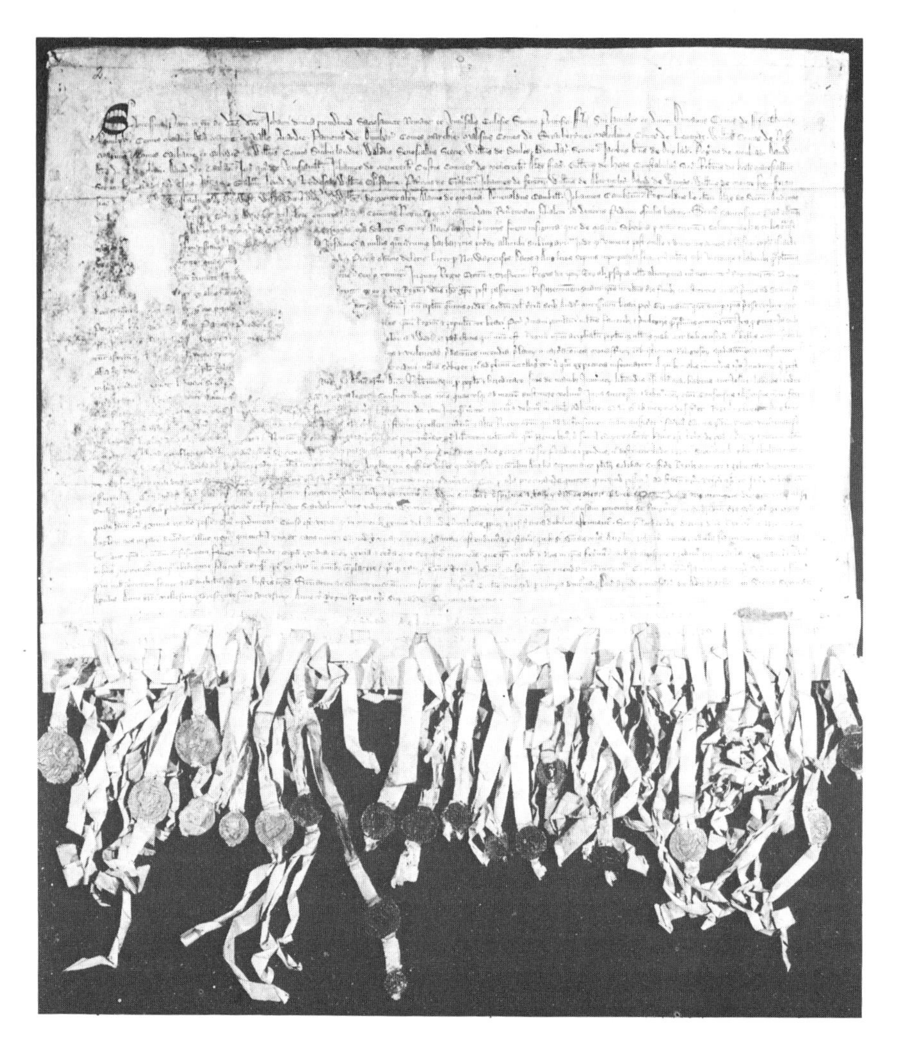

Above: The Declaration of Arbroath, 1320. This is one of the most important documents of Scottish history. In it a number of Scottish nobles appeal to the Pope to recognize the independence of Scotland and to accept Robert Bruce as their King.

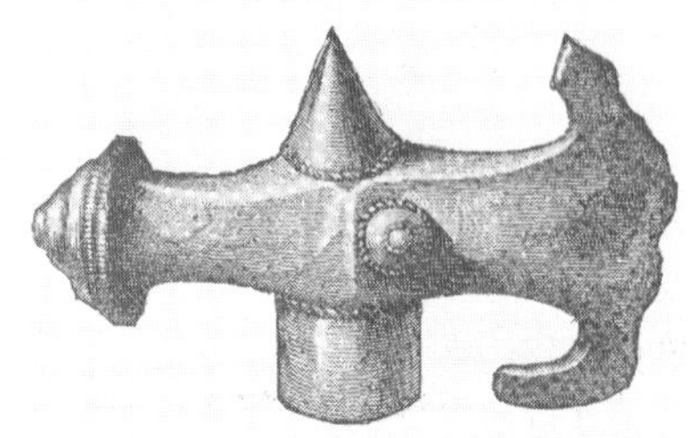

Above: This is the head of a battle-axe found on the site of the battle of Bannockburn in Stirlingshire. Bannockburn was the scene of a glorious victory by the Scots under Robert Bruce (1306–1329) against the English, in 1314, in the fight to maintain Scottish independence.

most Welshmen from Catholicism to Protestantism. They had clung obstinately to the older faith while England was turning Protestant, but the Welsh Bible, and the publication of a Prayer Book in Welsh, brought them into line with their neighbours.

Scotland

No sooner had Edward I of England conquered Wales than he turned his attention to Scotland. Here he was not so successful. Though he acted as king for about ten years, from 1296 to 1307, as soon as he was dead, the patriotic movement led by Robert Bruce began to chip away at the English administration. In 1314, Robert utterly smashed the English at Bannockburn in what must be one of the most glorious victories of any nationalist movement. Scottish independence began to become a reality and the country was able to go forward and develop in its own way under its own kings.

The war of independence had, however, left Scotland very weak and very poor. What the country needed was a succession of firm and just rulers like Robert, but it did not get them for some time – in fact, until the 15th century and the accession of the Stewart royal house. Scotland was a land of contrasts. It was also two countries rather than one—the upper, or Highland half, roughly above a line running from Glasgow on the Clyde north-eastwards to Aberdeen, and the Lowland half below this line. The Highlanders were a race apart. They lived in clans and accorded their clan chiefs the kind of reverence more usually given to gods or kings. Each clan loathed the next one, and inter-clan feuding and fighting was the order of the day. Few clansmen felt they had lived if they had not killed or injured at least one of their hated neighbouring clansmen. It was difficult in such conditions for the people to advance in civilization, and for a long while they were indeed behind their Lowland neighbours.

The Highland countryside was, right up to the 16th century, bare and without many trees. Hedges, dykes, and stone walls were few and far between. Although there were plenty of sources of stone for building, for some parts of Scotland are rich in granite and stone, most Highlanders continued to dwell in dingy windowless turf block houses or huts, trying to plough the slopes of the hills which were not rich in soil. The plains below were richer, but they were also waterlogged and no-one bothered to drain them. Where they did get results, these were not good, as they would grow the same crop time and again, say barley or oats, on the same land and never let the land lie fallow. Their ploughs were not very effective and some required teams of eight oxen to draw them. It is not surprising that they preferred to graze cattle and sheep on these unproductive acres.

And when they were not farming, the Highlanders joined their clan chiefs in one or other of the interminable feuds, or they descended in raiding parties on the Lowlands in search of anything they could use or trade with merchants elsewhere. They were indeed not far removed from their ancestors of the days of the Roman occupation of Britain.

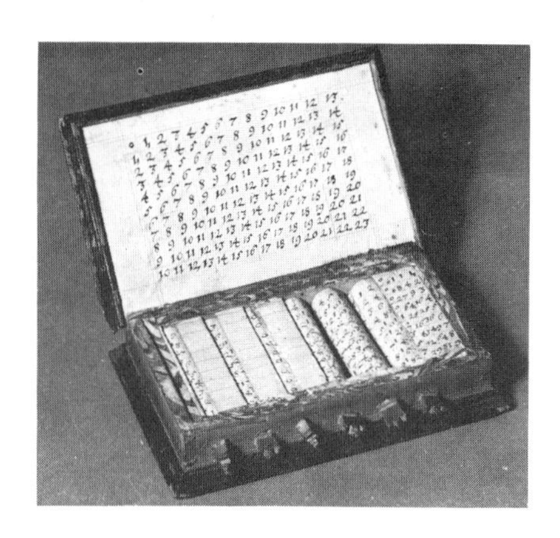

Above: John Napier of Merchiston (1550–1617) was the brilliant Scottish mathematician who invented logarithms. This revolutionized maths. He also invented the first calculating machine, which you can see. It was known as Napier's Bones. The rollers are made of ivory. Napier's work was recognized by leading scientific men of Europe, including Tycho de Brahe and Johann Kepler.

Right: Inside Parliament Hall in Edinburgh. It is a fine piece of architecture. When Scotland gets its own Parliament in a few years time, will the members meet here?

The Lowlanders were very different. Their lands were closer t England, and while they did not like the English, there were many things they had in common. They understood each other's languages. Malcolm III and his English wife had introduced many English customs, and the Norman type of feudalism was, in modified form, operating in the Lowlands. The picture was in fact a more encouraging one. The Lowland Scots advanced in civilizatior and culture, learning and building, at the same rate as their English neighbours – in some respects faster. What is more Lowland trade and commerce grew by leaps and bounds. Aberdeen for example, which had its own university by the end of the 15th century, had become one of the principal fishing ports in north west Europe, and it kept this predominance up to the Act of Unior of 1707.

The growing prosperity of the merchant class was reflected in the way in which they built themselves good homes. Stone house began to spring up, with vaulted cellars and what we call crow stepped gables. Many of these houses were put up round courtyards Edinburgh, for example, which became the official capital o Scotland early in the 16th century, was a fine city by that time Its houses had iron studded doors, and gardens stretched backward presenting an attractive prospect. But there was no proper drainage and rubbish had to be thrown into the streets, there to accumulate and fester.

Facies Civitatis Sancti ANDREÆ. The Prospect of The Town of St ANDREWS.

Above: The *Great Michael*, the model of which is in the Royal Scottish Museum, was built for James IV (1513–1542). It was in its time the biggest battleship afloat, some 72 metres (220 feet) long. It carried 300 sailors. It had been constructed from oak trees from Fife.

Above left: A panorama of St Andrews in the 17th century. It was here that the first Scottish university had been founded.

The town houses of the merchants and businessmen, the rofessional lawyers and scholars, were cheerfully decorated. Vooden rafters across the ceilings of the main hall were often ainted in gay colours. The walls were hung with tapestries vhich, on the whole, were imported from Europe rather than nade at home. The floors did not have carpets, but were covered vith dried rushes. Furniture was sparse, as in England. The main iece in the hall was a huge trestle table for dining or working, nd it might be covered in green cloth. There were one or two ther side tables with fixed legs, and some chairs, especially a ig one for the owner. Along the trestle table there would be enches with soft cushions. One or two parts of the wall between vindows would also have benches. Windows were usually glazed n the top halves only. Elsewhere in the hall would be chests or *ists*, and some had an *aumbry*, or cupboard. *Aumbry* is the same s *armoire*, the French for a cupboard which stands on its own, a iece of furniture that began to be made in central Europe in ie 13th century, chiefly for ecclesiastical use, for containing obes and vestments.

The hall had at one end a large stone-surrounded fireplace vith a mantlepiece. Logs were thrown onto the stone hearth, but iere was often nothing to stop burning logs rolling out into the ushes and starting fires. So someone thought of the fire dog.

At the table for meals, guests ate off fine silverware plates with poons. It seems they did not have forks or knives, though eople did carry knives about with them everywhere, for a variety f reasons. It was still not safe to wander about the streets and lleys of Edinburgh, Glasgow or Aberdeen in those days. Food as eaten using the hands, and you could wash your hands in a owl in the middle of the table, where there would be small towels rovided. If the meal was more casual, pewter or wooden plates ere used, for the Scots were not yet using china or glass.

A town house bedroom was thinly furnished and usually very raughty. The bed itself, a thick feather mattress in a wooden ame, and topped by a canopy with curtains of heavy cloth, was robably warm enough.

Scottish education

The Scots have long been famous for their learning and scholarship - and not without good reason. A native intelligence allied to a inbred disposition to work hard, probably the result of the long tempestuous history of the struggle to triumph over barbarism has made them among the brightest and most diligent people i the world. The long list of inventions and discoveries emanatin from Scottish-born men amply testifies to this – Napier (logarithms Watt (steam engine), Macadam (road surfaces), Kelvin (man electrical inventions), Fleming (penicillin), Simpson (chloroform and so on. Early in the 15th century, the first university in Scotlan was set up at St Andrews. Up to then, Scots who wanted to study wider range of subjects than Latin, elementary mathematic and their own language offered at the local grammar schoo went either to England or to Europe, chiefly to France. In Englan the father of King John Balliol (1292–1296) had founded Balli College at Oxford. In France a special school for Scottish pupi was set up in Paris.

French influence in Scotland was very strong, not least becaus Scotland and France had a common enemy – England. It wa not surprising that many French scholars came to teach i Scotland in the 14th and 15th centuries, about the time of th

The city of Glasgow from the north-east. This was engraved in the 1680s.

'undred Years' War between England and France. Scottish hurchmen used to go to France for further study. Scottish troops ften went to the aid of French armies, and the arrangement was eciprocated.

In 1451, Glasgow University was established by Bishop Turnbull, ho had obtained his own degree at St Andrews. And in 1495, berdeen University was founded. Its first head was Hector Boece, ho knew Erasmus (the amazing Dutch-born scholar who spent is life roaming the universities and learning capitals of Europe). 1505, James IV gave a royal charter to the College of Surgeons Edinburgh. By that time it had become compulsory for upper ass families to send their eldest sons to grammar school, until ey 'have perfect Latin', and then to a university to study law. ower down the academic scale, Scotsmen were always keen to nd their children to schools of one kind or another. This was eatly fostered by the marvellous Protestant reformer, John nox who, anxious to see Scotland quickly and properly converted the new faith that Calvin had been preaching at Geneva in vitzerland, sought to ensure that there would be no more norant' priests. The clergy would spread the doctrines and he id he would fill the country with schools, one at least for every rish, however small, so that everyone with any intelligence uld go to grammar school and then to university.

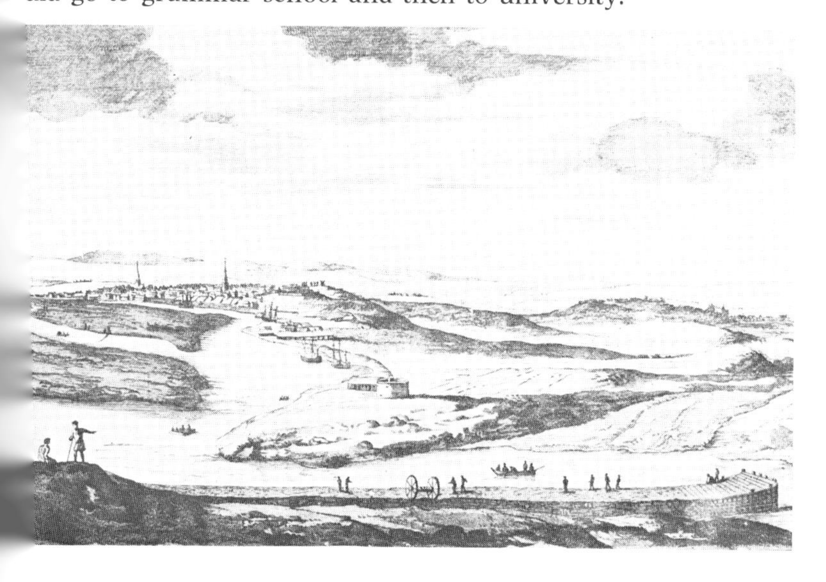

Aberdeen, as seen by the artist and map-maker John Slezar, towards the end of the 17th century. By then, the city was very prosperous, chiefly through the splendid fishing fleets harboured there, which went to sea and brought back catches into the docks.

On this cross you can see (left) a carving of a man playing a harp. The harp was the national musical instrument of Ireland. Indeed, for some time harp-players were the only musicians in Irish society who were considered free men. The national emblem today is the harp. The cross, a 10th century work, is at Castledermo

Union of the crowns

The union of the crowns of Scotland and England, brought about when James VI of Scotland, cousin and heir to Elizabeth I of England, succeeded her as king of both lands, did not do much besides uniting the crowns. Scotland kept its own Parliament, privy council, law and law courts, church structure, coinage, weights and measures, and its own army and navy. Even James' own efforts to promote free trade between the two was bitterly opposed by the English. But the Scottish Parliament had few teeth in any case because James managed to ensure that executive power remained in the hands of the special committee, founded about two centuries earlier, and called the Committee of the Articles. Before his time it had elected its own members. Now he appointed them. And this meant the Committee would do much as he ordered it to. There were other problems too, as we shall see in Chapter Thirteen.

Ireland

The Anglo–Norman invasion of Ireland in 1171–72 was the start of seven and half centuries of exploitation of one people by another, though it should be said that the first three hundred years were not anything like as ruthless as the ensuing four hundred and fifty. It was the opening of one of the ugliest chapters in the history of colonial dominion. The unfortunate people of Northern Ireland (Ulster) are still reaping the results of it today.

Henry II's conquest was quite rapid, largely because of the habit of the Irish of not co-operating between kingdoms, even between villages or families, making the job of the conquerors an easy one. Indeed, Dermot McMurrough, king of Leinster, had enlisted the help of an Anglo–Norman lord, Strongbow, against his fellow king, Roderic O'Connor of Connaught (who also claimed to be king of all Ireland). When Henry came over he received the submission of the Irish kings and lords, and the leaders of the church as well.

A favourite pastime of some Irishmen who were disinclined to work hard on farms and grow crops was cattle-stealing. They enjoyed it most if they could organize a raid on a neighbouring ranch. This engraving shows a raid in the 16th century.

The Anglo–Normans (or English as we shall call them from now on), found they preferred some parts of the country to others, particularly the area around Dublin and Wexford, which came to be called The Pale. They settled down there, introduced English law and customs, began to build in stone, and said to the native Irish, join us or go 'beyond the Pale'.

For the next three centuries or so, things remained more or less like that. Various efforts were tried to bring the native Irish to heel, but they usually failed. Irish chiefs attacked the Pale, and were beaten off. English landlords fought each other for lands or over their wives, and they used native Irish troops in their private armies, for the Irish were keen on fighting. The point was that the English stayed there largely because the Irish could not agree to combine and drive them out.

The English lived much as they had been used to in England, and they introduced changes into Ireland. But not all were acceptable, nor were they enforceable. The result was that the English way of life predominated in the towns, and the Irish way in the country districts. Irish law, for example, quite a different thing from English, was allowed beyond the Pale. The Irish language, another strain of Celtic, called Gaelic, and as old as Welsh, was spoken widely. On the whole the Irish did not care for towns. They were like their Welsh kinsmen, country people tending a few sheep or horses or cattle on the rolling hillsides or the rich green plains. They did not bother much about farming.

They did not trouble to trade. They were not interested in work or money. Cows remained a main article of currency for years, and as long as they could get by using cows to buy what they could not steal, they were content. They had their feasts which all classes shared. Kings and chiefs sat at the same tables as their servants and retainers. They all enjoyed music. And they loved the ancient sport of hurling, a game like hockey played with crooked sticks or clubs between two goals. Quite often people got badly hurt in this game as the teams played with great gusto and abandon. The English government tried to ban the game in the 14th century, but to no avail. The Irish just went on playing it.

The Irish also loved their drinking hours, quaffing whiskey in quantities that at first appalled the English. They spent hours and hours in alehouses of one kind or another.

Dunbrody Abbey. A Cistercian foundation in County Wexford, of the 13th century. It was inspired and largely built by the Norman settlers who came to Wexford following the invasion of Ireland by Henry II in 1171.

The English built towns in Ireland and surrounded them with walls and ditches. They put up stone castles, many of them on the coast, and constructed permanent buildings from which to administer the law. The attitude was that you could come and live in the towns, or in the country areas near them, submit to English feudalism which was modified, or you stayed in the peat bogs, the hovels and the marshy ground of the remoter countryside. Gradually, the English became more and more Irish, and the Irish in their turn took to many English customs. This served to make the Irish chiefs more powerful than before, and they began to deck themselves and their courts in the finery more appropriate to an English lord on the mainland. And the introduction of the wool industry, in which some of the chiefs got involved on an ownership basis, increased their status.

But the rural Irishman who did not want to be part of the English scene continued to live austerely and roughly. Irish houses, like those of the Highland Scots of the same time, were turf-bricked with no windows. Inside, there was hardly any furnishing and few kitchen utensils, for one or two pots would do for all needs. Bed mattresses were a luxury enjoyed by few. Most slept on straw or reeds on the earthen floor. Their clothes were rough, too, a sort of smock of linen with a cloak of wool, until in the 16th century they began to wear trousers which would not look out of place today.

In the mid-14th century, the English Government tried to do something to bring the Irish – and the English settlers – into line. Many areas of English dominion had been invaded by Irish chiefs and had fallen. Edward Bruce, Robert Bruce's brother, had in 1316 organized a huge uprising against the English in Ireland and had nearly driven them out altogether. It was a close thing. Worse, many of the English had become identified with the Irish and no longer looked to London for government. Some had even changed their names, such as Mortimer to MacNamara. There was an Irish Parliament, set up in 1295, but it legislated for the Irish as much as for the English and paid little heed to London or to the officials sent out to Dublin.

In 1367, this Parliament was persuaded to pass the Statute of Kilkenny which endeavoured to keep the two races apart – a kind of medieval apartheid. Among the terms was that it became an offence for any English settler to speak the Gaelic language, to wear Irish dress or to adopt any Irish customs. It did not work, of course. How could it be enforced?

Then Ireland was virtually left alone for another century or so, until Henry VII sent out a new Deputy in 1494, Sir Edward Poynings, an Englishman. The previous deputies had often been Irishmen, some of them members of the influential Geraldine family – that is, the FitzGeralds of Kildare. Poynings made the Irish Parliament re-issue the Statute of Kilkenny and ban private armies. Then a set of laws of his own were introduced. These made the Irish Parliament dependent upon Westminster. Before it could even be summoned, application had to be made to London, with the reasons for summoning it listed. Moreover, all laws passed at Westminster were now to apply to Ireland.

It was in the 16th century that the sufferings of Ireland really began, and we shall look at those in Chapter Thirteen.

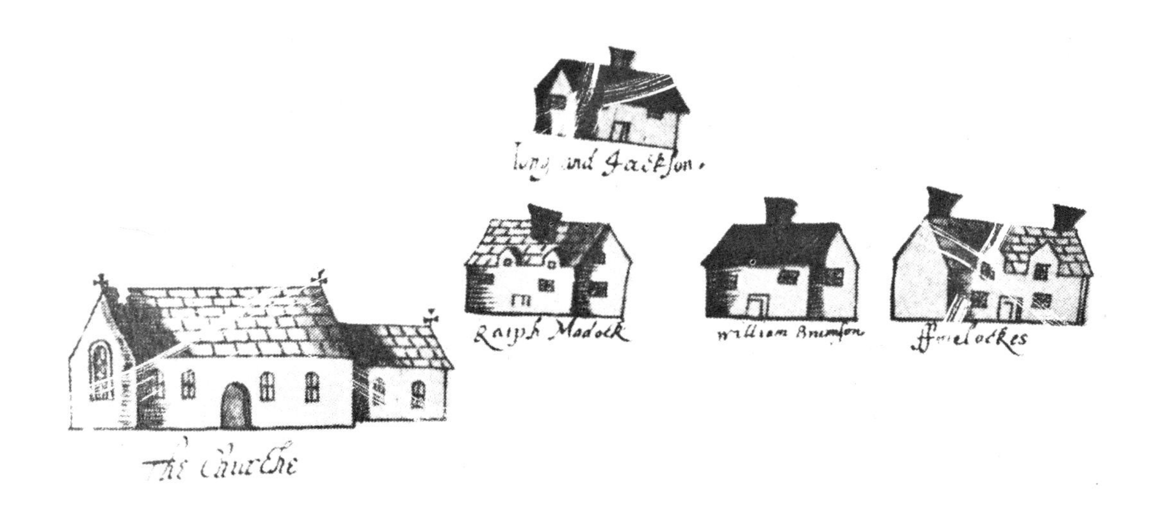

English and Scots people were encouraged to settle in Ulster in the late 16th and early 17th centuries. Here are some houses and a church which make up a small village in County Derry in the 17th century.

11 The Victorian Age

The nineteenth century has often been thought of as a time of glory, power, riches and comfort for the British people. Napoleon's dream of a united Europe was smashed, first by his defeat in Russia in 1812, and then by his defeat at Waterloo in 1815. Thereafter, except for the Crimean War of 1854–56, a relatively minor war, Britain was not involved in European conflict for almost a hundred years. In that time, the Victorians had their Great Exhibition of 1851 in Hyde Park, then the biggest ever show of its kind in history. Thousands of companies demonstrated millions of different products which they made or put together, from whole houses to small sewing kits inside mother-of-pearl eggs on stands, from traction engines to model steam locomotives. It was a huge propaganda exercise to show that Great Britain had become industrialized and led the world in engineering, scientific and material progress.

So far, so good, but the exhibition did not show what life was like for the people who made the exhibits. Many of them were condemned to live their whole lives in mean houses, monotonously strung out in endless rows in growing industrial towns, and to work in cold, badly lit, smoke-filled factories for the great majority of daylight hours, six days a week. That this was bad for any human being is obvious. One of the worst aspects was that these workers never met the men for whom they toiled, unless it was in time of trouble or unrest, when tempers were frayed, harsh words were uttered, voices raised, and violence was not unknown. There was, in fact, no communication between them. They did not even pass the time of day as farmers and their workers did in the countryside. Where there is no communication, there is no understanding, and that is what lay at the root of the industrial unrest of the 19th century, and lies at it still today.

The growth of industrial towns

At the beginning of the 18th century, the bulk of the population lived in the southern half of England, below the river Trent, which runs approximately through the Midlands. Below this line

Left: A view inside the Crystal Palace in Hyde Park, where the Great Exhibition was held in 1851. At right on the ground floor are the sections devoted to displays from India. The framed-glass structure was designed and built by Sir Joseph Paxton, who was by experience a gardener.

were the major towns – London, Bristol, Norwich, Exeter, Southampton, and numerous smaller towns still fat on the wool trade. Sussex and the Forest of Dean in Gloucestershire were still the principal areas of iron-making because of the charcoal. True, there was coal in the north, but it had not yet been employed in the production of iron.

A view of Brunel's amazing steamship, the *Great Eastern*. This was built over the years 1854 to 1859 and was the wonder of the shipping world. It was far larger than anything ever built before, and remained the biggest ship in the world for nearly 40 years. But it was not a commercial success and in 1865–6 it was converted for use to lay the first Atlantic cables. (Lord Kelvin, then William Thomson, had a major part in this adventure.)

A picture of slum dwellings in London in 1875.

This was all changed by the Industrial Revolution, particularly the development of the steam engine and the machines to which one could gear it to make production runs many, many times greater than those possible by hand- or foot-operated machines. Steam engines needed coal and they needed it to be readily accessible. Iron-making also needed coal, and supplies had to be close by. So the new industries began to operate where the coal was, in the north, and as the factories began to go up, the population also started to drift northwards. Added to this, the enclosing of land and the improvements in farming and farm machinery outlined in Chapter Eight drove many men off the land, in search of jobs in the new factories.

One result of this drift was the rapid growth of many midland and northern towns into great industrial centres. Among those that very soon changed from small market towns into sprawling factory-filled cities with endless streets of drab, characterless small houses were Birmingham, Manchester, Leeds, Sheffield, Derby, Liverpool and Hull (the last two were already important as ports), Newcastle, Darlington, Doncaster, Oldham, Rochdale and Nottingham. They soon outstripped the older cities which remained architecturally more interesting.

Conditions of labour

This development was one of quantity rather than quality. The first, and in so many cases the only, concern of the factory owners was to get as many people into them as possible, and to have

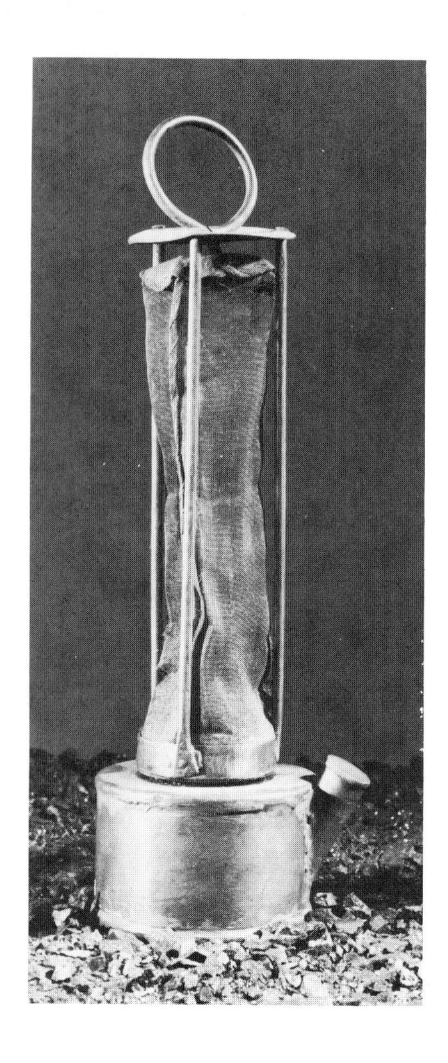

An example of one of Sir Humphry Davy's safety lamps for coal-miners.

them working for long hours all day, every day, except Sunday. Conditions of labour was a concept that did not bother them (there were some wonderful exceptions to this in the factories owned by Quaker families like Cadbury, Fry, Rowntree, and others). Nor, regrettably, did it bother the Government or Parliament. To increase the labour force, women and children were employed for equally long hours, shouldering jobs more suitable for men. And these unfortunate people had to take jobs to eke out the miserable wages paid to their menfolk.

To take a typical coal mine in Lancashire as an example; women were employed working as much as sixteen hours a day, most of them on all fours, dragging small coal trucks along rail tracks with long chains tied round their waists. While they did this, they had to watch their children standing about for hours in the cold, ill-lit gassy atmosphere opening and shutting ventilator flaps and doors to let the trucks through. These long hours were, it is true, interrupted with short periods for meals, but the food was usually so poor and there was so little of it that it often merely worked up an appetite for more, that had to wait several more hours before it could be satisfied. It is not surprising that whole families working in these conditions, and living, as we shall see, in terrible houses, aged rapidly, fell victims to colds, 'flu, tuberculosis, and, after the 1830s, to cholera when that dread disease first hit England.

Sir Humphry Davy invented the miner's safety lamp in 1816, and thus cut down the danger of explosion in a pit through the gases being ignited by the older type of lamp which had an unprotected flame. But many other accidents occurred against which there was no means of protection.

If a family decided not to risk all in migrating to a new industrial centre, it stood to fare little better by working in a local mill or iron forge. These nondescript buildings were badly ventilated and the light was poor. The owners were allowed to beat the workers, and often did. They could also pull their ears. If the family threatened to leave, they were told that there was a queue of people waiting to take their jobs. They were hemmed in by

A factory building of the middle of the 19th century.

numerous petty restrictions. They could not sing or whistle while they worked. If their hands were found to be dirty, money would be docked from their meagre wage packets. After years of this kind of servitude, some of the workers became deformed, like a 'crooked alphabet', as some observer once said. Many volunteered to join the army to fight against Napoleon, to escape such a life. When the press gangs roamed the streets of some towns looking for men to seize, kidnap or take to some ship or other for service at sea that might last several years, there were often men willing to be taken.

If the workers in a mine or a mill wanted to object to their conditions, they were told that the Combination Act of 1799 forbade the formation of any kind of union of workers to secure better terms, and that they risked severe penalties by threatening to combine. For twenty-five years they could do nothing, until the act was replaced in 1824.

Why did Parliament do nothing about this distress? There were many reasons. For one thing, England had been involved in a struggle to the death with France from the 1790s to the final defeat of Napoleon at Waterloo in 1815, and the statesmen who governed were too involved to see what was going on in their own back gardens. For another, the French Revolution, with all its ferocity, death, destruction and change, had thoroughly frightened them. They dreaded that if they did anything to make things better for the working people in Britain, these workers would, seeing they could get something, try to get more, if necessary by force. What happened in France would happen here.

And there was another thing. In the 18th century there had been little class hatred, even if there were sharp differences in standards of living. The jolly apprentice was still a common type, living with his master and hoping to marry his daughter and succeed him in his business. The master made a good living but he was never anything like as rich as the new breed of factory and coal mine owner which grew up in Britain in the 19th century. And here lay the difference. As the industrialist became richer, the poor worker who enabled him to get fat became poorer. By the 19th century, class hatred had got a grip on the lower classes – and with some reason. In return for being bondsmen under the old feudal system, serfs and villeins did get something, such as protection, a more or less guaranteed job, quite often a home. But those who became little more than bondsmen to the great industrialists got nothing. So there was nothing for which to be grateful, and no reason to love their employers. And when there is no love, there is only hatred, or at best sullen indifference. This class hatred, born out of the Industrial Revolution, is with us still.

The situation between the management and the workers was an explosive one, and it did not need much to set it alight. In those days, patriotism was still one of the highest ideals a Briton could aspire to, and so during the wars with Napoleon, men got on with their jobs in the national interest. But once Waterloo was over and Napoleon safely exiled far away in the south Atlantic, working men began to agitate for improvement in their conditions of work. The after-effects of the war had not been, as hoped, times of peace and plenty. Many soldiers, sailors and armaments makers were suddenly no longer wanted, and were thrown on to the labour market, swelling the ranks of the discontented. The next thirty or so years of industrial and social history are the story of the struggle of the working classes to get some redress for their very real grievances. Highlights of the struggle were the movement to get Parliament to do something, which meant the actual

There were riots in Lancashire over a cotton slump, in 1878. Angry workers forced out of jobs, burned down factory owners' homes in protest.

nside a workhouse in Bethnal Green, ondon, in the 1840s.

reform of parliamentary representation itself, the Chartist movement and its influence, the foundation and growth of trade unions, and the attempts of individuals, like Lord Shaftesbury, to make things better.

Need for parliamentary reform

More and more thinking people, not only among the working classes but more especially in the professional class, and even the gentry, were beginning to realize that no reforms would be of much use until the poorer classes themselves were represented somehow in Parliament. It seems astonishing to us today, when we have been used to the one man – one vote principle for as long as most can remember, that in 1815 the House of Commons did not represent Britain at all in any democratic sense. The distribution of seats at the time of Simon de Montfort had been

Mrs Emmeline Pankhurst, the great fighter for the right of women to vote at elections, arrested while demonstrating outside Buckingham Palace, 1914.

fairer. In 1815, towns like Manchester, Sheffield, Leeds, Birmingham, Oldham and Sunderland had no representatives, though they all had huge populations. Small villages like East Looe and West Looe in Cornwall, Wootton Bassett in Wiltshire, and Orford in Suffolk each had two members and Old Sarum, then only a clump of green mounds, also sent two members to Westminster. The boroughs with few electors were often the property of a local magnate, who not only could influence the way the electorate voted, but who could even stand for the seat himself. These boroughs were called 'pocket' boroughs, and where they were notoriously corrupt, 'rotten' boroughs. Opportunities for corruption were in fact frequent and they were often taken. Consequently, parliament was filled with members representing their own or their patrons' interests, and the great majority of the people of the country had no representatives at all.

The situation might well have gone on indefinitely had not the new businessmen in the big but unrepresented towns seen it was to their advantage to have seats at Westminster. Some joined the few radical Whig members who were already campaigning for electoral reform. In 1830, a general election resulted in the return of a Whig majority, for the first time in half a century. The new prime minister, Lord Grey, introduced a Reform Bill in 1831, and it was carried by one vote. As the votes were counted, the silence was electric. 'You could have heard a pin drop,' said Macaulay later Lord Macaulay, the distinguished historian, poet and exper on Indian affairs.

Unfortunately, the Tories managed to get the bill amended and Grey at once resigned, to appeal to the country through anothe general election. This time he won with an increased majority The bill was presented again and carried well. Then the House o Lords threw it out. This was the signal for an outburst of rioting and violence in places all over the country. The London mob stoned the Duke of Wellington's house, Apsley House, at Hyd Park, for he was the Tory leader of the Lords who had rejected the bill. They even threatened the great man himself as he rode stern, impassive and resolute, from Westminster to his home on

The "Peterloo massacre" took place at St Peter's Field in Manchester in August 1819. Here, more than 60,000 people had gathered for a demonstration of support for parliamentary reform. The authorities responded by sending in mounted troops to arrest the main speaker, 'Orator' Hunt, and in the resulting mêlée several people were killed and hundreds injured. It was called "Peterloo" because it was an engagement people wanted to compare sarcastically with the great victory of Waterloo, a few years earlier, which was still in everybody's mind.

evening. In Nottingham, mobs looted and burned shops, and in Bristol they sacked the centre of the city. Birmingham threatened to send 20,000 men to march on London. The country was nearer to civil war than it had ever been since the time of Charles I.

Grey tried again, but the Lords threatened to throw the Bill out once more. So he went to the king, William IV, 'Silly Billy' as he was called, whom the country quite liked, and who had some sympathy with the reform movement. He asked him to create enough peers to swamp the Tory majority in the Lords. William consented, and Grey began to draw up a list. Wellington, not at all anxious to have the Lords permanently swamped by a Whig majority, advised his colleagues not to vote at all if the Bill came forward again, and when it did come up, it was carried.

The Reform Act, as it became, abolished the pocket boroughs and gave the 140 or so seats thus released to counties and large towns. The vote was given to people owning land worth £10 or more a year, or to tenants of land worth £50. In the towns, it was given to householders whose property was worth £10. It was a mild measure by our day, but a sensational victory in those days for the forces of progress. It broke forever the monopoly of power held by the landowning classes.

It was the first stage in the movement to make Parliament truly democratic. The Second Reform Bill of 1867 extended the vote to all householders in towns who paid poor rates and to all lodgers who paid £10 a year rent, and in the counties to all occupiers paying rates on an assessment of £12 a year. This effectively gave the vote to nearly all working men. And in 1884 the Third Reform Bill gave the vote to agricultural workers. Every occupier in town or country paying £10 in rent received a vote. One man in seven of the population had a vote, which was much better than in 1832 when it was one in twenty-four. A fourth reform act of 1918 gave the vote to all men over 21 and, for the first time, to a section of the female population. All women over 30 were entitled to vote, and women were also allowed to stand for Parliament. Ten years later, all women were permitted to vote on the same terms as men. Universal suffrage had come, 96 years after the First Reform Bill.

With Parliament reformed, there seemed some hope of redressing the many outstanding grievances.

The Chartists

The First Reform Bill did not satisfy the more angry and extreme of the agitators. They wanted manhood suffrage straightaway. One could still not be a member of the Commons until one had estates worth at least £300 a year, which effectively cut out many men in the towns, especially at worker or foreman level. These men joined with those who had been greatly disappointed at the failure of the Grand National Consolidated Trades Union of 1834, organized by Robert Owen, and they formed the Chartist movement. This was so-called because they drew up their demands in a 'People's Charter', a kind of working-class Magna Carta. The Charter was revolutionary. It demanded votes for every man, parliaments to be summoned every year, members of Parliament to be paid, equal electoral districts, and no property qualifications for members.

The Chartists never found support in Parliament, even among the more radical members, and when they started to talk about the use of force—and actually organized a monster demonstration march from Kennington Common to Westminster, which was carefully but firmly dispersed by troops under the commond of Wellington, these members became alarmed. The London demonstration failed and this led to the collapse of the movement. The ideals, however, remained, and were in time realized more peacefully.

The famous gathering of the Chartists at Kennington, in 1848, before the march towards the Houses of Parliament. A drawing from *Illustrated London News* of the time.

Trade unions

The trade union movement, although much slower, was—and has been ever since—more successful. The Combination Acts were repealed in 1824 and working men were allowed to form trade unions to obtain better wages and easier hours. But it was a decade before any real progress was made. In 1834, Robert Owen created his Grand National Consolidated Trades Union, a combination of trade unions representing skilled and unskilled workers. He wanted the union to fulfil a dream of a vast workers' co-operative, where products were exchanged and not sold for profit. But extremists wanted the union to exist only to press for higher wages. The membership was over a quarter of a million, and the government became very concerned. In an effort to crack down on it, they prosecuted some farm labourers in the village of Tolpuddle in Dorset, for swearing men into a trade union which proposed to join the Grand National Consolidated. They did this under an old act of 1797, called the Unlawful Oaths Act, and the men were sentenced to transportation to Australia. A public outcry followed, with a monster petition bearing more than 200,000 signatures, begging for reconsideration of the case. The men had to go, but they were later pardoned. In the interval they came to be called the Tolpuddle Martyrs.

This led to the collapse of the Grand National Consolidated, and the extreme members joined the Chartists. Meanwhile, more moderate men tried to keep the trade union movement going, and in 1850 the first organized union was formed, the Amalgamated

Society of Engineers. This provided its members with constructive leadership which sought negotiation with employers rather than resorting at once to strike action, and which offered unemployment benefits. Other unions followed, and in 1868 the Trades Union Congress was founded in Manchester, consisting of a combination of this kind of union. It represented the movement in Britain and was active particularly in parliamentary circles.

In 1875 Disraeli's government passed the Employers' and Workmen's Act by which strikes were made legal. The Conspiracy and Protection of Property Act of the same year allowed peaceful picketing. The Trades Disputes Act of 1906 stated that trade unions were not liable for losses caused by illegal acts of its members, that is, losses of production and earnings through strikes. Meanwhile, to protect their interests, unions sent members to Parliament, paying them sums of money from union funds to keep them going. At the time members were not paid and trade union men usually could not otherwise afford to go to Parliament.

By 1910, over 2,500,000 men were members of unions, and four years later the total was over 4,000,000.

Shaftesbury

Conditions of workers and their families in factories, meanwhile, had steadily been giving great concern to many people. We have seen how children were employed under conditions that amounted to slavery. (Slavery throughout the British Empire, by which we mean the employment of negro slaves under degrading

Below left: A magazine picture of children working in mines, in 1842.

Below: Queueing up for a coal hand-out in Manchester during a cotton famine, 1862

Above: A power loom of the 1850s.

Above right: The first electric power station in England was opened at Deptford in the 1880s.

conditions, in chains, was abolished finally in 1833, the crowning work of William Wilberforce.) They received no education, had no hours for play, seldom saw the sun, and were doomed to a stunted existence in mine shafts, tunnels or factories. Strenuous efforts to do something for them had been equally strenuously resisted by the owners of mines, factories and mills. Then Lord Ashley (later Earl of Shaftesbury) stepped in on their behalf and campaigned vigorously. He had money to spend and he spent it freely in support of his ideals. He got the government to set up a Royal Commission to look at factories—that is, to get its hands dirty and see what was really going on behind the factory doors. Parliament was sickened by the Commission's report, and the Factory Act of 1833, passed in a general mood of reform, forbade any child under nine being employed at all, and cut the hours of those over nine to a maximum of eight a day. Inspectors were appointed to see that the Act was being enforced. Fourteen years later, Parliament passed the Ten Hour Bill fixing the limit for women to ten hours a day working, with a half day on Saturday. These Acts were chiefly for the textile mills, but others soon followed to cover other industries, and they embraced accident prevention and compensation, health standards, and so forth.

In 1834 a new Poor Law was passed. Up to then each parish looked after its poor, following the first act of Elizabeth I's reign. The rate had been paid out according to the size of the family and the price of bread. This new act had its degrading side, however. No able-bodied man could have poor relief unless he went to live in a special workhouse which belonged to one of 640 new Poor Law Unions set up throughout the country by Parliament. This meant that if he left the workhouse he risked starvation. But the law coincided with the rapid expansion of railway building, and many potential workhouse inmates got jobs as navvies on the new Great Western or the London and Midland.

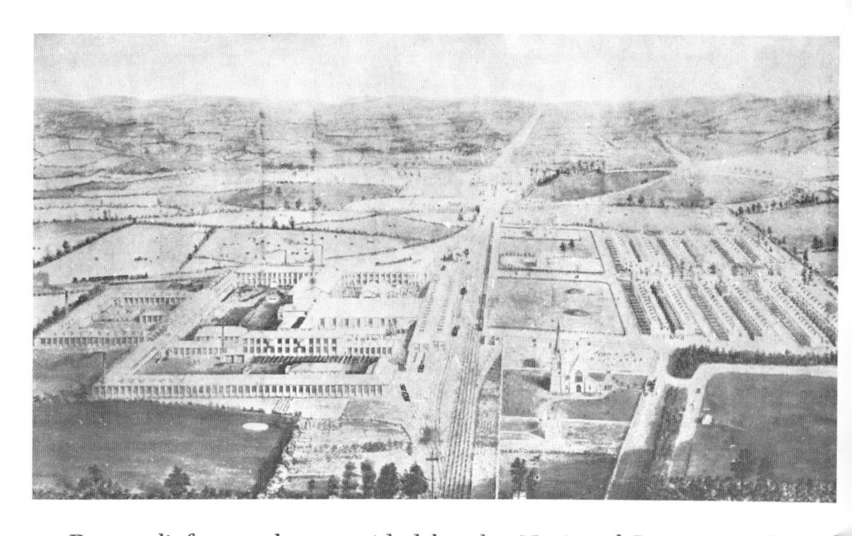

Above: Things may have been good for the upper classes in the time of Edward VII, but among the lower classes there were shortages of every kind. Here, people are queueing for bread, in 1910.

Above right: A painting of Brunel's railway village at Swindon in Wiltshire, in 1849. The village was threatened with demolition in the 1960s, but Swindon Borough Council, with magnificent public spirit, stepped in and bought the bulk of the houses from British Rail, and so saved them. Now they have been restored, and look much as they did in 1849.

Poor relief was also provided by the National Insurance Act of 1911 which entitled men earning less than £3 a week to free medical attention and to sick pay of 10 shillings a week. The same act also organized a contributory insurance scheme against unemployment, which gave men 7 shillings a week. The original weekly payment by an able bodied worker in a job was 4d a week for an insurance stamp. The employer also paid a contribution. This Act has been considerably extended. In the meanwhile, since the beginning of the 18th century, there had been private 'friendly societies' into which members paid subscriptions, so that if they were taken ill and so incapacitated for work, they received payments. These societies did a lot of good all over the country, and flourished right up to the present century.

The birth of the Labour Party

These and many other schemes helped greatly to make some, if not all, people less poor and distressed, and they gave some dignity to the working man. But more and more people realized that the battle would never be properly won while the campaigns were fought by the Liberal Party (which grew out of the Whig party), or by the Conservatives (Tory party). A new party was needed, strictly representing the working man with its members coming from his class. And this was the origin of the British Labour Party. The parliamentary Labour Party was not founded until 1900, but the movement towards it dates back further than that. Two miners had in fact got themselves elected to Parliament in 1874, and had sat as radicals. John Burns, a socialist, was elected as a radical in 1892, and he rose eventually to cabinet rank as President of the Board of Trade in a Liberal government in 1914. In 1906, twenty-nine Labour Party members were elected and they made enormously valuable contributions to debates

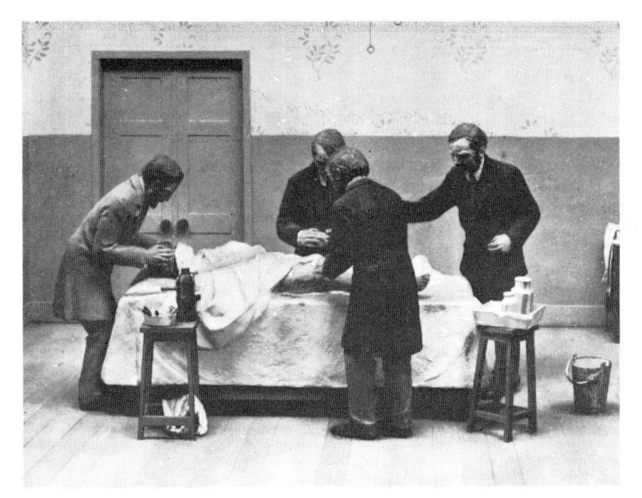

Above: Prince Albert, who was the prime mover of the Great Exhibition in 1851, took a close interest in designs for new houses for artisans. A block of these was displayed at the Exhibition, and can be seen in this picture.

Above left: Lord Lister introduced the antiseptic system into surgery in the 1860s, and so made surgery far safer than it ever had been. Surgeons and nurses in the operating theatre worked in an atmosphere heavily laden with carbolic acid liquid spray, distributed round the room with a spray gun, which can be seen on the small table.

because of their intimate knowledge of working conditions and working class aspirations. Many of these Labour members had stood against Liberal candidates and had beaten them. It was a surprise, for the aims of Labour and Liberal seemed very similar. In fact they were not. The Labour party wanted to pull the whole structure of government down and rebuild it. They sought state control of the means of production, distribution and exchange—that is, they wanted government ownership of factories, mines, farms, and private businesses, especially banks, insurance companies and retail concerns. Some of these aims have been achieved, as we shall see in Chapter Twelve.

Slums

We know about the wages, the hours, and the misery of the working man during these times of industrialization. But what sort of roofs did they have over their heads? The 19th century gave birth to many things, some of them good, and some of them regrettable. One regrettable product was 'slums'.

The word comes from an old English word 'slump' which meant marshy place. It refers to the rows and rows of cheap box-like houses built in a hurry to accommodate workers in the new factories. These factories were often sited near rivers and canals, for transport convenience, and the houses were put up equally close by, where quite often the ground was marshy and unhealthy. The individual houses were not well designed, amenities were almost totally lacking, and the layout of the streets was cramped and sunless. Many rows were built back to back. There was no water supply, no drainage and sewerage, and you had to empty your rubbish into a collective heap in the street. Before long the whole street became a breeding ground for germs, as there were no facilities for clearing it. Disease was a constant risk, especially cholera, which is so often fatal. It is amazing to think that this type of accommodation was built for over a century, that the only lavatory was an earth bucket in a shed in the area at the back.

It was not until the year of the Great Exhibition, 1851, that anything was done by Parliament. It should be remembered that slum properties were owned in whole rows by factory owners or other landlords and rented out to workers. The Common Lodging Houses Act made it compulsory to register the houses and submit them to inspection, but many landlords found ways around this. Twenty-four years later the Artisans' Dwellings Act tried to establish building standards for these places, but it was not easy to enforce it. Slum property was supposed to be pulled down and new homes built, but to judge from the fact that by the end of the Second World War in 1945 there were over 2,000,000 homes of the period prior to the Act still standing, it had not been widely enforced. It is said that even in 1974 over 1,000,000 homes still had no bath!

Model of a kitchen in a small house of the 1870s. You can see the kettle hanging over the grate in the black cast-iron range at the right.

Drainage and sewerage were tackled in the 1875 Public Health Act, which put the responsibility for collecting rubbish and keeping a sewer in working order on to local authorities, who were also to maintain a water supply and be answerable for the water's purity. Another Public Health Act at the end of the century made it the local authority's job to cleanse the streets.

Whole families lived out their entire existence in places like these all over Britain, from Newcastle to Exeter, from Cardiff to Liverpool, from Manchester to Northampton, from Glasgow to Hull. And these families often handed them on, with the owner's consent, to the next generation.

At the Great Exhibition some new designs for houses for working class families were shown, and here and there sympathetic landlords and property developers did try to produce new types of accommodation. But it was all too rare. At about this time – and over the next seventy years or so – some charitable trusts were formed purposely to build blocks of flats for these families. Among those whose names are well-known are George Peabody

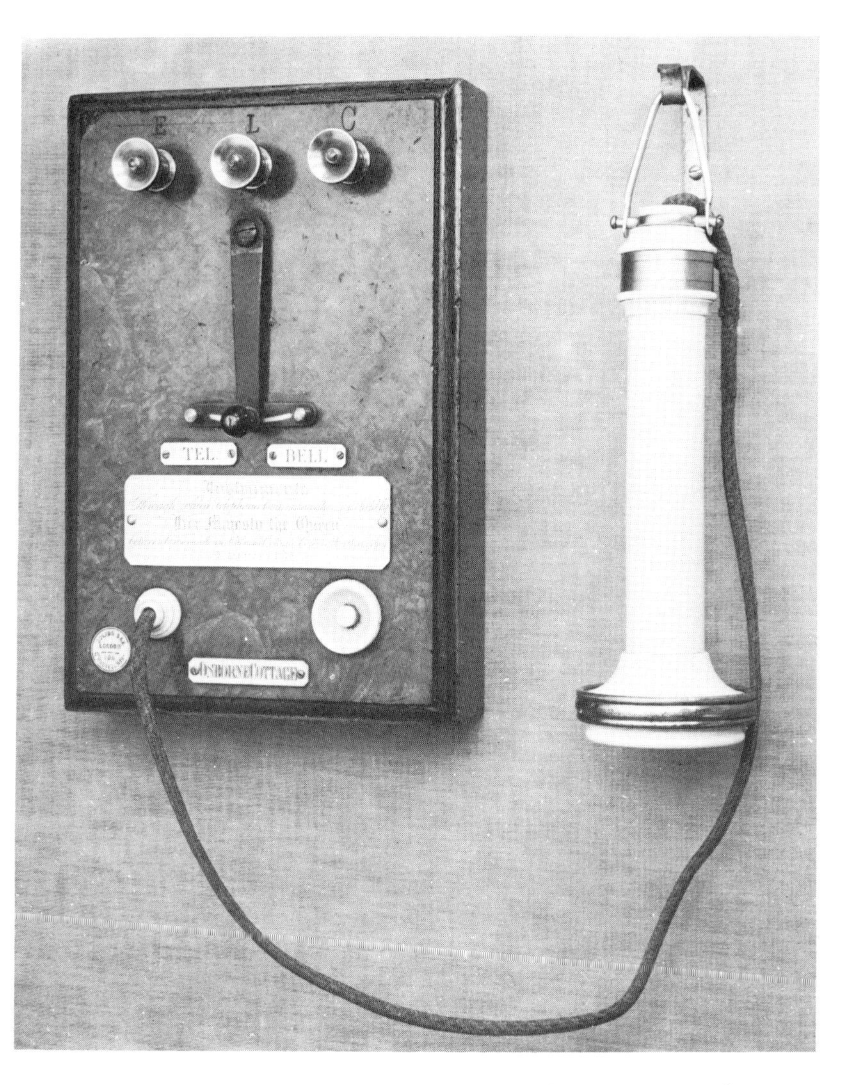

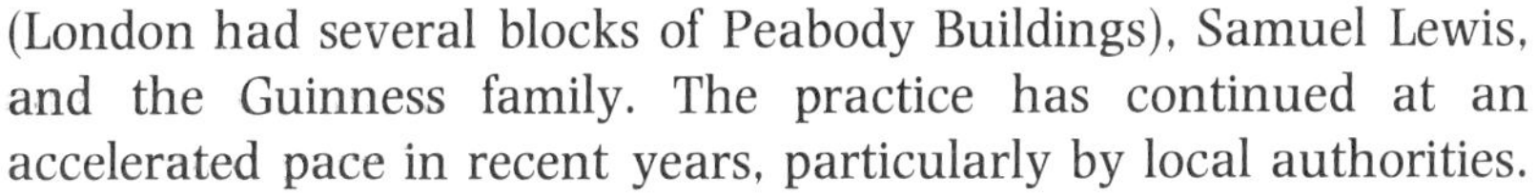

(London had several blocks of Peabody Buildings), Samuel Lewis, and the Guinness family. The practice has continued at an accelerated pace in recent years, particularly by local authorities.

In the countryside, meanwhile, the poorer man's cottage continued to be built in a more individual and picturesque way. There was of course much more room, and landlords did not need to build so many. The Quennells, in their *History of Everyday Things in England, 1733–1851*, mention a paper on designs for cottages and schools, dated 1825. In this are given the requirements for single and double cottages whose living rooms were to be 3 metres (9 feet) high, the upstairs bedrooms 2½ metres (8 feet), and which were to stand in plots of land of 1¼ acres. The rents recommended were 3 shillings (15p) a week. If you look about the countryside, you will see many of these cottages which conform a little to this idea. Every one of them seems to have individuality.

Above: The aerial in this picture is part of the apparatus set up in 1901 by Guglielmo Marconi at Poldhu, in Cornwall, with which he had a radio signal transmitted across the Atlantic to Signal Hill, St John's, Newfoundland, where he and colleagues were waiting to receive it. The success of the experiment was a landmark in wireless history.

Left: An early telephone instrument, based on Alexander Graham Bell's invention, installed in Osborne House, the Isle of Wight home of Queen Victoria.

Shops

The Industrial Revolution brought about a substantial growth in the quantity and variety of things that the ordinary householder could buy for everyday use or consumption. In the Middle Ages, people bought what they wanted at markets in the many market towns, or if they wanted craftsman-made things they ordered them at his workshop. But enclosures, new farming methods and industrialization generally denuded the countryside of people, and rural crafts and industries declined. Towns needed more and more display points for goods, and shops became an increasingly common feature in streets. Shops had already been equipped with glass window fronts by the early 18th century (before that they were exposed bottom halves of ordinary houses). In the 19th century the town began to enjoy the benefits of multiple stores. The first was probably Bainbridges in Newcastle-upon-Tyne. The next development was the chain store, and among the earliest were Boots (chemists), Liptons (grocers) and Woolworth's.

While the working classes worked and suffered to make Britain influential and powerful in the world, their masters had good lives, relatively trouble free. If the men had to put in an appearance in their

Some 18th-century shops, restored and displayed at the Castle Museum at York.

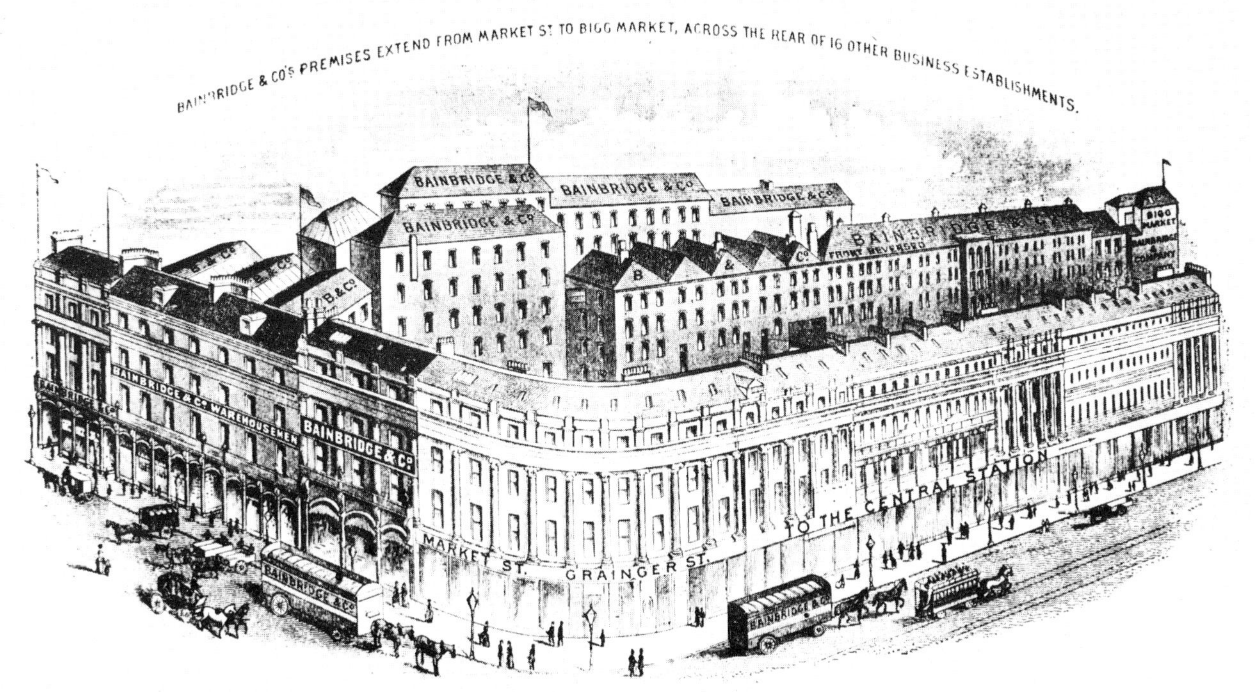

Bainbridges in Newcastle-upon-Tyne was the first department store developed in England (1849). It is still there today, though it is now part of the John Lewis Partnership.

offices, or look in at the factories to see how production was going, or spend some time travelling about the country or abroad getting orders the women and children seemed to want for little. Everything was done for them. An average businessman's household had more servants than members of the family. About ten per cent of the country's population was in service in some way or other by the end of the 19th century. The upper classes had never had it so good.

A 10 h.p. two-seater Rolls-Royce motor car, of 1904.

12 England since 1914

In 1914, Britain declared war on Germany because the German Emperor, Wilhelm II, had sent his armies to invade Belgium, a small kingdom on its western border. Few people at first realized what this war would do to England, Germany, Europe and indeed the world. Most believed it would last for a few months and then be patched up by a peace treaty. In fact, it dragged on for four and a quarter years, in which time millions of men were killed in the field of battle, at sea or in the air, and at the end of it Europe's face had changed. Nothing would ever be the same again.

The peace treaty at Versailles which followed left Germany humilated and economically distressed. Out of this grew the terrifying period of Adolf Hitler and his National Socialists, who made war again with quite appalling vengeance and ferocity, only to be defeated and leave all Europe shattered.

These two wars changed many things in England. So did the inter-war years and those that have followed the destruction of the Nazi regime in 1945.

More changes seem to have taken place in English social life in the past sixty years than in any similar period, or even in any century before. But if you look a little more closely beneath the panorama of marvels of science, engineering, medicine, law, politics, religion and environment, you can see that many human attitudes have remained the same. We may be able to land men on the surface of the moon, even enable them to drive a small truck across its plains, but we are still unable to settle industrial grievances without resort to strikes, with their attendant bitterness, picketing, even violence. We may be able to give people with arthritis of the hip new metal hip joints to relieve the pain and make them walk again, or to graft a new liver into a living person taken from someone who has just died, but more than a million people each year in Britain slowly destroy their livers by drinking too much alcohol, because they cannot stand the stresses of modern society. There are still some three million homes woefully below standard, with inadequate bathing and lavatory equipment, and there are over five million old people living alone or in pairs desperately short of money, food, coal, heat and, above all, hope. And there are more than

1,500,000 people out of a job, and living on the dole.

Peace and depression

The end of the First World War was greeted by everyone in England with enormous relief and expectancy. They hoped that peace would mean prosperity, for the nation had had to tighten its belt in the war years and go without many things. But prosperity did not follow. The country had had to borrow heavily from the vastly rich United States of America to see the war through, and when the time came to repay, the value of money had gone down. The demobilization of the armed forces and the stopping of armaments manufacture suddenly put millions of men out of work, and British industry was not geared to absorb them. At the same time, inventions in industry were making many kinds of work more automatic, many processes of production very much more rapid. For example, the growth of the motor car industry hit the railways, and the use of oil for heating and power struck at the demand for coal. Here were two major industries being severely dislocated and thousands of jobs threatened. But this in turn affected other industries, and by 1926, by which time there was still no improvement in the world trade position, the working men of England were in an ugly mood, ready to strike.

It began in the coal mines. More and more were losing work as the demand for coal went down. The pit owners decided to cut wages and hours of work. The miners retaliated by a big strike. At once the railwaymen and the engineers came out in support, and in days a large part of British industry was at a standstill. But it did not last, for the country was not sympathetic and many professional people took on the jobs of running the essential services, thus weakening the effects of the strike. Industrial unrest, however, was not appeased and the continuing decline in world trade, hastened by a terrible financial crisis in 1930–31, led to millions of men being unemployed in England. Several famous marches of hungry and jobless men from the north-east and the Midlands made their way towards London to protest.

Field Marshal Earl Kitchener was Britain's leading soldier at the outbreak of the First World War in 1914. As Secretary of State for War, he was the first – and at the time perhaps the only – statesman to realize that the war would last for three to four years, needing the services of millions more men than there were in the regular or Territorial army. So he organized a great recruiting campaign, and this was one of the posters used. The campaign eventually raised about three million troops. Kitchener was drowned at sea on a visit to Russia in 1916.

Slum housing did not disappear from the British scene in the 20th century. This is a drawing of how a poor family lived, in Southwark in London in the 1930s.

War and a new peace

A series of tough economic measures brought in by the Government stemmed the worst of the crisis. But in 1939 Britain went to war with Germany because of Hitler's invasion of Poland. Once again the nation had to tighten its belt, endure strict food rationing, aerial bombardment on a much larger scale, shortages of every kind, and borrow vast sums from the United States. The British spirit, personified in the magnificent oratory and leadership of Sir Winston Churchill, probably the greatest man England has ever produced, triumphed, and in 1945 the nation settled down to face the difficulties left by a shattering war in which over 50,000,000 men and women had been killed and thousands of cities and towns severely damaged or destroyed.

The British electors, though grateful to Churchill for leading them to victory, did not think he or his Conservative Party were the right people to get the country going again. There were still far too many social problems that had to be tackled, new areas of welfare to be explored, which they felt would be better done by a

In 1936 there was still severe unemployment in many British industries. The town of Jarrow, in County Durham, was one of many towns which had an acute problem, and the workless got together to march to London to protest to Parliament, gathering support from similarly affected people on the way. Here, the Jarrow marchers pass through Harrogate.

In 1926 there was a General Strike, when most of the workforce in Britain struck in support of coal-miners who were agitating for better conditions. Public services, however, had to continue, and people from many walks of life carried out jobs of which they had no experience. Here, university undergraduates man a railway signal box.

Labour Government. So they returned Labour to power in July 1945 with a huge majority, and in six years (it was returned again for a year, 1950–51) it achieved the biggest social revolution in the country's history. It nationalized the coal mines and railways, taking over the responsibility for running them from private owners. It created the National Health Service, which provided—and still provides—free medical care for everyone in the land who wants it. True, one has now to pay a contribution for dental treatment, drugs and one or two other things, but the price is a subsidized one, that is, it is only a part of the real cost, the rest of which is met by the Government. It also made national insurance compulsory for everyone, that is, payments are docked every week from salary cheques and pay packets to provide for sickness, unemployment, old age pension and maternity benefits.

Since 1930, many new welfare benefits have been instituted for the old, the crippled, the destitute and the unemployed. It must be remembered that we shall always have these less fortunate groups of people in our society, and any one of us could become one of them at any time. It is a far cry from the early days of the Industrial Revolution. Then, thousands who were glad enough to work could not get jobs and often died of starvation. Today no one need starve. If they do, it is because they choose to.

There have been so many other advances that it is not possible to list them here. Perhaps the most important fields in which they have been made are education, medicine, public health, building standards (though not necessarily architectural design), transport, public services, energy supplies and entertainment.

Sir Winston Churchill (1874–1965). Statesman, soldier, author, painter, his many-sided genius was equalled in English history only by that of Alfred the Great. Churchill held most offices in government in a career spanning half a century. His supreme moment came in 1940 during the Second World War when, as prime minister, he rallied the nation by his oratory and by his skilled handling of government, the forces and the public, and led it to victory in 1945. Although he is best known for his war services, in his earlier days he had been responsible for many social reforms. He created labour exchanges and also suggested to Lloyd George the foundation of national insurance.

Education

The Elementary Education Act of 1870 had set up school boards which could establish elementary schools by using local rates and getting assistance from the Government. These boards had the power to compel the attendance of children between 5 and 12. The act was strengthened in 1880 by another which made attending school compulsory up to the age of 10. If a child had attended often enough he could leave at 10 with a certificate, but if he had not, he had to go on until he was 13. The Education Act of 1902 put an end to the boards set up in 1870 and transferred the responsibilities to the local authorities.

In 1944 more changes were made. One of the most important was that secondary education from the age of 12 was made free for everyone who wanted it. A ministry, called the Department of Education, was set up inside the Government and it has lasted ever since. Later developments included the creation of the comprehensive school.

At the higher level, there has been an enormous expansion of universities and technical colleges. In 1914 there was only a handful of universities in England, but today there are more than forty.

Public health

We have seen that there was a Public Health Act in 1875 geared to improving the conditions in 'slum' dwellings. Some time in the

Part of Edinburgh in 1939.

reign of Edward VII (1901–1910), a very good king, who is all too often written off as a playboy, someone said to him, 'A lot of illness among the people could be prevented.' To this he replied, 'Then why not prevent it?' He remembered how Lord Lister had saved his life in 1902. And from this remark stemmed many improvements in public health services. Today, school medical examination is compulsory, and there are clinics to deal with school illnesses. Indeed the state does what it can to ensure the maintenance of the good health of the population.

But public health goes further than people's illnesses. Conditions in housing are important. In 1936 a Public Health Act reinforced standards of building required in new dwellings, and there have been other Acts, including the Building Regulations (1965). London has had its own, much higher, standards set by its own building bye-laws, and so has Liverpool.

The improvement in building standards has gone hand in hand with changes in architecture and design. The architecture has not necessarily been better, nor more handsome, though it has taken into account more amenities for the people who are to live in the homes. Up to the end of the First World War, emphasis in big houses was on size—huge rooms, tall ceilings, vast windows, staircases, and doorways, with the whole structure set in big surroundings. In smaller houses the emphasis was in the opposite direction, as many rooms as you could fit into a small total space, as box-like in shape as possible. Now, big houses are seldom built at all. There are no servants to run them. Rich city tycoons who want vast mansions as a sign of their wealth buy up old stately homes from families who have perhaps owned them for generations but can no longer afford to keep them. The endless rows of small slum houses, however, are now no longer built. In their place are tidier and more roomy rows of modern houses, each with its bit of garden around it, or in front and behind it. These are often landscaped in pleasant areas, with room for playgrounds, trees, paths and car parks.

As well as small houses, the flat has come into its own for accommodation on a large scale. Blocks of flats, some as tall as

The new Roman Catholic cathedral at Clifton, in Bristol.

A view of the new town at Cumbernauld, which lies midway between Glasgow and Stirling in Scotland. Already it has a population well over half the target figure of 70,000 people. It is a key centre of industrial growth.

thirty storeys or more, are put up in, or on the outskirts of, major cities up and down the country. Either they are built of brick, or concrete and steel. These have been built by both local authorities and private developers. Many building systems have been used, not all of which have been of the best quality or standard of safety. In 1967 a block put up by a London borough partly collapsed into the street when a gas pipe burst. A whole family was killed and others were injured.

Energy

The industrialization of the countries of the world has meant that nations need various sources of power to make their machines work. The principal sources are coal, gas, electricity, oil and, in recent years, nuclear energy. Coal was the first, and its use in the steam engines of Watt's day was essential. It was hewn out of the ground in two main kinds of mine, the open cast pit, that is, where the coal is near the surface, and the deep-seated pit, where you have to go down a lift shaft several hundred feet below the surface and along tunnels to chop away at coal seams. Then, men discovered that engines could be run on oil or products produced from oil. Oil is expensive to get out of the ground, but it is not so dangerous an occupation drilling for it as is cutting out coal. Once oil production became a possibility, whole areas of industry went over to its use, which of course hit coal mining. But it was still needed for producing coal-gas for lighting in home and street,

A Shell company oil rig in the North Sea. The self-propelled, semi-submersible drilling platform "Ocean Voyager" on station in Block 205/21 – 1A is buffeted by heavy seas.

heating and cooking, until in recent years gas was discovered under the North Sea and piped ashore.

Electricity is another vital energy source. It is produced on a national scale by means of electric power stations which are huge factories where vast turbine generators convert power to electric current. These generators are driven by coal burning, oil burning, hydro-electric force, or by nuclear energy. So coal still has a vital role to play in national energy production.

Once upon a time, coal, electricity and gas were provided by private enterprise undertakings. Today, they are all the responsibility of the state. Oil is still in the hands of private companies which buy it in its crude state from the Middle East, Nigeria and Venezuela, and refine it in refineries in Britain. There it is made into whatever is wanted—petrol, diesel fuel, paraffin, lubricating oil and so forth.

Nuclear power is provided by the continuous reaction of the nuclei of uranium atoms being split, releasing vast quantities of energy which drive turbine generators that supply electricity to the national electricity grid. There are several nuclear power stations in Britain, at Hunterston in Scotland, Wylfa in Wales, and Berkeley in England to mention but three.

Top: The nuclear power station at Trawsfynydd in Merionethshire, north Wales. At the time of building it, much distress was caused to local people, but now it seems to have settled into the beautiful scenery.

Above: A coal-powered electric generating station, at Eggborough in Yorkshire. The vast buildings are a blot on the landscape, but they have to be lived with if we want the benefits of electric power.

The provision of electric power led to the invention of a multitude of gadgets for the home, including electric cookers, fires, vacuum cleaners, mixers, washing machines, refrigerators, razors and so on.

Transport

Perhaps the most remarkable developments of the century have been in transport. The motor car has probably been the greatest of all the inventions, and in its way has brought us the biggest number of problems. The petrol engine had been invented by Gottfried Daimler in 1885. In the next few years, motor cars and motor bicycles were tried out in Germany, France and the United States. In 1895, F. W. Lanchester formed a company in Birmingham to build motor cars. Other makers followed, including Herbert (later Lord) Austin and William Morris (later Viscount Nuffield). Both men mass-produced cars after the First World War, following the example set in America by Henry Ford.

When motor cars first appeared in England, the law of 1865, which said that road vehicles powered by steam should keep to 6 km.p.h, and be preceded by a man carrying a red flag, was applied with vigour. This lasted until 1896 when it was repealed, and the repeal has been celebrated every year since by the London to Brighton rally of veteran cars. But for some years after there was a speed limit of 32 km.p.h. (20 m.p.h.).

There had been horse-pulled omnibuses in London and some other cities from the 1830s. But in 1898 the first motor-driven buses appeared. Thirteen years later the horse bus disappeared altogether. Trams pulled by horses along rail tracks sunk into the road were introduced in 1861, and by 1880 there were 500 trams in London. By this time there were steam-driven trams in Govan in Glasgow. In 1884 the first electric trams were tried out in Brighton. But trams could never equal the flexibility of buses, and in 1952 London's last tram was run along the Embankment. Another public vehicle that was popular between 1910 and 1950 was the trolley bus. The first was run in Leeds, and by 1941 trolley

Opposite top left: The first British 'Concorde' supersonic airliner took off from London Airport in January 1976 on its first commercial flight. 'Concorde' is a triumph of British and French aero-engineering genius, and demonstrates clearly that technology of this advanced kind is not limited to the largest and richest nations of the world.

ıses were covering over 400 kilometres (250 miles) of routes in ɔndon. Today, there are none. They had been limited by the ct that they could only travel within the length of the electric ɔnductors to the overhead cables, and all this apparatus was xpensive. But they were quiet, clean and quite fast, and it is erhaps to be regretted that some more economical means of ınning them cannot be found.

There have been many new kinds of transport invented in this eriod. Perhaps the most successful have been the helicopter, the overcraft, the supersonic airliner (*Concorde*), and the airship, ıough the last one had a chapter of disasters in the 1930s that d to its being discontinued. Another important introduction was ıe jet propulsion principle for engines. This was brought to ıccessful application (though not invented) by Sir Frank Vhittle who, in the late 1930s, managed to get a jet engine to work.

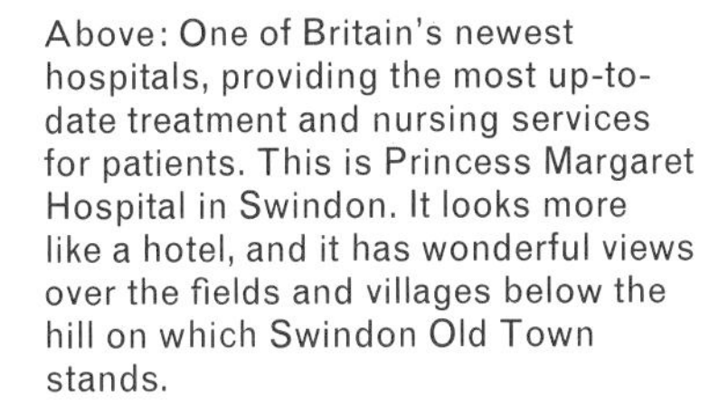

Above: One of Britain's newest hospitals, providing the most up-to-date treatment and nursing services for patients. This is Princess Margaret Hospital in Swindon. It looks more like a hotel, and it has wonderful views over the fields and villages below the hill on which Swindon Old Town stands.

Below left: The new West Dock at Bristol, which provides for ships of about 70,000 tons carrying capacity.

Below: London Airport is now the biggest and most complex airport in the world. There is an aeroplane taking off or coming into land every few minutes of the day.

This motorway network, on the outskirts of Birmingham, is popularly known as 'Spaghetti Junction'. You can readily see why. It is where several main roads, including motorways, merge, and while the junction is quite safe to navigate, it does require skill and sharp attention.

In 1941 the first jet aeroplane was successfully flown. Today, most airliners, bombers and fighter planes are jet propelled.

Entertainment

Another field of human activity where there has been a real transformation in the present century is in entertainment. Using the word in its widest sense, it embraces amusement of all kinds—sport, dancing, radio, television, cinema, theatre, high-fidelity record-playing, newspapers and magazines, and local shows, carnivals and so forth. Up to the First World War most of the entertainment varieties were available chiefly to the upper classes who had the money and the time to enjoy them. For the hard-working lower classes, like factory workers, labourers in the fields and domestic servants, there were games like football there were public houses where they could while away hours drinking, and playing darts or shove-halfpenny or bar billiards and the occasional variety show at a local theatre. In the country-side, labourers would spend their leisure time indulging in some

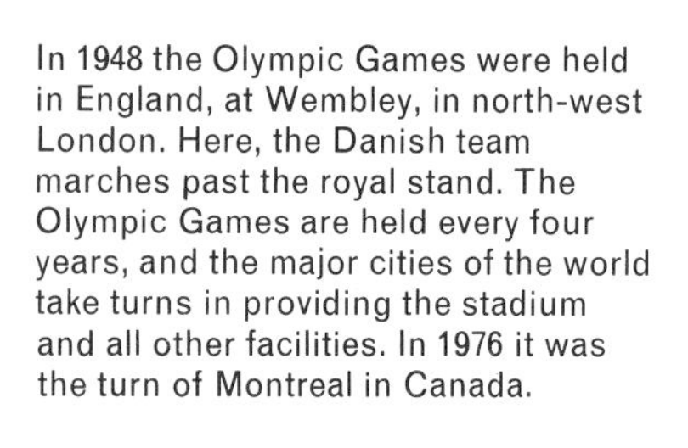

In 1948 the Olympic Games were held in England, at Wembley, in north-west London. Here, the Danish team marches past the royal stand. The Olympic Games are held every four years, and the major cities of the world take turns in providing the stadium and all other facilities. In 1976 it was the turn of Montreal in Canada.

handicraft as a hobby, for the town amusements were not readily accessible to them. The best they could enjoy was the village carnival or fête which took place once a year, lasted only a day or two, but which often took weeks to prepare.

This century has seen all that change. Football, for example, a game played in the Middle Ages and often banned because of its violence, did not come into its own until the middle of the 19th century. Then it was limited to public schools until some enterprising clergymen began to organize it for poorer families in their parishes. Early teams of this period are now household names—like Everton, Aston Villa and Bolton Wanderers. By the 1890s the Football Association and the Football League were both organizing regular matches, with proper rules of play, timetables, competitions and so forth. But the greater part of the famous clubs of today are of 20th-century foundation.

Men and women have danced in some way or other probably since the days of the ancient Egyptians (beginning in the 30th century BC), when the first musical instruments were made. Dancing was very popular in the Middle Ages among all classes. In the countryside, Morris dances, which are still held in the counties, were held on festival days like Christmas and May Day. By the present century, the upper classes enjoyed dancing regularly. Society hostesses held dances at their homes or in fine ballrooms for their daughters and their guests. It was a way to be launched into London society, to have your first dance to which you asked a host of eligible young men, one of whom might be interested enough to want to see you again. The lower classes danced in pubs, until after the First World War when dance halls were built all over the country. The 1920s saw a great era of dancing. Village halls and town halls held them; dance halls were tightly packed several days a week. From America came the Charleston and the Black Bottom, jazz and the foxtrot. These were followed by the quickstep, the jitterbug and swing. One dance enjoyed in England in the late 1930s was the Lambeth Walk. Swing, so well played by bands led by men like Glenn Miller and Benny Goodman, carried on through the Second

Dancing in the 1930s.

World War. After that there were more changes. In the 1950s, famous American singers like Elvis Presley, and band leaders like Bill Haley introduced rock 'n roll, which was followed by the twist. Then came the 'pop' revolution heralded by four young men from the Liverpool area, the Beatles (John Lennon, Paul McCartney, Ringo Starr and George Harrison), who introduced new musical sounds and melodies with their unique type of singing, harmony and words. They were copied by thousands of other groups of singers and players or individual artists, the instruments being chiefly electric guitars, drums and saxophones. Many played good music, but some merely made a lot of noise. And the revolution goes on. It has been helped by the invention of the gramophone record player, the wireless set—and their developments, the high-fidelity disc player and the transistor set.

In the intervals, older dances continued to be enjoyed, and country-style dances from the American west of the 19th century have been extremely popular.

The craze for dancing was accompanied by a rapidly growing enthusiasm for individual singers—like Bing Crosby and Frank Sinatra. They held the day for a generation, from the 1940s right

This is a night club in London during the Second World War. The lights have been switched off because of the 'black-out'.

Above left: The first television films were shot before the Second World War. This is an early postwar picture of television cameras filming some dancing artistes for a variety programme.

Above: In 1937 a TV film was made of some fire-fighting drill. The man actually jumping down towards the blanket is Leslie Mitchell, a radio and TV commentator who was among the very first TV stars after the war.

into the 1960s, followed by more emotional singers like Frankie Laine, Johnnie Ray and England's Cliff Richard. The 1960s produced a great variety of 'pop' singers like Adam Faith, Lulu and Mary Hopkin, and groups like the Rolling Stones, the New Seekers and the Supremes. Records, or discs as they are called, of these and many other performers' numbers began to sell by the million, and in countless homes you could—and still can—hear the beat of the latest 'top of the pops' discs, played on shining new noisy high-fidelity stereophonic record playing apparatus.

The advent of radio in 1922 had become national by 1927, when over two million radio licences had been issued. This helped enormously to spread these forms of entertainment. By the 1950s, when small transistor sets were in mass production, half the population had wireless sets.

After the Second World War, television, first tried out by the Scottish electrical engineer John Logie Baird in 1925, became a major influence in British lives. The BBC had the monopoly of broadcasting TV programmes until 1955 when the Independent Television Authority was formed and two companies began to broadcast other programmes on rival networks. Now, with colour television a reality, there are over twelve million sets in homes throughout the country. Television has rightly or wrongly become an integral part of our lives. You can be educated by watching special schools programmes. You can see and hear the latest news, brought to you by reporters on the spot. You can see old feature films, new plays, Shakespeare productions, comedy programmes, quiz games, documentary films and a host of other things.

Another field of entertainment that is peculiarly 20th-century, although it was invented in 1889 by William Friese-Greene, is the cinema. A cinematograph machine, that is, one which projects moving pictures, was in public use before the end of the century, and by 1902 there were several music halls where from time to time you could see a short silent film. By 1912 there were more than a hundred special houses for film showing, called cinemas.

The age of silent films lasted until the late 1920s when 'talkies' were invented and were naturally much more popular. Films came into their own as a dominating form of entertainment in the 1930s, when colour pictures were made, and directors began to film epics lasting two hours or more. A landmark was reached in 1939 when *Gone with the Wind*, a fine story set in America during and after the 1861–1865 Civil War, was produced. It lasted for over three and a half hours and had some of the best actors and actresses in the world playing the leading parts.

After the Second World War, new techniques were introduced, including 3-dimensional films for which you had to wear special spectacles, Cinemascope and stereophonic sound tracks. But films had to compete with the rapidly growing popularity and ease of viewing television. Many famous cinemas have disappeared to become office blocks, bowling alleys, supermarkets and bingo halls.

Our lives have certainly become fuller, as the increasing boredom produced by working on mass-production lines has been balanced by a growing variety of entertainments and leisure pursuits. But are we any happier than, say, the simple, hard-working medieval villeins on the manors? This is the problem of the present time. Mankind has certainly advanced materially and technologically. An enormous number of labour-saving devices are available to him which were unthinkable even a century ago. But what has this produced? There is still great discontent among working people. There are still strikes, which are pressed home with every familiar bitterness, sometimes affecting the whole nation. There is still a great gulf in communication between the various parts of our society. Will the next generation see the answers to it all?

13 Wales, Scotland and Ireland since the 17th century

So many things happened in the three Celtic countries in the years from the 16th century, that it is not possible to do more than select one or two major features in each land. In Wales, country life did not change much. The most important developments were in education and religion, and of course it is necessary to look briefly at the effect of the exploitation of the coal and iron industries in the south Wales valleys. Perhaps it is this last picture that has led to the growth of a nationalist movement in Wales, *Plaid Cymru*, which means Welsh Party, that seeks self-government on the simple ground that it believes it could do better for Welshmen than a government centred in London.

In Scotland, a great and proud nation failed to yield to England in war, only to find itself united to England by an Act of Union in 1707. This Act did not bring to Scotland the benefits its originators expected. The emigration throughout the 19th century of Scottish people, especially Highlanders, to countries overseas was extensive, and it hurt the development of this tough, hard-working and upright people. Yet, today Scotland's whisky production is the biggest dollar earner in the whole United Kingdom export trade. The off-shore North Sea oil exploration bids fair to making Aberdeen, and the rest of Scotland, more prosperous than ever. And its nationals are still to be found in many leading positions in Government, the professions and private industry throughout Britain.

Ireland has had one of the most tragic histories of any nation in history. The great famine of 1845–49 effectively cut its population from about 8,000,000 to a little over 4,000,000, but the country survived this to win independence in one of the most gloriously successful wars of liberation in recent times, to split into two parts—Protestant Ulster and Catholic Eire.

Wales

Perhaps you would not be surprised to know that the Welsh way of life has not changed a great deal in the last three centuries or so. Although large areas of the south, particularly the valleys,

Gwynfor Evans, Welsh Nationalist (Plaid Cymru) M.P. for Carmarthen, is president of Plaid Cymru. Here he is at a party rally. He is one of the three Plaid members at Westminster. They stand for self-government for Wales, and the administration at Westminster has, for the first time in 700 years, recognized that Wales should have some self-government.

have been turned over to coal and iron production, the Welsh still sing in choirs, go to chapel regularly, take their education seriously, read and write verse and speak their ancient tongue. They have done this for hundreds of years. Two of the main features of Welsh life are the chapels and the schools.

Part of the national costume of Wales is the tall hat, worn by girls at choir-singing festivals, eisteddfodau and other enjoyments.

Edinburgh from the air in the mid-1970s.

Religion

In the 17th century, the Welsh, who had with great enthusiasm accepted the reformation of Christianity that had spread to many western European countries, bitterly opposed the high church ideas of Charles I and his archbishop of Canterbury, William Laud, in the 1630s. Many of the clergy refused to put them into effect, and they were expelled from the church. But the people still wanted to listen to sermons and have the services. So their clergy began to hold them in private houses, barns and even in the fields and woods where they thought they would be safe. This process spread throughout Wales, and it was encouraged by fresh arbitrary church rules put out during the reign of Charles' son, Charles II (1660–1685). Like the Scots, the Welsh did not want bishops. Nor did they like the English Book of Common Prayer. And many clergy who had not yet been expelled resisted. They, too, were now expelled and some were sent to prison. Others escaped to America. Still others fled to the countryside, and they came to be known as non-conformists, because they would not conform to the official religion.

The non-conformists created their own church organization later in the century. Its main features was the setting up of special chapels under preachers who had not been ordained in the Church of England. The first chapel was established in Monmouthshire. Others soon followed, in Carmarthenshire and Glamorganshire.

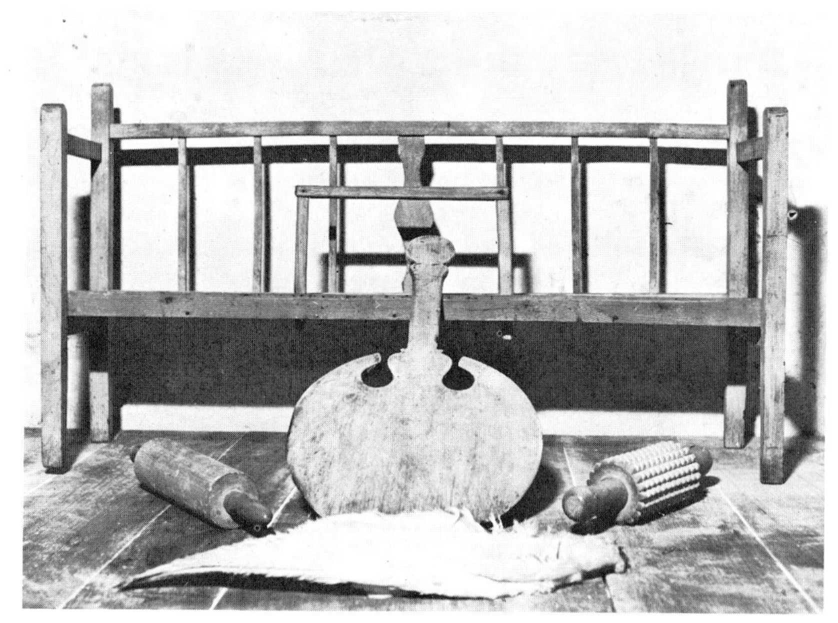

Above: Llandaff Cathedral, near Cardiff. The sculpture in the centre is called Christ in Majesty and was the work of Jacob Epstein, perhaps the greatest of all British sculptors. Llandaff was severely damaged in the air raids on Cardiff during the Second World War and much had to be rebuilt.

Above right: Some implements used in making oatcakes, from the Welsh Folk Museum.

And over the next two centuries the Welsh church expanded. It was greatly helped in the middle of the 18th century by the amazing career of John Wesley who had founded what came to be called the Methodist Church in England.

The orthodox church in Wales meanwhile continued, though its support was drawn chiefly from the upper and richer middle classes. In 1920 the Welsh church was disestablished, which meant it could have its own structure, with an archbishop and five bishops. The six dioceses are Bangor, St Asaph, Monmouth, Llandaff, Swansea and St David's. And an archbishop is selected from one or other of these in rotation.

Education

Until the period of the Tudors (1485–1603), there were very few schools in Wales. You learned elementary subjects at home, and then if you were really bright someone might pay for you to go to an English or Scottish university. Then, in the Tudor and Stuart ages, grammar schools, already thick on the ground in England, were opened in Wales. An early one was Carmarthen, and there were others at Ruthin in Denbighshire and Beaumaris in Anglesey. But these schools were meant for older boys, ready to go on to university, and the Welsh language was not taught there. You will remember that Henry VIII, in his Statute of Wales, had attempted to stamp out the ancient tongue.

In the 18th century, a splendid vicar from Llandowror in Carmarthenshire, Gruffydd Jones, set up a few schools where young children could learn elementary subjects and also be taught Welsh properly. The idea caught on and soon there were hundreds of small schools all over Wales. There, children were taught to read the Bible in Welsh, to learn Welsh grammar, and to write in the Welsh language. When Gruffydd Jones died in 1760 the language had been saved from extinction.

In the early 1800s, the Church of England, which was having a revival, founded National Schools, basically to give religious teaching to young people but also to improve education. From 1833 they were aided by grants from the government. These schools were introduced into Wales as well, but of course, as they were run by the English, Welsh was not taught. Indeed, it was prohibited and you could be punished if you were heard even speaking it in class or on the games field. Most of the teachers did not understand Welsh. Then, when the law of 1880 made education compulsory up to the age of 10, new schools were built wherever they were needed. Again, Welsh was not taught, and the language was threatened with extinction once more. This time, it was saved by the Sunday Schools. Today, the language is safe. Parliament accorded it equal status with English in 1967, and more and more people are learning it.

A harpist performs at the Powis Eisteddfod of 1820. A national eisteddfod is now held every year in Wales, and each year in a different town. Usually the towns chosen alternate between the north and south of Wales.

Industry

The valleys and hills of Wales are among the most famous in the world. They are also, in some cases, the most infamous. At Aberfan, for example, in 1966, a huge, black tip of wet ash and slag slid down the hillside and crashed into a school, engulfing it and smothering to death 144 children and adults. It was a most ghastly tragedy for the Welsh people, but only one more in a long histories of accidents involving whole communities. As all too often in the past, insufficient attention had been paid to safety.

The hills of Glamorganshire were once covered with woods. When iron was made in places like Sussex and Gloucestershire, the ironmakers used local timber. But as the demand for iron grew, the makers had to look elsewhere for timber, and one place they used was the Glamorganshire valley and hill district.

A familiar sight in south Wales, a beautiful valley surrounded by hills but marred by ugly buildings around a coal-mining complex. This one is Ogmore Vale, in Glamorganshire.

At the same time it was discovered that under many of these hills were rich coal deposits. Here were two sources of material for industry in one area, and on a big scale.

By the end of the 18th century, the valleys had been transformed from a beautiful and quiet landscape into a bustling, thriving, smoky, black hive of industry. Over the empty rolling grass plains and lower slopes of the hills were built rows and rows of workers' houses, slums like those in industrial England and Scotland. Towns grew up, like Aberdare, Merthyr Tydvil, Tredegar, Pontypridd and Ebbw Vale. And the mine and ironworks owners and the landowners became very rich indeed. Some found their way to the House of Lords in London!

It was very different for the workers and their families. Their homes were every bit as bad as the worst ones in England, and they had the additional misery of living in continual fear that the piles of slag and ash built up on the hillsides close to the mines and ironworks might at any time crumble and slide down the hill and smash them. The disaster at Aberfan was perhaps the worst of its kind, but it was by no means the first. And in many coal mining villages, the families lived in terror of the pits becoming flooded or the shafts being blocked by rubble from an explosion of gas. They never really knew whether their husbands and children would come home. At Senghenydd, in the early part of this century, a whole village of miners and their sons was all but wiped out by a terrible pit explosion.

The masters of these works were often Englishmen who did not speak or understand Welsh. They paid the men very badly for long hours. They also kept the only shop in the village and so compelled the men to pay whatever price they asked for goods. And if a workman could not pay, he had to mortgage his next week's pay, and so on until in many cases a man had sold himself into virtual slavery for the rest of his working life to ensure his family would eat.

Above: The Menai Suspension Bridge was designed and constructed by Thomas Telford (the Scottish engineer) in 1826. It is over the Menai Straits between Caernarvonshire and Anglesey in north Wales.

Above right: On the sea front at Aberystwyth in Cardiganshire is the Victorian building which houses part of the University of Wales. This is the oldest foundation of the university of of Wales, and was established in 1871.

For centuries the Welsh nation has been governed from Westminster, and more often than not the officials have not been Welsh and have not understood the basic differences between Welshmen and Englishmen, their cultures and their aspirations. In this century, these differences have become even more marked, and a movement for Welsh independence has grown up, mounting steadily in strength since 1966 when Gwynfor Evans won the first seat for the Welsh National Party (Plaid Cymru) at Westminster. In the 1974 general election, Plaid Cymru won three seats (and came second in several others), and this prodded the Labour Government into looking seriously at giving Wales a lot more say in the running of its affairs. Plaid Cymru wants Wales to remain in the United Kingdom, but with the kind of self-governing powers which Northern Ireland was given in the 1920 Government of Ireland Act.

Scotland

The Stewart kings of England and Scotland—James I, Charles I, Charles II and James II—seemed almost to forget they were Scottish at all. James I only visited Scotland once after his accession to the English throne. Charles I's visits were usually accompanied by trouble, such as when he tried to force the Scottish church to accept a new high church Prayer Book, and Charles II and his brother James II paid very little attention to the land of their forefathers. But you will remember that the king had acquired power over the Committee of Articles, and this meant he controlled the

In October 1913, a coal mine at Senghenydd in Wales was rent by a series of explosions and for the most part collapsed. 413 miners were trapped and died. It was the worst pit disaster in coal-mining history. Questions were asked at the time about the safety arrangements, but they were never satisfactorily answered.

Scottish Parliament. The result was that, in doing as it was told, it was not representing the views of the electors. For a century the country did not have good government.

Meanwhile, the nation tried to get on with the business of developing trade, the professions, education, local government, crafts and industry. But it was hampered by the association with England. While trade and industry were beginning to grow in the last years of the 16th century—for example, soap, glass and leather were being manufactured in Scotland for the first time—there were results of the union of the crowns which affected this growth sharply.

First, Edinburgh, which had been Scotland's capital for a century and the home of the royal family and the court, declined rapidly in importance from 1603 onwards when James VI became James I and moved to London. The court went with him, and as a result Edinburgh shopkeepers and traders lost a lot of business. The court also attracted many Scottish nobles to England for long periods, some of whom bought homes in the southern country, and this, too, deprived traders of business. And after the union, Scottish exporters who had previously only had to pay low duties on the goods they sold in France now had to pay the same as traders in other lands. Then, if England embarked on war, the Scots had to contribute money and men to the war effort, even though they were not consulted.

The church

There were other disadvantages. James, once king of England as well as Scotland, tried to make the Scottish Reformed Church accept bishops as representatives of the church in Parliament. The Church objected to bishops. They had a new structure based on a General Assembly of representative clergy. Prayer books which bore any resemblance to the Roman Catholic books were banned. Churches in Scotland had been whitewashed inside, stained glass windows smashed and replaced by plain glass, and the high altars removed to make way for round tables in the centre of the church, around which minister and congregation gathered.

James had wanted to alter all this, but was wise enough to try a little at a time, hence his success with the bishops. He also got the Assembly to agree that it should be compulsory to attend services at Christmas, Easter and on Whitsunday. Bishops were also allowed to confirm children.

James' son, Charles I, as he did in everything else, went at the church in a bull-headed fashion and tried to foist a new Prayer Book on it. A rebellion resulted, which eventually led to war. The king had to withdraw. Charles II, restored to the joint thrones in 1660, also imposed bishops on the church. The result was that hundreds of Scottish ministers abandoned their churches and held services with their congregations in the fields. The Government tried to stop this by imposing stiff penalties, but in 1679 a dangerous revolt broke out in which the Archbishop of St Andrews was murdered.

When William III accepted the throne from the English Government in 1688, the Scottish Parliament offered the Scottish throne to him as well, but on certain conditions. One was that there should be no bishops in the Scottish church, and that demand was granted. There has not been a bishop in the Scottish church since. William also agreed to the abolition of the Committee of Articles which, in effect, freed the Scottish Parliament.

Stagnation

Scotland did not change a great deal in the 17th century. The

The City Hall at Cardiff, Wales' capital.

Scotland has for centuries been famous for its silversmiths and their fine craftsmanship. Today, the skill is still very evident among present time silversmiths.

Life was very hard for children in Glasgow in the days of the Industrial Revolution. Janet Cumming was only 11 years old, but she had to carry 'large bits of coal from the wall face to the pit bottom', as she described the job, in a coal-mine. She said her loads weighed 1 cwt or more.

Here is a kind of aerial map of Edinburgh, as it was drawn by de Wit in 1647. It is in the Central Library in Edinburgh. You can see what a large and crowded city Edinburgh was, even 300 years ago.

crop fields remained huge, unenclosed and still erratically ploughed as in earlier times. The country cottages were the same, low-roofed turfed huts with trodden earth or clay floors, the smoke going out through unglazed windows as well as clumsy chimney stacks poking through the thatch. Trees and hedges were still rarities, except round the homes of the nobility and rich merchants. The laird's house was usually a fortified manor house, a style of home abandoned in England by the time of the Tudors. These Scottish manor houses are often called castles, because they were covered with iron barred windows, built of granite or stone, equipped with gun loops, and decked with pepper-pot turrets with pointed roofs. In the second half of the century some owners tried to make them more comfortable and they panelled the walls in oak, put up portraits of the family ancestors, and introduced glass drinking vessels, glazed earthenware plates and dishes, marble fireplaces, and here and there rich pile carpet. More chairs were introduced in the styles already enjoyed in England.

Union

In the last years of William III's reign, moves were made between England and Scotland to make a political union, that is, to unite the two countries properly by joining the Parliaments. The English

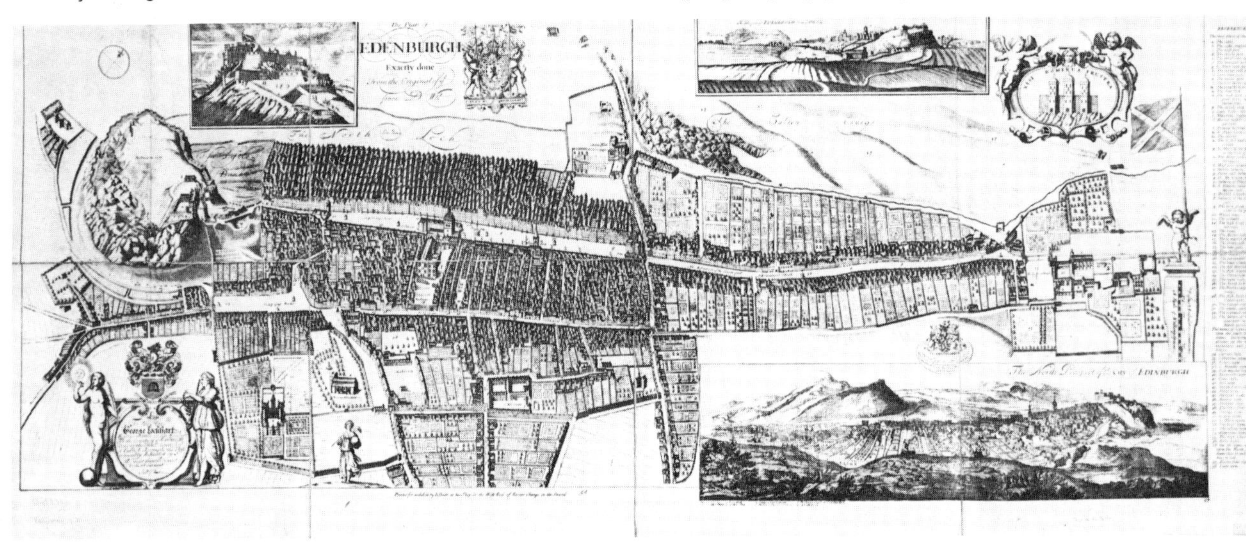

were all for it—naturally, as in any agreement they stood to gain so much. Their population (5,000,000) was five times as big as Scotland's. The Scots were not so keen. And when Queen Anne succeeded in 1702 they felt the time had come to state more clearly on what terms they would consider it. By the Act of Security of 1704, if Anne should die without heir, her successor was to be chosen within twenty days. He must be a Protestant and a member of the House of Stuart. But he must not be the same person as chosen by England, unless they agreed to give Scotland freedom of religion, free government and freedom of trade.

The English dreaded a different king in Scotland. So they bullied the Scots by passing the Alien Act at Westminster, which said that if the Scots would not accept their choice of monarch on Anne's death, no Scottish goods would be allowed into England. Bitterness increased and the two countries almost went to war. Then, some statesmen on both sides met to see if they could resolve the differences. They met at Westminster in 1706 and drafted a Treaty of Union, and this was put to both Parliaments in 1707. Both accepted it.

By the treaty, the Scottish Parliament abolished itself. In its place, sixteen lords and forty-five commoners were given seats at Westminster. Scotland kept its church, its law courts and law, and its education, but it lost its coinage, and its independence.

Some houses in Glasgow in the early 19th century. Note that one or two are thatched.

Walking in the streets of Glasgow in the early 19th century was not safe. Here, a gentleman looks on horrified as some street bullies attack passengers boarding a coach bound for London.

The Gorbals district of Glasgow was for years the worst slum housing area in all Britain. Nothing was done to improve conditions, and the illness rate among the tenement dwellers was very high. Then in the last decade or so, local authorities began to clean the whole area up, pull down the blocks and build new ones. This picture was taken in the Gorbals in the 1950s.

Inside the laboratory of Lord Kelvin, OM, GCVO, FRS, at Glasgow University, towards the end of the last century. Kelvin was Scotland's greatest scientist and inventor, and possibly the most brilliant man of science in all British history, apart from Sir Isaac Newton.

The Scots had been enticed into union by free trading rights, which seemed to promise economic wealth. But as many Scots had feared this did not materialize. The trading advantages were all England's for many years, and the deception—for that is how many Scots viewed it—was soon made clear. Taxes were to be collected in Scotland by English collectors. Parts of the treaty promised certain payments to Scotland, but these were a very long time in coming.

There were many more objections to the union. One was that Scottish lords who had negotiated the deal had been bribed with large cash sums, and there was some evidence of this. Another was that the English adopted an extremely patronizing attitude towards Scotsmen, not unlike their dealings with peoples all over the world whom they cajoled or forced into submission.

The leaders of the Jacobite cause—that is, the party which wanted to restore James Edward, the son of James II, to the throne—seized on the discontent, and in the Highlands found strong support for the rebellions of 1715 and 1745, both of which failed, however, to unseat the Hanoverian monarchy in London.

Growth and development

By the middle of the 18th century, things were beginning to look up for Scotland. The little town of Glasgow, whose population was only 12,000 at union, had become the leading port for tobacco imports in the United Kingdom, and millions of pounds of leaves were being delivered, chiefly for re-sale in Europe. Huge quantities of sugar and rum were also being imported and re-exported. Other goods exported, which were produced in or around the coasts of Scotland, included cloth, knitted wools, wrought ironwork, leather, pottery, crystal glass, and salted fish. Perhaps the most important export of the 18th century was linen, made from flax and spun, woven and dyed in hundreds of cottages throughout the land. Linen factories were also set up later in the century at Glasgow, Paisley and Dundee.

In the 1770s, the newly-developed cotton industry in England was introduced into Scotland, and it soon thrived. Again, Glasgow was a main centre for factories, and before long there were mills along the riversides of Scotland producing cotton in great quantities. The wool industry was greatly expanded by the introduction of knitting machines.

The Industrial Revolution, which had transformed England, also transformed the Lowlands of Scotland. But it brought the same miseries, the slum housing (which was worse in Glasgow than anywhere), the long hours, and women and children in the factories and mines. The first coal mine was opened at the end of the century, and the owners sacrificed safety to productivity.

Cotton remained the dominating industry in Scotland until the 1850s. The introduction of powered looms and spinning machines put the hand weavers out of business, though the fine shawls produced at Paisley with the world-famous designs were always in demand. The American Civil War (1861–1865) abruptly cut down the quantity of cotton raw material coming into Scotland (and to Lancashire in England, too). When it was re-activated, it was too late for Scotland. What Scotland lost in cotton it gained, however, in iron and steel production, engineering and shipbuilding. Everyone knows that a Clyde-built ship is the best thing afloat in the world. It has been for a hundred years.

The Highlands

The Highlands were a different matter. There, the majority of the support for the Jacobite rebellions had been found, and when these were crushed, the English Government dealt harshly with the survivors. Highlanders were not allowed to carry arms. Their tartans and kilts were banned. Their chiefs could no longer raise their own regiments. This struck at their authority. Some

A view of a Clydeside shipyard. The ships built on the Clyde over the last century or so have been among the best-constructed ships anywhere in the world. The industry has been run down over the past generation, tragically for the Scottish economy, and this is but one of the many grievances voiced by the Scottish National Party, which in the 1974 General Election won eleven seats at Westminster.

A famous drawing, now in the Mitchell Library in Glasgow. It illustrates the 'Clearances' policy, when Scottish clansmen and others in the Highlands were driven out of their lands by big landowners.

chiefs decided to rear cattle or sheep for sale in Lowland towns. They rented huge areas of farmland to enterprising Lowlanders and to Englishmen. But this put the clansmen out of work, as only a few were wanted to manage the grazing. So the clansmen had to go south to find jobs in the industries in Glasgow, Paisley, or Motherwell, or cross the border into English cities, or emigrate to America, Canada, Australia, and, in the 19th century, South Africa. Some joined the army and provided the best fighting troops the British forces ever had. Highland regiments won battle honours on nearly every important battleground where British troops were engaged.

In the 1800s, distress in the Highlands was aggravated when landlords began deliberately to clear the lands of clansmen remaining. These 'clearances' are a bitter memory in Scotland. In whole areas families were evicted from their cottages (which were burned), and driven to the coast where they were expected to find work in the fisheries or sea shore crafts. Many landlords shipped whole families out of Scotland to America. For those allowed to remain there was some work to be done in the great road-building programme and the canal-cutting projects, especially the Caledonian Canal from Moray Firth to Loch Linnhe.

For a long time the Scots have seen their affairs handled from offices in London by people who have not always understood their problems, and still treat them with patronizing attitudes. At the same time, they have made—and are still making—astonishing contributions to many areas of British achievement, providing the best administrators in the old British Empire and today in the present civil service, and leading the U.K. in the scientific world for generations. Scottish demands for self-government have been growing since the Depression of the 1930s, which hit Scotland worse than anywhere else in Britain. In the 1974 general election the Scottish National Party won eleven parliamentary seats at Westminster, and is currently the most widely supported political party in Scotland. The U.K. Government has taken note, and has made definite proposals for devolving domestic government to a Scottish national body of elected representatives.

Weaving has been a Scottish craft, as it has been among nearly every race sometime or other in history. The Scots have been very fine weavers, particularly with heavy wool

The Caledonian Canal was an engineering project, planned and directed by Thomas Telford (1757–1834), the famous Scottish civil engineer. The canal, opened in 1822, is 96 kilometres (60 miles) long (including 37 km (23 miles) of artificial cutting) and stretches from the Moray Firth to Loch Linnhe.

Ireland

The first thing to hurt the Irish very deeply in the 16th century was the Reformation. In England, Scotland, and later in Wales, men had seen that the old Roman Church needed reform. But in Ireland, the native people, and the Anglo—Catholic Irish families, remained fiercely Catholic. They hated the dissolution of the monasteries, the defacing of churches and the giving up of the old forms. This united all Irishmen against their English overlords.

Religion

The result was a string of rebellions. The English thought that one way to deal with them was to parcel out parts of the country to Protestant noblemen and courtiers, and let them build their own petty kingdoms there, in which they could take what measures they liked to crush the Irish and stamp out the Roman faith. This was the beginning of the plantations, as they are called, in which the new owners undertook to employ only Englishmen on the land, thus putting the native Irish out of work. Settlements were made in the old kingdom of Ulster in the 1570s, and in the 1580s more were made in the old kingdom of Munster.

This policy was extended in James I's reign. Nearly all Ulster was divided into estates of 1,000 or 2,000 acres, and sold to English or Scottish settlers who were encouraged to expel the native Irish. Those who stayed could only do so if they agreed to accept servitude as 'hewers of wood and drawers of water'. You can see how the present troubles in Northern Ireland began, so long ago, and why antagonism between Protestant and Catholic is so intense even now.

The second half of the 17th century was worse still for Ireland. The English Government crippled Irish trade by forbidding Irish merchant ships to trade with the colonies in the New World. Both sheep and cattle, which the Irish pastured on the rich, green grass of their land, were not allowed to be exported. And the sale of wool abroad was also banned. It could only be sold to England. But the same government would not import butter or cheese from

Above: A cottier was a kind of free-lance farm labourer who owned his own land but worked for other people, sometimes on a day-to-day or week-to-week basis. It was an insecure life, he was for the most part extremely poor, sometimes starving, and he was never able to improve his lot. This is a cottage of one of them in the 18th century. Its style was scarcely different from that of several centuries earlier.

Right: The Four Courts in Dublin. This splendid building houses the Irish Law Courts. It was originally built towards the end of the 18th century, was almost completely destroyed during the Civil War of 1922, and has since been restored.

Ireland. What was the farmer to do to make a living? Well, he joined the flourishing smuggling business, getting his products out to Europe on a wide scale, but this was only possible for the bigger farmer with the necessary cash to pay what bribes were required by corrupt officials. The smaller holders—and they made up the majority of farmers in Ireland—suffered very great hardships.

When James II (1685–1688) tried to restore Roman Catholicism in England, it was a chance for the Irish, who had been reduced almost to slavery by the Protestant landowners, to get some redress. But James was forced to abdicate in 1688, and the war which ensued between him and the followers of William III was a disaster for the Catholic cause.

Discrimination

The Treaty of Limerick of 1691 was, it is true, more generous than the Irish Catholics expected. No lands were forfeited; Catholics could continue to worship in their own way. But the treaty was also more generous than the English Parliament liked, and the next year it began to introduce fresh measures to make the Irish Catholics powerless in every way. They were stripped of almost every elementary right. There followed what are called the Penal Laws. Some set down definite penalties for practising the Catholic faith. Others merely set out disabilities. Catholics were barred from being members of the Irish Parliament, and they could not hold any government post. All Catholic bishops and monks were banned from Ireland. If they were caught, they were to be hanged,

THE ILLUSTRATED LONDON NEWS

Above: The grievances of the Irish peasantry against the British and Anglo-Irish landlord class were numerous and long-standing. By the 1870s, fierce fighting was a frequent occurrence on small properties where the poor occupants, unable to pay rent, were driven out and their houses burned down. This is a drawing from *Illustrated London News*, of 1887, showing a disproportionate number of troops and police guarding the landlord of a house while he sets fire to it after evicting the tenant. The troops were there in case there was trouble.

Top right: William Gladstone (1809–1898), who was prime minister four times, was the champion of the Irish Home Rule movement. But he could not get a Home Rule Bill safely through Parliament. Here he is urging members of the Commons to accept the proposals.

drawn and quartered. No Catholic could carry a sword or ride a horse worth more than £5. His Protestant neighbour could offer him £5 for it and then legally take it, and he (the Catholic) could not go to law to recover it. Catholics were not allowed to vote, nor could they be citizens of towns with borough charters. They could have leases on land for not more than 31 years and two-thirds of the profit had to be paid to the lessor. They could not practise law. The universities were closed to them. They could not start schools or teach. The aim was to exterminate them. An English lord chancellor of the time actually said, 'the law does not take into account the existence of such a person as an Irish Roman Catholic.'

What did these terrible laws do to the Irish Catholic peasantry? They drove them to live in the humblest possible surroundings, where they ate a diet of roots, and coarse unpleasant bread washed

Irish tenants who could not afford to pay their rent or do the work on their cottages needed to keep them in good order were driven out, or evicted. Even during the terrible Potato Famine of 1845–8, which gave rise to the Great Hunger and the deaths of over 1,000,000 people, landlords still turned tenants out. This is a harrowing scene of such an eviction, in 1848.

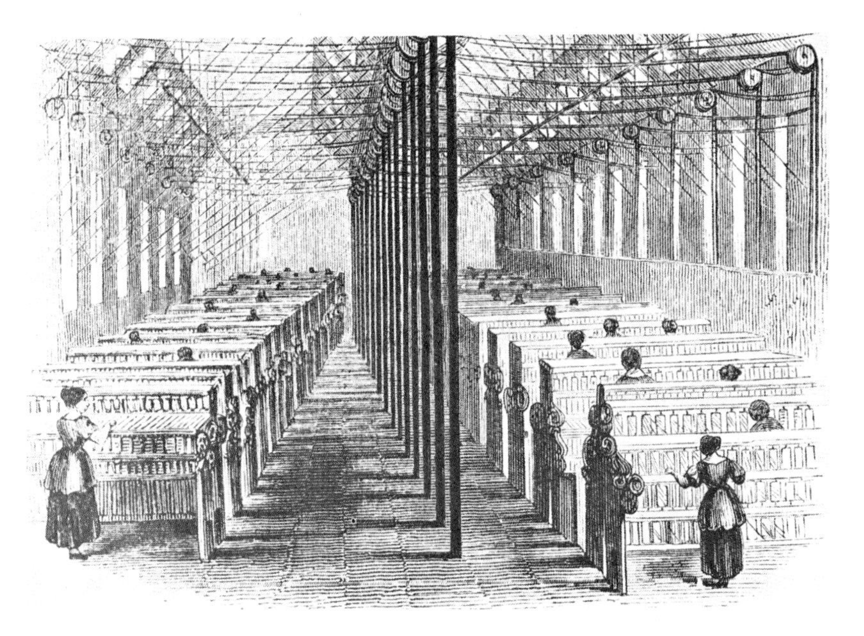

down with milk. Their houses, if you could call them houses, were cabins in plots of land of about half an acre, with a pile of turf, some corn and some oats. Much of the land was given over to planting potatoes, some cabbages and so on, the green food mostly eaten by one or two scraggy ill-nourished calves or piglets. The peasants had little meat for themselves. In very bad times, it was customary to tie a lump of boiled meat onto a piece of string. The other end was fixed to the ceiling over the box at which the family sat down to a meal, and the members grabbed the lump and brushed it across the top of a plate of mashed potato to give it a tiny trace of meat flavour.

These cabins were made by laying long sticks across a ditch to a mud wall on the far side of it, weaving them together with wattle and covering them with heather, straw and earth to make a sloping roof. In this primitive hut a whole family of, perhaps, father, mother and six children lived.

This condition of the poor did not alter much for a century and a half, during which time the rich Protestant landlords and their agents built themselves magnificent country homes in the latest architectural styles, like those in England, in estates with rolling lawns and parkland, or in Dublin, in its rows of beautiful town houses. When the appalling famine of 1845–1848 struck the country, the peasantry were in no condition to resist the privations it brought and the sickness which resulted. It is little wonder that very deep resentment burned. There was parliamentary representation in Ireland it is true, but it was Protestant only and so it in no way represented the great majority of Irishmen. Even when it had broken away from the grip of Westminster in 1782, when Poynings' Law was repealed, the new independent Parliament was still

Above: In the early years of the present century many people in Ulster, that is Northern Ireland, did not want Home Rule for Ireland. They wished to stay part of the United Kingdom. They organized many demonstrations of their loyalty, as they called it. One of their leaders was Edward Carson, later Lord Carson, who was a senior statesman in the British government, and in this picture he is addressing a rally

Above left: Inside a thriving linen mill in Belfast, in the 1850s. Linen was one of the major industries in Northern Ireland.

Protestant. There was no alternative but civil war at the end of the century. But this was crushed, and in 1800 the English Government passed an Act of Union with England, closing down the Irish Parliament. 28 peers and 101 commoners were to be sent from Ireland to Westminster. In 1829, the Catholic Emancipation Act enabled Catholics to stand as members for Ireland at Westminster. This was a great advance, but it was too late to remove the long-standing bitterness between Irish Catholics and the English Protestants living in Ireland.

Disaster

In the 1840s, Ireland was to endure yet another time of agony—the most frightful in all its history. The population had been rising steadily since the beginning of the century. By 1841 it was over 8,000,000, which was getting on for three times that of Scotland. This population was unevenly distributed, however, and in many cases thousands of people lived packed together in areas on the coast where the soil was most unproductive. Of the 8,000,000, only about one million lived in towns of any size, a fair proportion of them in Dublin. That left 7,000,000 in the countryside trying to eke out a living from the land. As the population figures rose, the small landholdings were further sub-divided and then broken up again, so that by 1840 many of the potato patches—for that is all they were—were too small to support even the holder and his family, unless the harvest was a good one. If there was a bad harvest, or if there was potato disease, famine would follow as surely as night follows day. It had done so several times before, but not to any alarming degree.

Then, in 1845, a fresh blight appeared on the potato plants, and the year's crop was a disastrous failure. Famine followed with a vengeance, and for the first time the results were widespread. Starvation was the order of the day everywhere. This was aggravated by the re-appearance of the blight in 1846 and 1847, so that for three years the potato crop literally ground to a halt. Worse followed. Smallholders who did grow corn as well were

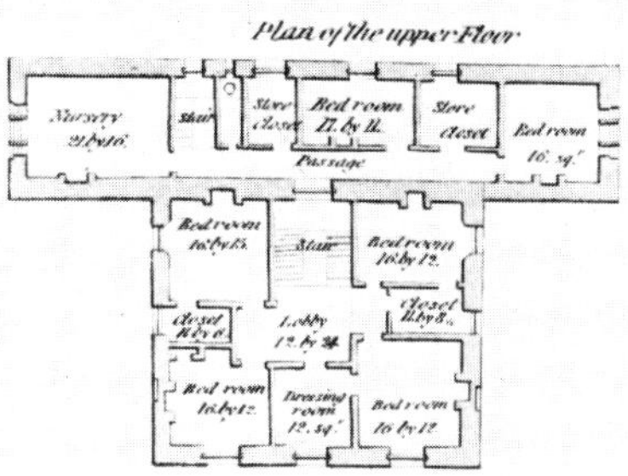

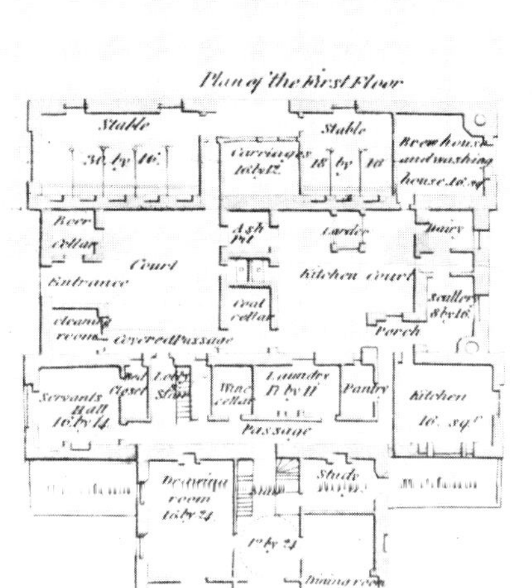

A design for a Scottish gentleman-farmer's house. This one would have cost about £3000 in 1814, when it was drawn.

obliged by statute to give two-thirds of their yield to the landlord, generally an Englishman who lived in England and managed his estates through an agent.

The English Government failed utterly to comprehend the size of the disaster. And when finally it did, it still failed to do anything on any scale to help. Because one or two areas were found to be relatively unharmed, the English Government, given the details from these areas, imagined that the tales of death and suffering from a great many areas elsewhere were exaggerated.

The result of the famine was that more than a million people—one seventh of the total population—died in their homes or on their land. That is the equivalent of *eight million* people dying out of

today's United Kingdom population. Another 750,000 peopl
piled into boats and ships heading for the New World, or fo
England and Wales, ready to emigrate wherever the navigato
would take them. They arrived at these places in the grip of one
or other of the diseases that follow starvation. Ships reached port
in America and Canada with their holds filled with people, a
least twice the number considered safe for crossing the Atlantic
Half of these unfortunates were found to be dead, even putrefying

Independence

The miseries which this terrible series of disasters produced, an
the failure of the British Government to remedy them or t
alleviate the awful disabilities of the Irish peasant, led to th
growth of the Irish nationalist movement from one seeking Hom
Rule within the U.K. into a republican one bent on total independenc
from England. A serious rising at Easter 1916, in which patriot
like Padraig Pearse, James Connolly, Eamon de Valera and Michae
Collins battled with Government troops in Dublin, was put down

But the Irish fought on, brilliantly led by Collins (for Pears
and Connolly had been executed in 1916), until 1921 when th
Irish Free State was created by the British Government, and late
came to be called Eire. Northern Ireland, however, remaine
within the U.K.

Today, Northern Ireland, still intensely loyal to the Unite
Kingdom, produces linen on a large scale, builds ships for nation
all over the world, has rich farms and encourages the developmen
of British industries which seek more congenial surroundings wit
lower expenses and government financial aid for improvement. I
Eire, the industries remain what they have been for centuries
farming, livestock rearing, whisky, stout, wool and hair. Dubli
is still the largest city by far in the south, and is a major touris
attraction not only because of its unique Georgian architecture
but also because the very best of Irish art and culture are o
display or performance all the time, emulating the splendi
glories of the 6th to 9th centuries when Ireland was the centr
of western European learning.

Further Reading

This outline of twenty centuries of British social history may have encouraged readers to look further into the subject. It is a very wide field, already covered by numerous books, with, doubtless, many more on the way. Specialized works on individual aspects will be found in most libraries and bookshops. Reference can also be made to back numbers of newspapers and magazines, some going back to the 18th- and even 17th-centuries.

Among the more general works devoted wholly or partly to the social history of the four nations are:

England

Arnold, Ralph, *Social History of England (55 BC to AD 1215)*, Constable, 1967; Bagley, J J, *Life in Medieval England*, Batsford, 1960; Bryant, Sir Arthur, *The Age of Chivalry*, Collins, 1963; Dance, E, *Britain in World History*, Longmans, 1932; Derry & Blakeway, *The Making of Britain*, 2 vols, John Murray, 1969; Feiling, Sir Keith, *History of England*, Macmillan, 1963; Foote & Wilson, *The Viking Achievement*, Sidgwick & Jackson, 1970; Gardiner, S R, *Student's History of England*, 3 vols, Longmans, 1904; Green, J R, *Short History of the English People*, Macmillan; Harrison, M, *How They Lived, 1485 to 1714*, Blackwell; Hassall, W O, *How They Lived, 55 BC to 1485*, Blackwell, 1962; Marten & Carter's *History: Vols 1 to 4*, Blackwell; Mitchell & Leys, *A History of the English People*, Pan Books, 1967; Oman, Sir Charles, *History of England*; Quennell, Marjorie & C H B, *History of Everyday Things in England*, 5 vols, Batsford; Quennell, Marjorie & C H B, *Everyday Life in Roman and Anglo-Saxon Times*, Batsford, 1959; Rayner, R, *Short History of Britain*, Longmans, 1944; Seebohm Rowntree & Lavers, G R, *English Life and Leisure*, Longmans; Trevelyan, G M, *History of England*, Longmans; Trevelyan, G M, *English Social History*, Longmans; Warner, Marten, Muir, *Groundwork of British History*, Blackie, 1943.

Wales

Cordell, Alexander, *Rape of the Fair Country* and *Song of the Earth*, two novels of 19th-century industrial Wales, Gollancz; Davies,

I M, *Roman Villa to Norman Castle*, GWASG, Aberystwyth, 1957; Ellis, P Berresford, *Wales, a Nation Again!*, Tandem Books, 1968; Jackson, K H, *A Celtic Miscellany*, Penguin Books, 1971; Lewis, E & P, *The Land of Wales*, Batsford, 1945; Lloyd, Sir Edward, *History of Wales from the Earliest Times to the Edwardian Conquest*.

Scotland

Brown, Hume, *Short History of Scotland*, Oliver & Boyd; Glover, Janet, *The Story of Scotland*, Faber, 1960; Donaldson, G, *Mackie's Short History of Scotland* (edited), Oliver & Boyd, 1962; MacLean, Sir Fitzroy, *A Concise History of Scotland*, Thames & Hudson, 1970; Mackie, J D, *History of Scotland*, Penguin Books, 1969; Menzies, G, (edited) *The Scottish Nation*, BBC Publications, 1972; Prebble, John, *The Highland Clearances*, Secker & Warburg, 1963; Smout, T C, *History of the Scottish People*, Collins, 1969.

Ireland

Beckett, T C, *The Making of Modern Ireland, 1603–1923*, Faber, 1966; Chauvire, R, *A Short History of Ireland*, Devin-Adair, USA, 1965; Cullen, L M, *Life in Ireland*, Batsford, 1968; Curtis, *History of Ireland*, Methuen, 1936 edition; Henry, F, *Irish Art in the Early Christian Period*, Methuen, 1965; Moody, T W, & Martin, F X, *The Course of Irish History* (editors), Merceir Press, Cork, 1967; Woodham-Smith, Cecil, *The Great Hunger*, Hamish Hamilton, 1963.

Index

This Index excludes terms that appear frequently throughout the book, such as British, Anglo-Saxon, Normans, Christianity, etc.

Page numbers in italics indicate illustrations.